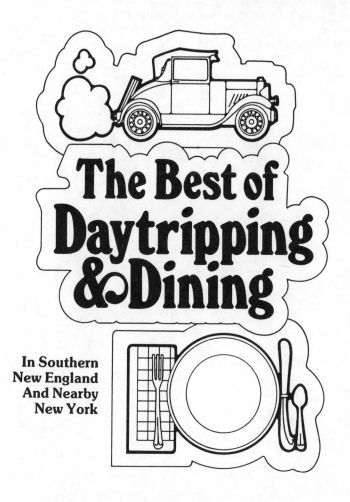

The Best of Daytripping &Dining

In Southern New England And Nearby New York

by Betsy Wittemann and Nancy Webster

Wood Pond Press
365 Ridgewood Road
West Hartford, Conn. 06107

Also by Betsy Wittemann and Nancy Webster:
Daytripping & Dining in Southern New England.
Daytripping & Dining 2 in New England.
Weekending in New England.

Readers should bear in mind that prices, especially in restaurants, change seasonally and with inflation. Prices quoted in this book were correct at presstime. They are offered as a relative guide, rather than an absolute.

First printing, June 1985.

Contents

MASSACHUSETTS

1 Hancock Shaker Village, Pittsfield **1**
Zanadu Garden Cafe, New Lebanon, N.Y. **5**

2 Naumkeag and Chesterwood, Stockbridge **9**
Embree's, Housatonic **13**

3 Historic Deerfield, Deerfield **17**
Deerfield Inn, Deerfield **20**

4 Laughing Brook, Hampden **25**
Salem Cross Inn, West Brookfield **27**

5 Higgins Armory Museum, Worcester **31**
Struck Cafe, Worcester **34**

6 Fruitlands Museum, Harvard **39**
Chez Claude, Acton **42**

7 Peabody Museum, Salem **46**
The Lyceum, Salem **49**

8 Isabella Stewart Gardner Museum, Boston **53**
Cafe Budapest, Boston **55**

9 The Computer Museum and Boston Children's Museum, Boston . . . **59**
A Family Potpourri, Boston **62**

10 Whaling Museum, New Bedford **66**
The Candleworks, New Bedford **69**

RHODE ISLAND

11 Sakonnet Vineyards, Little Compton **73**
Cafe in the Barn, Seekonk, Mass. **76**

12 Slater Mill Historic Site, Pawtucket **80**
Hurricane, Providence **83**

13 Green Animals, Portsmouth **87**
The Black Pearl, Newport **89**

CONNECTICUT

14   Caprilands Herb Farm, Coventry **93**
Mansfield Depot, Mansfield **95**

15   Gillette Castle, Hadlyme. **99**
Fine Bouche, Centerbrook. **102**

16   Thimble Islands, Stony Creek. **106**
Friends & Company, Madison **109**

17   Whitlock Farm, Bethany. **114**
Britannia Spoon Company, Yalesville **116**

18   Mark Twain Memorial, Hartford **121**
Standish House, Wethersfield. **125**

19   Sloane-Stanley Museum, Kent **129**
Holley Place, Lakeville. **131**

20   Aldrich Museum, Ridgefield **136**
Stonehenge, Ridgefield **138**

NEW YORK

21   Roosevelt Sites, Hyde Park **142**
Culinary Institute of America, Hyde Park **146**

22   Sleepy Hollow Restorations, Tarrytown **151**
Tappan Hill Inn, Tarrytown **155**

23   Bronx Zoo, The Bronx. **160**
The Lobster Box, The Bronx **162**

24   Brooklyn Botanic Garden, Brooklyn. **166**
Raintrees, Brooklyn **169**

25   Walt Whitman Birthplace and Old Bethpage Village, Long Island . . **174**
The Great Dane, Huntington **178**

To Our Readers

A daytrip, with lunch or dinner out. What more refreshing mini-vacation is there?

We've been writing about daytripping and dining since 1978 and we're still having a great time doing so. This third book is special because in it we focus on places to visit and restaurants that are among our favorites. We think these daytrip destinations — and the accompanying dining selections — represent the best in Southern New England and nearby New York.

You will find some of our old favorites: the Isabella Stewart Gardner Museum and the Cafe Budapest in Boston, or the Green Animals topiary garden and the Black Pearl in Newport, for example. You'll also discover some marvelous new destinations: the Brooklyn Botanic Garden and Raintrees in Brooklyn, N.Y., or the Franklin and Eleanor Roosevelt historic sites in Hyde Park, N.Y., and the great restaurants at the Culinary Institute of America nearby.

The book is designed for picking and choosing, mixing and matching. You may want to take a picnic with you to the Hancock Shaker Village in the Berkshires on one visit, and go back another time to dine at the nifty new restaurant in nearby Housatonic, Embree's. Or you may find yourself some evening in Worcester, Mass., and wonder where in the world to eat (perhaps you'll be amazed by all the good new restaurants we've found there).

Some of our readers tell us they keep these books in the glove compartments of their cars for just such occasions. As they drive around Southern New England or New York, they use them for reference.

Others keep these guides on their coffee tables or bedside tables at home — at the ready for planning the next jaunt.

Whichever you do, we're delighted to have you join us in this adventure called daytripping and dining. We wish you successful trips, marvelous meals and happy memories.

Betsy Wittemann
Nancy Webster

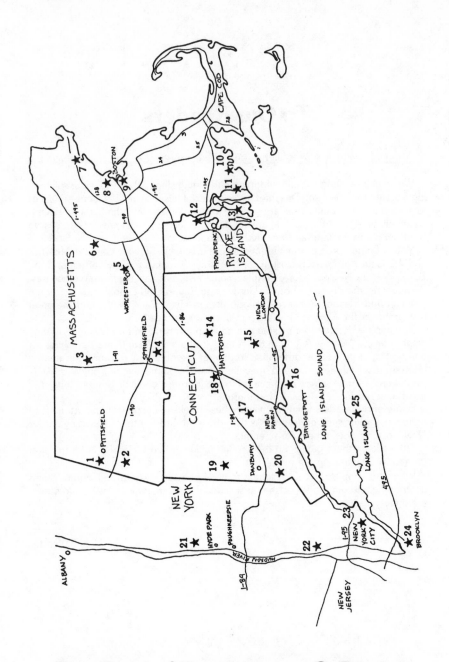

The Best of Daytripping & Dining
In Southern New England and Nearby New York

1830 kitchen at Hancock Shaker Village.

The City of Peace

Hancock Shaker Village/Pittsfield, Mass.

There are no living Shakers at the Hancock Shaker Village, which celebrated its 25th anniversary as a museum in 1985, but visitors sometimes get confused. That isn't hard to understand if you've spent a few hours in the bucolic setting where interpreters (women wearing aprons and men in smocks) work in the kitchen making Shaker foods, in the herb garden tending Shaker herbs, in the barns caring for sheep or horses, or in the blacksmith shop forging a piece of iron.

The recreation of this 19th century Shaker village is so authentic, in fact, that the staff purposely does not wear the full Shaker dress in an attempt to keep the confusion to a minimum.

The United Society of Believers (as the Shakers are officially known) lived in community at Hancock from 1790 until 1960, when the last three elderly Sisters were moved to another Shaker site and the Hancock property put up for sale.

Fortunately, locals who cared about the Shaker heritage were able to drum up the needed resources to buy the extensive property and turn it into a museum.

It is a great place. Much of its greatness, of course, stems from the fact that it is a real place, a recreation of the way things were *where* they were. The visitor not only gets to walk through several restored structures (20 in all) but to do so in the environment in which they always existed. He can understand the relation of one building to another, and appreciate the practicality of the placement; get a feeling for the closeness that these Shakers had with the natural world around them, and still understand that they were not off in the wilderness (Route 20 being a reasonably well-traveled road and the Shakers having conducted business with "outsiders" as a help with financial survival).

Hancock was an agricultural community. The imposing and famed round stone barn at its center serves as a symbol of that commitment. While some Shaker communities were making chairs and others were sewing cloaks on a commercial basis (Hancock Shakers did these tasks, but not commercially), those in western Massachusetts were dairying and planting and harvesting. The cycle of the seasons determined their yearly activities and the Hancock Shaker Village museum is faithful to that calendar.

Of the single special events for which Hancock is known, possibly the most famous is the Shaker Kitchen Festival held in late July or early August each year — call for exact dates — when culinary experts prepare foods and discuss various cuisines for an entire week. Visitors get tastes, but not full meals. And not all of the preparations are of Shaker foods.

Other special events draw people to the village from Memorial Day Weekend, when it opens, through late October. A special Christmas weekend in December brings them back to share in Shaker preparation for the holidays. Throughout the season, and depending on when they come, guests might avail themselves of special children's tours, candlelight tours, blacksmithing workshops, the World's People's Dinners usually served in conjunction with the Kitchen Festival, and two popular fall weekends: the Annual Festival of Shaker Crafts & Industries in September and the Antiques Show and Autumn Weekend over Columbus Day.

But everyone who visits Hancock should allow himself a "normal" visit as well, a leisurely time to stroll through the complex and really get the feeling of what it was like to be here as a member of the community. There are two ways to do this: one is to do an entirely self-guided tour with the help of a very good visitor's map; the other is to hook up with one of the two daily guided tours (at 10:30 a.m. and 2 p.m.) when an interpreter will take you through the major buildings, ending at the Meeting House for a brief demonstration of Shaker music and dance.

Even if you decide to do it on your own, however, interpreters in the main buildings are on hand to answer questions.

A day (or at the very least, a half day) at Hancock Shaker Village begins in the contemporary administration building, where tickets are purchased. From here you go through the tiny garden tool shed into the herb garden. Herbs were extremely important to Shakers for medicinal purposes, and at Hancock two young herbalists grow herbs the way the believers did: in long straight rows. Specifically Shaker herbs in the herb garden at Hancock include dandelions (dandelion extract was used as a diuretic and to purify the liver); elecampane, which looks like a sunflower and was used in various ways, and calendula, which was made into a salve for cuts and bruises (you can buy some in one of the stores on the site).

The Poultry House on the property is used to display the Shaker spirit drawings in Hancock's rich collection. The original of the famous Tree of Life drawing, which is so widely reproduced, is at Hancock. Other changing exhibits are sometimes mounted here.

The five-story Brick Dwelling House, erected in 1830 when the 200-member Hancock community was at its height, is an exceptional place. Here is the ground-floor Shaker kitchen where someone is usually at work baking or preparing foods the way the Shakers did; the dining room and meeting room for the community; the bedrooms of the Sisters and the Brethren, and the specialized workrooms such as a sewing room, tailor's room, deacon's office, pharmacy and nurse shop.

The wide hallways, polished wood floors and pegboard along every wall made this an exceptionally beautiful, simple and orderly place. The Shaker stoves in all rooms, familiar taped rockers, simple rope beds, gorgeous cupboards, all attest to the Shaker practicality and simplicity of design; the furniture collection here is priceless.

In the nurse shop you may at first be amused to see enormous adult-sized cradles on the floor. But the Shakers were an understanding people, and when members of the community were ill, they were often "rocked" to soothe them. "It's something we all need a little of at times," noted the guide who was touring us through.

Several beautiful Shaker cloaks hang in one of the tailor's rooms and the pharmacy is where the herbal medicines were concocted. The bedrooms typically housed two to four of the Brethren or the Sisters; clothes were hung from the pegboards, and life was kept simple in line with the Shaker motto "hands to work and hearts to God." At Hancock it is not difficult to believe in a life lived devotedly and contentedly.

The round stone barn is noteworthy and served as the center of the Hancock Shakers' important dairy business. Built in 1826 to house a large herd of milk cows, the barn features an unusual design which allowed horse-drawn wagons to bring hay into the upper level where it was unloaded into the central haymow at the level where the cows were kept. In 1864 a cellar was dug beneath the milking floor and used for the storage of manure until it was needed to fertilize the fields.

Other houses open to visitors include the Sisters' House, where churning, weaving and spinning were done by the women of the sect, and the Brethren's Shop,

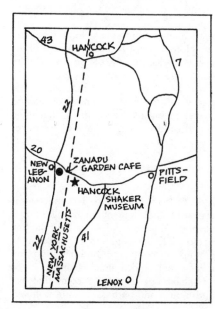

Location: Route 20, 5 miles west of Pittsfield, Mass. Mailing address: P. O. Box 898, Pittsfield 01202.

Open: Daily, Memorial Day weekend through Oct. 31, 9:30 to 5. Guided tours daily at 10:30 and 2.

Admission: Adults, $6; children 6 to 12, $2; under 6, free; family rate, $15; senior citizens and students, $5.50.

Special Events: Shaker Kitchen Festival, a week of events in late July or early August, including several special World People's Dinners featuring Shaker foods; Candlelit Tours of the village, offered several evenings during the season; Special Children's Tours; Crafts Weekend in September; Antiques Show and Autumn Weekend in October; Christmas weekend with special workshops early in December. Call ahead for schedules of all special events, including new ones scheduled each year. A complete schedule can be requested.

Telephone: (413) 443-0188.

where the men made brooms (those at Hancock being somewhat famous) and oval boxes and also were involved in tinsmithing. At Hancock today, craftspeople work in these shops; a visitor on any day might see a blacksmith, tinsmith, weaver or chair taper.

The Ministry Wash House used by elders and eldresses of the Ministry for laundry and bathing has been most recently under reconstruction, giving visitors a chance to see the exceptional care being taken to make the museum authentic.

The Trustees Office and Store is the only Victorian-style building at Hancock and visitors are sometimes surprised at the flowered wallpaper and stuffed furniture; a store exhibits items similar to those which might have been sold by the Shakers in the late 19th century.

For the visitor who wants to take home some memories of a visit to Hancock, there are ample opportunities. A bookstore in the Administration Building (where you began your tour) offers books, posters and pamphlets; the Good Room in the Brick Dwelling House is a spot to buy jams and jellies and other items to eat; the 1910 barn has housed, since 1981, the largest shop on the property, where museum-quality Shaker reproduction furniture made at Hancock is sold, as are herb products, cards, books and other appropriate gift items.

Across the road from the main complex exists the very important Meeting House, where the Shakers had their Sabbath services. Note the two entrance doorways, one for men and one for women; upstairs were living quarters of the Elders and Eldresses of the Ministry (in essence, the four people who managed the community). Nearby is the Shaker cemetery, where more than 250 Brethren and Sisters are interred; the last burial was that of Sister Frances Hall in 1859. Only a single monument, in the center of the fenced area, remains to commemorate the Shakers who lived at Hancock.

The horse barn houses a couple of workhorses which are used to plow the fields; on this side of the road is also the tiny schoolhouse where Shaker children attended classes for four months each year (girls in the summer; boys in the winter). Because they were a celibate community, the Shakers' only way of propagating was to take in orphans or other children who were given into their care to raise. While many of these children later left the community, many records indicate they had a happy, loving life in places like Hancock.

Hancock was the third of the eventual 18 Shaker communities formed around the country. The village was never seen by Mother Ann Lee, the foundress of the sect, who died in 1784, although it is said she traveled past the site on a missionary tour of New England several years before its founding.

After your tour of Hancock — or possibly at the midpoint — you may want some lunch. An attractive lunch room, furnished with reproduction Shaker chairs and tables, offers sandwiches, soups and Shaker rosewater ice cream, at the main building. However, picnickers are welcomed, and there are many picnic tables around the site.

Also in the Area

The Shaker Museum, Old Chatham, N.Y. (518) 794-9100. This museum is located across the New York State line, west of Hancock by about 18 miles and a trip of less than a half hour. Annual Festival of Antiques and Art is held the first Saturday in August and usually draws a big crowd. Exhibits are housed in a complex of eight buildings that includes a library, museum book store and gift shop and education center. There is a cabinet maker's shop and a small chair factory; a blacksmith's shop and a craft gallery. Other exhibits describe Shaker community life and period rooms are reproduced. An herb house and herb garden are popular.

Open daily, May-October 10 to 5. Adults, $3.50; senior citizens, $3; students 15-21, $2.50; children 6 to 14, $1.50.

Arrowhead, 780 Holmes Road, Pittsfield, Mass. (413) 442-1793.This is the house where the American author, Herman Melville, lived from 1850 to 1863 and where he wrote *Moby Dick*. The house was beloved by the author, and contains a few items of family furniture. The second-floor study is the jewel of the house for those who admire Melville; a simple and pleasant room, it allowed Melville a view of Mount Greylock which he found inspiring. The massive central chimney of the house was another favorite feature of the author. Outside the house is the red barn where Melville and friend, Nathaniel Hawthorne, often had philosophical discussions. Open daily, June-October, Monday-Saturday 10 to 5, and Sunday 1 to 5.

 # Dining 1

Colorful house is home of Zanadu Garden Cafe.

Zanadu Garden Cafe/New Lebanon, N.Y.

Inside and out, Zanadu is a colorful spot. And it's no wonder it's called a garden cafe, this unusual restaurant just across the New York state line from the Hancock Shaker Village.

The Victorian frame house is purple with yellow shutters, a black door and a green awning. The two small dining rooms inside (one on a back porch) are a blaze of hues, with striking black, orange and green tablecloths topped by straw mats, beaded lamps, fringed orange sheer curtains, distinctive soft fabric sculptures on the walls and arrangements of silk flowers everywhere. The Samuel Taylor Coleridge poem, from which the name is taken, is framed and hung on one wall.

Add the striking sculptures by Arline Peatree Shirlman on the back lawn (which you can see from the porch and where there is outdoor dining at umbrellaed tables in summer) and you've got a lot to look at!

Be advised, however, this is a crowded place. Some of the eight tables in the front room are almost on top of each other and seem congested because of the large floral pieces. Beyond is a work room with refrigerator, through which you pass to get to the back porch and which a more conventional restaurant would long since have used for extra tables. The rear porch has three tables and a corner service bar.

But the food is so well thought of that for many the congestion doesn't matter. On the afternoon we visited, at least three people were lunching alone — Zanadu is the sort of place where solitary lunchers do not feel conspicuous.

The feminine touches and the names of some of the dishes (Cleopatra salad rather than Caesar) might tell you that this restaurant is owned by women — and it is. Says Peggy Reynolds, "my daughter Deborah and I sat down one day five and a half years ago and thought of all the names we could call our place. When she said Zanadu, I said that's it!"

The luncheon menu of soups, sandwiches and salads is augmented by several daily specials. On our visit, they were beef stew, cold poached salmon and a curried chicken plate, all $7.50. We tried the last and it was a nice mix of chunky chicken, with much garnish of vegetables and fruit.

The quiches, Lorraine or broccoli, were served in generous wedges with salad and were remarkably good. A soup of the day, leek and vegetables, was light rather than thick, and well seasoned. Salads arrive in gigantic glass bowls and our spinach salad with anchovies was almost too much to tackle.

The rolls are heavenly, steaming hot, some studded with poppy seeds and some filled with sunflower seeds. It's too bad they come with aluminum pads of butter atop some crackers in cellophane.

"There's no such thing as a plain sandwich here," says Peggy Reynolds. Indeed they come on all kinds of bread and with all kinds of garnishes and side salads in the $4 to $5 range.

There is a full service bar and an unusually good bound wine list with labels.

At night the menu is rather formal, with a very large selection of entrees, from $14.95 for chicken stuffed with lemon and topped with lemon sauce, to $19.50 for extra thick lamb chops served with Parisienne potatoes. Rainbow trout with a spinach and mushroom stuffing, moussaka, chicken a la Tahiti (with sweet and sour sauce, peppers, onions, snow peas, pineapple, mandarin orange, bananas and coconut, served in a pineapple shell), four preparations of veal, three of filet mignon, pork oriental, and roast duck with apricot and honey sauce are some appealing choices.

The Reynoldses' desserts are well known and customers often buy a pie or such to take home. Things like rum cake, apricot torte, chocolate kahlua cheesecake and chocolate mousse pie are specialties. Often augmented by cherry or cranberry bog cheesecakes, carrot cake, black bottom cake with chocolate chips and cream cheese, and even a beer cake Mrs. Reynolds describes as spicy, the day's offerings are on display on a table in the edge of the front dining room as well as in the work area.

When we were there, a pie topped mile high with meringue had just come out of the oven and the four women having lunch at the next table had cast lustful eyes at it as they entered. To no avail, because, said Mrs. Reynolds, it was too hot and if cut then, the meringue would collapse. They would just have to come back later.

Zanadu Garden Cafe, Routes 20 and 22, New Lebanon, N.Y. (518) 794-9971. Open daily from 11:30 for lunch, dinner, and afternoon tea or coffee and desserts. Reservations recommended. No credit cards.

Also in the Area

Shuji's, Rtes. 20 and 22, New Lebanon, N.Y. (518) 795-1333. Across from Zanadu Garden Cafe is the large and very Victorian 1897 home of former New York Governor Samuel J. Tilden which, for the last 16 years, has been the home of Shuji Uchiyama and his wife, who have made their Japanese restaurant fit extremely well into the space. You may dine in one of several paneled downstairs dining rooms including a spacious front porch or, up a stately oak staircase framed by priceless Tiffany stained-glass windows, in tatami rooms where you take off your shoes and recline on pillow chairs. A full Japanese gourmet dinner for $23 includes soup, sushi, lobster, tempura, teriyaki, dessert and a glass of plum wine along with a lot of other dishes. Dinners (including an appetizer, salad and rice) are from $9 for vegetarian tempura or teriyaki to $30 for Shuji's king of the sea platter. Sushi and sashimi dinners are $16. Mt. Fuji, a rum sponge cake topped with ice cream and whipped cream, is a popular dessert. The menu for the tatami rooms is slightly different, with shabu shabu and king crab tempura as additions. Everything is served on handsome Imari and other Japanese pottery. And of course you can get sake, $1.75, and Kirin or Sapporo beer, $2. Dinner only, from 6, from 5 Saturday and Sunday. Closed Monday.

The Coach Lite, 1485 W. Housatonic St., Pittsfield, Mass. (413) 499-1523. Everybody in Pittsfield loves the Coach Lite, we're told, and with good reason. It's an elegant, proven establishment out Route 20 west not far from Hancock, with an ambitious menu at pleasing prices. You enter through the trolley car that was the diner from which the restaurant evolved. The place appears much larger than its 125 seats in two dining rooms, thanks to well-spaced tables and luxurious appointments. In the 14 years that chef Paul Bock has owned it, the Coach Lite has changed the eating habits of Pittsfield, according to his wife Patty. "Probably only two or three items remain from our original menu," she says. Now, dinner entrees aspire to frog legs, sweetbreads, veal Oscar, scallops Antoine and brace of quail grand marnier at prices from $8.75 to $15.75. With most appetizers $3 to $4 and desserts $2 to $3, why not start with brie in beer batter with strawberry sauce or oysters on the half shell and end with chilled strawberry souffle or creme anglaise? "The natives come here for special occasions and the tourists think it's a gold mine," says Patty Bock. A surprising number of good wines are under $10 or in the low teens. The vast luncheon menu contains many of chef Bock's specialties, with sandwiches from $1.95, entrees from $3.50. Lunch, Tuesday-Saturday 11:30 to 2:30, dinner 5 to 10, Sunday noon to 9:30.

The Dragon, 478 W. Housatonic St., Pittsfield, Mass. (413) 442-5504. In a teeny red and white diner, Kim Van Huynh, who used to run a restaurant in Saigon, serves up some exceptional Vietnamese and oriental food. Booths topped with red formica make up the decor; a small room added in back has a few tables with flowered cloths covered with glass. You may bring your own wine or beer, and the prices are certainly right — lunch entrees $5.75 and under; dinner entrees $5.95 to $7.50 (except for sauteed shrimp, Vietnamese style, for $10.95). Two Vietnamese spring rolls (more crisp and delicate than the Chinese egg rolls) are $1.75. Chicken with lemon grass, ginger chicken, spicy pork with broccoli, shaking beef, and scrod crisped with fresh tomatoes and onion sauce are some of the good choices; dragon burgers on steamed buns are a special, and you can top your meal off with lychee nuts or ice cream and a pot of the excellent Vietnamese coffee, done in French cafe-filtre style ($1.50). The Dragon does a lot of takeout business as well. Usually open from 10 a.m. to 10 p.m. or midnight, but sometimes closes during off-season. No credit cards.

Duck Soup, Route 7, Lanesboro, Mass. (413) 443-1106. Another small place with a big personality is Duck Soup, located right beside the highway in a gray house with mulberry shutters. Much of the personality comes from gregarious owner and chef Doug McClelland; his wife Betty does the baking and her cinnamon toast loaves, muffins, and pies (like blackberry or raisin walnut) are famous. Roast duckling a l'orange with a brandy sauce is $12.95 at night; you have to reserve it in advance. The drippings, broth and bits of meat form the base of the very good duck soup, 75 cents or $1.25. A roast goose dinner, $38 for two, includes half a ten-pound goose, chutney, rice pilaf, french bread and salad. Dinner entrees are $6.50 to $12.95; the more interesting are printed on a blackboard menu and included, on our visit, shrimp scampi bianco, bluefish provencale and veal, Greek style. An asparagus and Swiss cheese omelet at lunch was $4.95, bay scallops in herb butter with rice and salad, $4.50. Breakfast is a good bet here, with things like the Brodie Mountain omelet (Swiss cheese, fried potatoes and grilled ham) $4.50, corned beef hash with two eggs, pimento and parsley, $2.75, and two fried eggs with home fries ("they really have personality, with garlic, onion and thyme," says McClelland), choice of grilled ham, bacon or sausage, toast and jelly, for $2.75. Decor consists mainly of red booths and black naugahyde seats; you can bring your own wine or beer (small corkage fee), and you can order, for dessert, a piece of the fabulous cheesecake made by the nuns of New Skete near Saratoga Springs, N.Y., (the kahlua cheesecake is legendary). Breakfast daily (Sundays only in winter), from 8 a.m., lunch and dinner, closed Tuesday.

Day's Catch at Pontoosuc Landing, North Street (Route 7), Pittsfield, Mass. (413) 499-FISH. The plant-filled, glass-enclosed porch with the smashing view of Lake Pontoosuc is everything at this large new establishment, one of several run locally by Donald Gallagher and Michael Hendler. Well, not exactly everything. The fresh fish is the rest: the usual plus the exotic like Alaskan kingcrab, Gulf shrimp Clemenceau, Nantucket bluefish, Idaho rainbow trout and lobster fra diavlo. The "Admiral's Cache" is steamed lobster, broiled and fried seafoods in a pu-pu style platter, $28.95 for two. The prices are reasonable (Louisiana crabmeat casserole and cioppino are both $11.95). Bouillabaisse makes a fine lunch for $6.95; eggs St. Charles, shrimp Creole and seafood tempura are offered at Sunday brunch, as is an impressive buffet for $9.95. The wine list is serviceable if a bit strange, and the main interior dining room is ordinary-nautical. But it is, after all, the fresh seafood and the view from the lakeside porch that matter; get there early for the best seats. Lunch, 11 to 5; dinner, 5 to 11; Sunday brunch, 11 to 3:30.

Truffles & Such, Allendale Shopping Center, Route 9 east, Pittsfield, Mass. (413) 442-0051. Breakfast, lunch and early supper are served up by Irene and Michael Maston, she a Culinary Institute of America grad, in this crisp contemporary place opened in early 1985. The long narrow room has a patisserie in front, chrome and bentwood chairs and one wall of mirrors, the other with arty posters. Stained-glass lights (which Michael made himself) hang from chains over the tables topped with white linen, blue mats and pink napkins. Classical music plays as patrons dine on hummus or shrimp remoulade, eggs benedict or pasta, Mediterranean torte sandwich, mixed grill or scrod duglere. Sandwiches and salads are $3.25 to $3.75, the six entrees $4.50 to $6.25. Everything is made on premises and available to take out. Open Monday-Friday 9 to 7, Saturday 9 to 5.

Main house at Naumkeag.

Houses and Gardens

Naumkeag and Chesterwood/Stockbridge, Mass.

It was the view of Monument Mountain in the Berkshires that attracted them both. Lured by the beauty of the hills, the promise of cooler summers than those in the city, and the fashionableness of summer cottages in western Massachusetts, New York lawyer Joseph Hodges Choate and famed sculptor Daniel Chester French chose sites in Stockbridge for their turn-of-the-century retreats.

This was the Gilded Age, but both houses are less than imposing. Naumkeag, the Choate home, was designed by Stanford White in the "shingle style" popular in the day. Its 26 rooms are built on a human scale and it was a comfortable summer house for the Choates and their five children. Built in 1884, it was used by the family for many years, and then by one of the Choates' children, a daughter, Mabel, until 1959.

It was Mabel who was the gardener. She added the extensive and unusual gardens to the hillside site, and so interesting are they that some visitors never even stop inside to see the house.

The house is nestled below the road on Prospect Hill, and the shrubbed and planted areas lie to the west, clinging to the rather steep hillside which faces Monument Mountain across the Housatonic River. Nathaniel Barrett, a pioneer in landscaping, fitted the house and the gardens to the difficult piece of land by creating two broad grassy terraces.

After her parents died, Mabel Choate engaged the distinguished Boston landscape architect, Fletcher Steele, to extend Barrett's original concept and to redesign

9

a portion of it. This was done gradually over a 30-year period; Steele became such a frequent visitor to the site that a room was reserved for him.

To the south, or left, as you exit the rear of the house, are the Outdoor Room and the Afternoon Garden. Oak pilings dredged from Boston Harbor were carved and painted to resemble Venetian posts. The marble chip walks and four small fountains make for an intimate and picturesque spot. Wrought-iron furniture invites the visitor to pause and enjoy the views of the Berkshire hills. There are more elaborate and dramatic areas at Naumkeag, but this was our favorite spot, a perfect marriage of form and function, both romantic and restful.

From the Afternoon Garden, walk down several grass steps to a Chinese pagoda surrounded by Japanese maples. The pagoda was fashioned from a cast-iron veranda support of a house in Washington, D.C.; its grapevine relief was actually painted and gilded by Miss Choate.

The Linden Walk, planned by the wife of Joseph Choate, is shaded by an archway of 60 trees. Beneath your feet the ground is spongy and soft with moss. Here, even on a golden autumn day, the sun barely filters through; the woods are deep and ferny and one can imagine the relief from summer's heat.

Back toward the house, running down the center of the hillside, is an imaginative series of terraced steps known as the Fountain Steps. The sound of trickling water as one pool flows to the next level, and the shimmering of birch leaves from the trees flanking the steps, add to the experience. Beyond, and below, are the orchard, greenhouses and hidden farm buildings with hay fields glistening in the afternoon.

A huge evergreen garden close to the house and a rose garden, carefully manicured, were part of the original plan. But the Chinese Garden is a magical world, set apart from the rest. Brick walls enclose the stone Buddhas, lions, dogs and other carvings brought back from the Orient by Mabel Choate in 1935. A stand of nine gingko trees stood in a golden pool of fallen fan-shaped leaves when we visited. The garden invites repose and contemplation in the Eastern tradition.

From the Chinese Garden, the visitor can return to the house via the circular Moon Gate in the brick wall. The guided tour through the 26-room house encompasses all three floors, furnished as they were when the Choates were in residence. Throughout are Stanford White-designed fireplaces — almost one per room.

Many of Miss Choate's oriental porcelain pieces are displayed in the dining room; portraits of her and her father by the American artist John Singer Sargent in the library across the way. Paintings by both mother and daughter are to be seen in the schoolroom. Possibly the most surprising room is Joseph Choate's own study: a very simple place with a plain desk and bookcase-lined walls where he worked while in residence.

The Choates enjoyed the low-key social life and the beauty of the Berkshires, we're told, so much so that they couldn't bring themselves to return to New York until November, after the bright golden days of fall had passed.

Daniel Chester French, the famed sculptor of the seated Lincoln in Washington's Lincoln Memorial, felt similarly. He and his family summered in a gracious home from which they also could see Monument Mountain, and we're told the families knew one another. French loved partying and playing during the six months of the year he claimed to reside "in heaven" but he worked at his summer home, **Chesterwood,** as well. In fact, the sculptor's studio and the gardens he designed around it, are the highlights of a visit.

French summered at Chesterwood from 1897 until his death in 1931. The house and studio at Chesterwood were designed for him by his architect friend, Henry

Skylighted studio at Chesterwood.

Bacon, with whom he shared many commissions, including that for the Lincoln Memorial.

While the first floor of the house is visitable, it is not especially important. The one memorable item is a dried rose which was given to French from the casket of Abraham Lincoln.

Next door to the house is the splendid skylighted studio (granting French the north light which most sculptors prefer). The studio itself is a 30-foot cube, the height called for because of the very tall equestrian statues popular at the time.

In the studio are the three increasingly larger working casts done of the seated Lincoln; the marble statue, Andromeda, on which French was working at the time of his death; several of his tools, and the like. An ingenious arrangement allowed the sculptor to have his statues taken from the studio into the light of day in order to view them in natural light. He had railroad tracks placed beneath the wooden floor of the studio (trap doors lead to them), upon which was a flatbed train. Any sculpture could be easily placed on the train car and rolled out into the light, and French could stand on the lawn below the building to see how the sculpture would appear to someone looking up at it.

The wide porch of the studio building, with its view of Monument Mountain, is lovely. It was here that tea was served on Friday afternoons to friends and visitors like the Choates or author Edith Wharton, who summered in nearby Lenox and was known to French.

Outside, to the rear of the studio building, is the garden designed by French himself. When we visited in early May, the borders were filled with daffodils, tulips, myrtensia and violets; later in the year summer flowers provide color. A semicircular marble structure with benches is in the more formal Italian tradition; leading from this is a walkway flanked by peonies.

The walk leads directly into a wooded area, where wildflowers and naturalized daffodils are found in spring beneath the thick stand of trees. This is the nature trail

11

area, also planned by French, and once you are a few feet away from the house, you are in a different world. A small statue of a cherub in repose is dedicated to someone who, the sign says, loved the garden.

For a student of sculpture — and anyone who visits should become one temporarily — the Barn Sculpture Studio to the rear of the property is important. Our well-versed guide took us through highlights of French's life and career, pointing out memorabilia and describing the symbolism or the design of famous statues as he did.

Born in New Hampshire, the sculptor was the son of Henry Flagg French, who was the first president of the agricultural college in Amherst, Mass.,which is now the University of Massachusetts. His mother died when he was a young boy and he was brought up by a stepmother who encouraged his artistic bent.

The family lived, during these formative years, in Concord, Mass., and it was the town of Concord that gave French his first — and still one of his most important — commissions. Though he had not yet had formal training in sculpture, the town fathers asked him to do a Minuteman statue to commemorate the Centennial of the Revolutionary War.

Then in his early 20s, French researched the situation carefully before designing the bronze Minuteman statue which today stands at the famous North Bridge in Concord. Next to the Lincoln Memorial, it is, perhaps, his best known work.

After studying in Italy, French returned to become one of the most prominent sculptors of his day. In the barn studio at Chesterwood one sees the working model of the standing Lincoln which the sculptor did for the city of Lincoln, Neb.; a model of the Dupont Circle fountain in Washington, D.C., for which French did the bas relief; the two allegorical statues, one representing Manhattan and the other, Brooklyn, which stood at the approaches to the Manhattan Bridge (they are now in front of the Brooklyn Museum). A particularly lovely statue is his marble Endymion, done when he was 24 and studying in Florence, Italy; for many years it was in his family's yard in Concord.

Now a property run by the National Trust for Historic Preservation, Chesterwood was lived in by French's only child, Margaret French Cresson, until her death in 1973. Also on the property are a nice gift shop and a picnic grove.

Location: Naumkeag is located on Prospect Hill in Stockbridge, just north of the center of town. To reach Chesterwood, take Route 102 from the west end of Stockbridge's Main Street until you reach Route 183. Turn left and travel one mile to the Chesterwood sign at Mohawk Lake Road. The house is about a half mile farther.

Open: Naumkeag is open weekends and Monday holidays from Memorial Day weekend through Columbus Day. From the last Tuesday in June through Labor Day, the house is open daily except Monday. 10 to 5; last house tour at 4:15 p.m. Chesterwood is open daily May 1 through Oct. 31 from 10 to 5.

Admission: Naumkeag, $3.50, house and garden; $3, house alone; $2, garden alone; $1, children 6 to 16. Chesterwood, adults, $3.50; children, $1.50.

Telephone: Naumkeag: (413) 298-3239. Chesterwood: (413) 298-3579.

Also in the Area

The Mission House, Main and Sergeant streets, Stockbridge. (413) 298-3239. Mabel Choate is responsible for the endowment and preservation of this interesting old house, built in 1739 by John Sergeant, a missionary to the Indians, for his new bride, the former Abigail Williams. The house was unusual for its highly ornamental entryway, known as a Connecticut Valley entrance, and for its curious placement of two chimneys behind the ridge line of the house, giving the rooms great depth. Miss Choate bought the house in 1948 and had it taken, piece by piece, from the hillside where it had been built to a corner in the center of town. The house, like Naumkeag, is under the jurisdiction of the Trustees of Reservations, a non-profit, private conservation organization. Open daily Memorial Day weekend through Columbus Day, Tuesday-Saturday 10 to 5; last house tour, 4:30; Sundays and holidays 11 to 4; last tour, 3:30. Adults, $2.50; children 6 to 16, $1.

Bartholomew's Cobble, Off Route 7A, Ashley Falls, Mass.(413) 229-8600. This is a garden of a different sort, a natural rock garden, if you will, overlooking the serpentine Housatonic River. Here are 200 acres of rock garden with some 500 species of wildflowers, 100 species of trees, shrubs and vines, and no fewer than 40 species of ferns. So important is the flora in the area that it's been designated a National Natural Landmark. There are six trails and a small museum, and it's possible to spread your blanket and have a picnic amid all this glory. Open daily, 9 a.m. to sunset. Museum open Wednesday-Sunday and holidays, 9 to 5. Adults, $2; children, $1.

 # Dining 2

Embree's/Housatonic, Mass.

In front of one of the Berkshires' newest restaurants in out-of-the-way Housatonic, burgundy awnings shade masses of impatiens in wooden boxes.

Plate-glass windows that front right onto the sidewalk are softened by enough plants to furnish a florist shop. Fans and turn-of-the-century lighting fixtures hang from the high ceilings.

Open shelves at either side of the large square room hold artistic arrangements of the glasses and plain white pottery used in the restaurant. Walls are a deep burgundy-rose, which softens the prevailing expanse of wooden floors and tables.

If all this seems theatrical, that's because the design of Embree's (in a space occupied for 50 years by a hardware store) is that of Jay Embree, a former scenery painter in New York theater (his last show was "Sophisticated Ladies," but, says he, "I spent a lot of time in the unemployment lines").

With his sister, Joan Spence of Stockbridge (a former chef at Wheatleigh), he opened Embree's in August 1984 and, mostly by word of mouth of delighted repeat patrons, has been doing a fine business ever since.

They're attracted not only by the handsome room with its polished wooden floors and tables topped with burgundy napkins, but by the menu (sort of nouvelle international), sensible prices and, usually, good service by women in long blue aprons over white shirts and dark pants. Weekend nights can get hectic, however, and the earlier you eat, the better you're likely to be served.

From the interesting list of appetizers ($2.50 to $6.75), we chose nachos with

Old hardware store shelves remain at Embree's.

salsa verde, a colorful and delicious melange of crisp, homemade tortilla chips, melted cheese, red onions, sour cream and a spicy salsa. This could have made a meal, but was just right when shared by two. Equally good were mushrooms stuffed with a pungent mix of mozzarella, goat's cheese and herbs.

Antipasto, chicken wings marinated in ginger sauce, meat loaf terrine with pine nuts and basil, and a spicy, homemade sausage with peppers were some other appetizer choices from the autumn menu. The next spring, there was a cold butterfly shrimp with a dijon-aioli sauce and a delightful Japanese vegetable sushi ($5.25), garnished with bits of radish and long strands of scallions and served on a butcher block, but without the pickled ginger which usually accompanies sushi.

A small salad of mixed greens, including spinach, was tossed with a good, slightly sweet vinaigrette. A loaf of dense bread came with a soft, zesty tarragon butter.

The dozen seasonal entrees are priced from $7.25 (stir-fried vegetables with curry, ginger and cashews) to $14.75 for filet mignon. Vegetarians appreciate changing items like the tempeh and vegetable shish-kebab, tofu sauteed and served with a coriander yogurt sauce or, on our spring visit, homemade tomato pasta with tofu, red pepper, ginger root and bean sprouts in a red wine tamari sauce.

We certainly appreciated our entrees: a tender breast of chicken coated with a crisp batter and topped with a lemon sauce, a sensational grilled bluefish spiced with ginger and strands of scallions, and — one of the best dishes we have had in ages — babotie, little balls of ground lamb and almonds, highly and heavily spiced, atop a delicate custard and accented with chutney. With melt-in-the-mouth new potatoes cooked in their red jackets plus crisp zucchini, this was a meal fit for a rajah.

Other interesting entrees might be a Mediterranean fish soup, filet of sole with smoked mozzarella and a vermouth and sweet butter sauce, filet of beef with ginger, cilantro and saffron in a vermouth and lemon butter sauce, and veal paupiettes stuffed with garlic, bread crumbs, parmesan cheese and raisins.

The wine list is small but adequate and also very fairly priced. One time we had a fine Charles Pax Cote du Rhones and another time an excellent Graves, each $9.50. Pre-dinner drinks also are ample and served in over-sized glasses.

Desserts (by Ronnie Roisman of Stockbridge) change nightly. There are usually three kinds of cheesecake including chocolate, and on the first night we were there, poached pears in champagne, peach tart and, our choice, a Hungarian nut torte that was out of this world, accompanied by fragrant coffee in large white cups.

Adding to the dining pleasure at Embree's are votive candles flickering on each table, flowers in vases or floating in small, clear bowls, and classical music on tape. The candles are hand-carried and lit by Jay Embree, who leaves the bar clear across the room to greet and seat arriving patrons.

Day trippers who prefer not to drive home after dinner can get a taste of Embree's fare at Sunday brunch, when seven entrees items are offered in the $5.50 to $8.95 price range.

All in all, Embree's is one of the more appealing places at which we've eaten, the kind of restaurant to which we'd return again and again.

Embree's, Main Street at top of Pleasant Street, Housatonic, Mass. (413) 274-3476. Dinner, Wednesday-Sunday from 6 to 10 or 11; Sunday brunch, 11 to 2. Major credit cards. Reservations suggested.

Also in the Area

Red Lion Inn, Main Street, Stockbridge. (413) 298-5545. Whenever one of our brothers from Montreal is on his not-infrequent business trips to the Berkshires, he stays and dines at the Red Lion Inn. So does almost everyone else from around the world, it seems. Such is the draw and the name of the Red Lion, the quintessential New England inn. Since 1773, it has dominated Stockbridge's Main Street, guests rocking on the wide front porch or sipping cocktails in the front parlor. Public rooms are filled with antique furniture and china, and in one corner the inn's gift shop, the Pink Kitty, is just the ticket for doting grandparents and selective browsers. There's elegant dining in the spacious main dining room, where seafood is featured and entrees run from $9.50 for a vegetarian plate to $18.50 for roast prime rib or double lamb chops. Even more appealing is the dark-paneled Widow Bingham Tavern for a tete-a-tete meal. In warm weather, canvas deck chairs dot the popular outdoor courtyard lined with spectacular impatiens, a colorful and cool spot for lunch, dinner or drinks. The same menu is served inside or out. For lunch ($4 to $8.50), you can get almost anything from creamed chicken or Welsh rarebit to smoked haddock with dill, a sampler of tuna, seafood and turkey salads, or a stuffed potato. Desserts range from rice, bread and Indian puddings to pecan ball with butterscotch sauce and chocolate chip pie. Lunch, daily noon to 2; dinner 6 to 9, Sunday noon to 9, summer 5:30 to 9:30. A light menu is available between meals in the tavern or on the courtyard.

Church Street Cafe, 69 Church St., Lenox. (413) 637-2745. At their small but expanded "American bistro," co-owners Linda Forman and Clayton Hendrick offer fresh, light cafe food inside by the ficus tree or outside on pleasant decks. Blackboard specials supplement the seasonal menus. Lunch items ($3.95 to $5.25) include black bean tostada, a tortilla sandwiched with pinto beans, green chiles, cheese, salsa and sour cream, and an interesting oriental salad of broccoli, water chestnuts, mushrooms, tofu and scallions in a ginger-sesame dressing. The dinner menu is slightly larger and more ambitious. You might start with black bean nachos with salsa and sour cream, grilled chicken satay with spicy peanut sauce, or Nantucket bluefish or smoked Maine trout with horseradish cream. Entrees range from $6.50 for pasta of the day to $13.95 for grilled sirloin steak. Other favorites are grilled lamb chops with pear-ginger chutney, chicken saute with ham, shrimp, white wine and garlic, New Orleans shrimp saute and baked polenta. Huevos rancheros is the most interesting item at brunch. Open daily from 11:30 to 11, to midnight on weekends.

Shaker Mill Tavern, Route 102 and 41, West Stockbridge. (413) 232-8565. A spacious outdoor deck is especially popular at this large, two-story affair with several dining rooms and a greenhouse section filled with plants at one end. The menu is a casual mix of burgers (one has sour cream, avocado and havarti cheese; another guacamole), salads, nachos, chicken wings and stuffed potato skins. Dinner entrees range from $8.95 for baked lasagna to $18.50 for filet mignon in herb butter. Chicken oriental and swordfish kabob are popular. The beer list is extensive and the wines reasonable, and live entertainment is featured frequently. Open seven days in season for breakfast, lunch and dinner; dinner only in winter.

Truc Orient Express, off Main Street beside the Williams River, West Stockbridge. (413) 232-4204. Who wouldn't like this sleek yet charming Vietnamese restaurant which stays open all day year round, whether any patrons are there or not (in the dead of winter, they're often not; in summer, the place is popular at all hours)? Vietnamese music plays in the background and wonderful aromas based on garlic waft from the open kitchen. The occasional communications gap with the Vietnamese family which runs the place is bridged by pointing to the numbers of the 47 items on the exotic menu. The perfectly prepared dishes are as spicy as you like; prices are about $6 at lunch, $8 to $10 for dinner. The "singing chicken" and Mongolian hotpot are great. Open daily from 11 a.m. to 11 p.m.

Sullivan Station, Elm and Railroad streets, Lee. (413) 243-2082. Trains on the old New York, New Haven and Hartford line still pass, delighting diners at this cute, reasonably priced place. The menu is limited mainly to sandwiches, burgers and quiche, served day and night, plus blackboard specials and entrees like veal parmesan with pasta or baked stuffed sole ($7 to $11). A mini-salad bar comes to your table. The railroad theme lovingly executed by Marilyn and Dan Sullivan and their family carries into the ladies' room, which has a plant in an old engine model, and to the new Caboose Gift Shop. In summer there is outdoor dining on the station platform. Open daily, 11:30 to 10; Sunday brunch, 11 to 3.

Noodles, 12 Railroad St., Great Barrington. (413) 528-3003. Founding chef Anthony Cerruto of the popular 20 Railroad Street restaurant moved a couple of doors down the street in 1985 to open Noodles with three young partners. The name indicates the theme — pasta and informality — but hardly prepares you for the prices. We thought we were looking at the lunch menu when we saw the dinner blackboard: appetizers like escargots, mushroom pate, lamb jo-jos and smoked duck with mango ($2.50 to $3.95), four pastas ($3.95 to $4.95) and entrees including four variations of veal, Greek swordfish, sole Jerome, trout with walnuts and Italian fishermen's platter (pasta with swordfish, scallops, mussels and olives), $5.95 to $7.95. Lunch prices are even more remarkable, $2.95 to $5.95. How do they do it? "Volume," answers partner Phil Zagran, and the small place has been crowded since it opened. A huge polished brass espresso machine is perched atop the bar near the entrance; seating is at wooden banquettes or tables in the main dining room, or at a few tables outside on a sidewalk cafe and in the bar. Open daily from 11:30 to 10.

16

Ashley House at Historic Deerfield dates from 1730.

A Village Restoration

Historic Deerfield/Deerfield, Mass.

Something new has been added to Historic Deerfield and naturally it's something old. This restored village in the sleepy Connecticut River Valley — our favorite such spot in all of New England — has been known for years for its beautiful 18th and 19th century buildings. Those buildings have been carefully researched, restored, furnished and opened to the public as museums.

Now there's a new kid on the block — the Ebenezer Hinsdale Williams House — which was opened in the fall of 1984 as a restoration-in-process and will continue as such until it's finished.

It's a first for Historic Deerfield, but it doesn't surprise us. The care with which this historic place is run, and the creativity with which new projects are approached, keep it from getting stale. Visitors who return time and time again, and many do, will tell you the same.

The E.H. Williams House is a pre-Revolutionary building dating from around 1740 and built by the Rev. Ebenezer Hinsdale. It passed into another family but in

17

1816 was bought by Ebenezer Hinsdale Williams, a grand-nephew of the original owner. This descendant modernized the old house lavishly, adding a fashionable low-hipped roof, Federal detailing and a fan-light front doorway, plus meticulously carved interior woodwork.

All of these features survive but have been obscured by subsequent layers of paint. Visitors to the E. H. Williams house have an unusual opportunity to see how the architectural details are featured and salvaged as a building is restored. In order to focus attention on the restoration in progress, the house is being shown empty of furniture.

Yet it is the furnishings — and the textiles, the silver, the ceramics and all of the other rich collections at Historic Deerfield — that cause some visitors to drool when they visit. For others, the construction details of these gorgeous old homes and shops are the drawing card.

We think that the whole is greater than the sum of the parts — particularly here. Deerfield is an extraordinary village to start with, scene of the famed Indian massacre of 1704, home to fine private schools including the renowned Deerfield Academy, beautifully situated among the rich fields fed by the Connecticut River.

Early on, it was attractive to settlers because of its natural endowments. Those settlers, many of them successful farmers, built homes of taste and character. In the 1940s a couple from Greenwich, Conn., Mr. and Mrs. Henry N. Flynt, fell in love with Deerfield and decided it should be preserved for future generations.

The Flynts had come to Deerfield, as so many other families do, to bring their son to school at Deerfield Academy. But they stayed on, for more than 20 years, and painstakingly acquired houses and buildings in the sleepy village — which they restored and filled with outstanding collections of period furnishings.

Unlike other restorations we have known, that at Deerfield is special because the buildings, by and large, are on their original foundations. While many of them flank the village's main road (called simply "The Street") they are not the only ones there. Families, most of them academicians at the three private schools in the village, also live here, work here and play here. There is life going on, just as there is history being preserved.

The Flynts' original purchase was the Deerfield Inn, now a hostelry of some note, but then a sleepy country inn only open during the summer months. They hired a manager to run it, true, but it started their involvement in the village. In fact, they liked Deerfield so much they bought themselves a house — an antique saltbox on The Street, which they restored in the mid-1940s.

In succeeding years the village became their overriding passion. They bought properties, restored them and filled them with antiques of all sorts. They had the advice of experts and the means to purchase extraordinarily valuable items. In a total of about 25 years they personally selected and acquired more than 10,000 different items for Historic Deerfield.

Their selection of a place to do all of this, if somewhat accidental, was brilliant. Bypassed by the progress somehow connoted by highways (Interstate 91 to the west and busy Route 5 to the east), Deerfield was already something of an anachronism when the Flynts "discovered" it. And it was already conscious of its unusually rich historic heritage, from its settlement in 1669 through the massacre of 1704, rebuilding, involvement in the Revolution, and finally serious attempts to preserve the past started in the late 1800s by Deerfielder George Sheldon and his Pocumtuck Valley Memorial Association. (Memorial Hall is open as a separate museum in Deerfield.)

All of that the Flynts had to build on, and they did. They rebuilt, resituated (the Hall Tavern and the Dwight-Barnard house were moved from other locations) and restored. They soon had a pretty big hobby on their hands and they figured they ought to do something about it. While the Allen House was their own personal residence in Deerfield they could, after all, only live in one house. So in 1952, in an upstairs room in their own lovely home, Historic Deerfield was born and set up to protect and continue their efforts.

Houses, a silver museum and tavern have gradually been opened to the public since then. In November 1977, the house in which the Flynts themselves lived was opened to the public to celebrate the 25th anniversary of the association's founding.

Altogether, 12 buildings are exquisitely restored and opened to the public and the historic area is considered by director Donald R. Friary to be more or less complete. As it is, the buildings maintained by Historic Deerfield take a full three days to see and contain 12,000 objects in all.

There is enough at Deerfield to satisfy the most avid collector. While the furniture of Deerfield is known nationwide (the March 1985 issue of Antiques magazine devoted its cover story to the collection), other collections which are exceptionally strong are textiles (Mrs. Flynt's personal interest) and ceramics. "Leading authorities on ceramics come here and are floored," says Friary with conviction.

Something else about Deerfield is special. Its entire collection is always on display. While that makes for a bit of crowding in some rooms in some houses, it means you won't travel all the way from home to view a rare sunflower chest in the Ashley house and not find it. At least under ordinary circumstances, "99 per cent" of the collection is always on view.

You can "do" Deerfield in a variety of ways but you can't in any case see it all in one day. The staff recommends three houses (and various combination tickets for

Location: Deerfield, Mass. off Routes 5 and 10, south of Greenfield. I-91 Exit 24 (northbound) or Exit 25 (southbound).

Open: Year-round, Monday-Saturday 9:30 to 4:30, Sunday 1 to 4:30. Closed Thanksgiving, Christmas Eve, Christmas Day and New Year's Day.

Admission: Varies, depending on houses you wish to visit. Combination tickets to tour three houses are $4.50; a ticket to tour all 12 buildings and valid for one week is $15. Individual admissions to houses — ranging from $1.50 to $3 — can be purchased at the particular house. Children pay the same except in the Hall Tavern and the Frary House, where there are children's tickets at 50 cents each.

Special Events: The Fourth of July is celebrated with a parade and a special program in the Brick Church. Since this is not always held on the Fourth itself, call ahead for details.

Tours-by-Appointment: Groups ranging in size from two to six can have a special tour catering to special interests. These cost $12 per person for a half-day, $20 for a whole day. Reservations are required and may be made by telephone.

Telephone: (413) 774-5581.

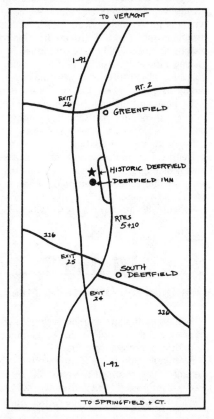

three are sold), but the director says you can possibly do five in a day "if you really push." Don't plan to try unless you're visiting off-season (which means not October, when fully one-fifth of Historic Deerfield's yearly visitors come to enjoy the foliage along with the furniture, or on summer weekends, which are also likely to be busy).

Deerfield is lovely in almost any season, including winter, when the Christmas wreaths stay up on the doors for some time after the holiday, and when you're likely to wind up with a personal tour at a leisurely pace.

First stop is always the Hall Tavern, which serves as a visitors' center and where you can purchase tickets. If you decide on a combination ticket, the "Deerfield Sampler" is a good one for first-timers. Or you can buy tickets to individual houses.

Deerfield recommends the Wells-Thorn House if only one can be seen. It not only happens to be the oldest house in the historic Deerfield restoration but interprets two periods of time, one earlier (1717) and one later (1751), giving a perfect on-site opportunity to compare.

If you've children in tow, by all means visit the Frary House, which is the only building of the 12 not restored by the Flynts but by Miss C. Alice Baker, a cousin of the indomitable George Sheldon and a character in her own right. The Frary House has 14 rooms and 11 fireplaces, and there's a ballroom on the south side, the part of the house once used as a tavern. Best for the children is the "touch it" room, where they are encouraged to explore in their own favorite way every item in the room, including 100-year-old candles made from fat. (They feel just as you'd expect — greasy.)

If you're a collector, a fine furniture enthusiast, or if you'd just like to get a feel for the way the Flynts lived during their years in Deerfield, go to the Allen House, which is individually priced at $3 but well worth it. Here is a treasure trove of furniture, much of it 18th century Connecticut Valley pieces in which Deerfield excels, and you will be open-mouthed when you've finished. The Rev. Jonathan Ashley House is another one for leaving you stunned with the richness of the collection. Its front parlor with matching shell cupboards is, according to some authorities, one of the most beautiful rooms in America.

You can find sustenance during all of this walking and seeing at the Deerfield Inn or in good weather you can picnic outdoors at tables behind the Hall Tavern. Free daily presentations of a slide show are a good orientation to the entire town and help put the pieces together.

Deerfield is one of our favorite places because it's done so well, remains so uncommercial (no advertising, for one thing) and because it genuinely succeeds at what so many have attempted: preserving the past. We've never forgotten the words of one elderly lady, spoken to her companion late one summer afternoon in Deerfield. "It's just a privilege to be here," she said. And so it is.

 **Dining 3**_____

Deerfield Inn/Deerfield, Mass.

It's hard to imagine anyone raising his voice, shrieking with laughter or dropping his cutlery at the Deerfield Inn — the atmosphere is simply too refined for anything more than a discreet murmur.

Seemingly light years from busy Interstate 91 barely a mile away, the serenely elegant dining room of the inn, built in 1884 and rebuilt after a disastrous fire in 1979, is an oasis of graciousness in a bustling world.

With its muted oriental-type carpets, gleaming brass chandeliers, striking Colonial

Main dining room at Deerfield Inn.

cutlery and heavy glassware on the polished mahogany tables, reproduction Chippendale and Duncan Phyfe chairs, portraits on the cream colored sage-trimmed walls, and sconces flanking an antique sideboard, the spacious main dining room seems like that of a private club.

Adding to the club atmosphere is the clientele, which in the fall, winter and spring seems to consist mainly of preparatory school students and their well-heeled parents. A few skiers in the winter find their way to the inn, as do many tourists passing through in all seasons.

The menu, too, is quite dignified, especially at night, when 15 entrees plus specials are offered. They range in price from $12.95 to $17.95 (including soup of the day) and include such specialties as devilled quail, a rack of lamb for one or two, seasoned with tomato and basil, veal masson sauteed with lobster tails, and carpetbag steak stuffed with oysters, among old New England standards. Nantucket smoked mussels and Virginia ham with fresh pears are two of the more unusual appetizers, $3.95 to $5.95.

At noon the menu is more informal with ample sandwiches from $4.25 to $4.95, nicely garnished with cantaloupe slices and potato chips; chef, fruit and spinach salads for $6.95 and a dozen entrees, served with salad and rice pilaf or potato and vegetable.

When we last visited for lunch, feathery hot biscuits were served with a ramekin of sweet butter as we sat down. Drinks came in large glasses and the house wine, a French bordeaux for $3 a glass, was a most generous serving.

One of us made an entire lunch out of the appetizer of New England pate and a hearty French onion soup, almost a meal in itself with plenty of onions, sealed with a thick layer of cheese. The pate, a crumbly combination of veal and chicken liver seasoned with herbs and brandy, also was an ample portion for $3.95. Garnished with fresh mushrooms and julienned carrots on a bed of ruby lettuce, it was served with English mustard and slices of rye toast.

Among entrees, we tried scallops Florentine, a special of the day, a delicate dish accented with garlic and served with spinach. Mixed sauteed vegetables and rice pilaf accompanied, as did a mixed green salad with a creamy house dressing.

From the dessert list, you won't go wrong ordering the apple crisp ($2.50), just like your mother used to make. Piping hot, with a scoop of vanilla ice cream melting into it, it made a soul-satisfying ending, as did strong coffee (served in a silver pot that was left on the table for refills). Coconut cream pie, Indian pudding, bread pudding, pecan pie and grand marnier torte were some other choices.

Other luncheon entrees ($5.25 to $7.95) include fried oysters, lemon sole with lobster newburg sauce, breast of chicken with raspberry sauce, panfried veal liver with shallots and sherry, and a "crepe of New England" combining lobster, scallops, shrimp, crab and haddock in a lobster sauce with sherry, cream and dill havarti.

Downstairs is a coffee shop, where breakfast and lunch are offered cafeteria style. Lunch on the adjacent outdoor patio is popular in summer; you can get hot dogs, hamburgers, french fries and such.

The inn's recently opened bakery offers a selection of pies, cakes and other desserts to go.

Rebuilt and expanded following the 1979 fire, the inn has 23 attractive guest rooms, each with private bath, in the original white frame structure and a barnwood structure out back. The antiques-filled lobby, the yellow Beehive Parlor and the bar with Windsor chairs at old tables of assorted shapes and sizes are inviting as well, and antiques lovers cherish the selection of furnishings from the private collection of Mr. and Mrs. Henry N. Flynt, founders of Historic Deerfield and the force behind the restoration of the inn.

Altogether, the Deerfield Inn is a fine place for a leisurely meal enhanced by a genteel air and a profound sense of history.

Deerfield Inn, Main Street, Deerfield, Mass. (413) 774-2359.Open daily, lunch noon to 2, dinner 6 to 9. Reservations recommended. Major credit cards.

Also in the Area

Bricker's, Intersection of Route 2 and I-91, Greenfield. (413) 774-2857. In the old Turnbull's Green Mountain Ice Cream factory and aptly named (thousands of red bricks inside and out), Bricker's opened in 1984 and provides a more casual alternative for dining near Deerfield. To the left as you enter is a sunken lounge with many couches and upholstered chairs in dark blue Laura Ashley-like fabric. A stunning iron chandelier has a twin in owner Herm Manacity's restaurant in the middle of town, Herm's. On the right is the dining area, filled with handsome booths and bare wood tables, and an airy dining porch in front. Apricot fabric hanging from polished brass rails separates some of the spaces. The same menu is used all day, with dinner entrees available after 4:30. A plain hamburger is $2.95; many add-ons are 30 cents to $1.05. Sandwiches include hot pita pockets, scallop or clam rolls, reubens and clubs and you can get tacos, omelets, quiche and salad plates (Caesar is $4.95). Dinner entrees are $7.95 to $14.95 (for filet mignon with bordelaise sauce) and prices include the salad bar. Scallops marengo, sole Florentine, roast duck and veal castelli romano (with mushrooms, Italian sausage and Madeira sauce) are a few. Among light dinners ($3.95 to $6.95) are liver and onions, an eggplant casserole and a broiled six-ounce sirloin. The wine list is fairly extensive and reasonable. Open daily, 11:30 to 9:30 or 10:30.

Famous Bill's, 30 Federal St., Greenfield. (413) 773-9230. Famous by virtue of longevity, if nothing else, is this crowded establishment of the old school. The sign outside proclaims jumbo shrimps, lamb chops and lobster. The large, family-style dining room with booths and tables is congested and noisy, but the crowd doesn't seem to mind. Lunch specials might be baked scrod with potato and cole slaw or sirloin tips and rice in burgundy sauce, both $3.95. Ten early bird special dinners from $4.95 for chicken cordon bleu to $7.95 for mini prime rib draw crowds Tuesday through Friday from 4 to 6. There's a children's menu, plus a no-nonsense dinner menu offering everything tried and true at reasonable prices. Open daily except Monday from 11a.m. to 11 p.m.

Plumbley's Off the Common, 30 Boltwood Walk, Amherst. (413) 253-9586. A large, strikingly yellow Georgian-style frame house, just off the main green in the college town of Amherst, houses Plumbley's and, in the basement, a more casual establishment called Webster's. Appropriate, for the land the restaurant stands on was once the garden and orchard of Noah Webster, who lived here from 1812 to 1822. Five rather ornate rooms (mirrors, floral wallpaper, glass-covered tables with burgundy napkins) seat 145 diners who can choose from a somewhat casual menu. Omelets, stuffed baked potatoes, sandwiches (the Amherst club is an educated turkey club) and salads are moderately priced; dinner entrees are from $7.95 for broiled orange whiskey chicken to $12.50 for prime ribs or Webster's plate, sliced tenderloin topped with crabmeat, broccoli and hollandaise sauce. The three or four seafood entrees change nightly, depending upon availability. Sunday brunch (from 10 to 2) features an always-changing menu. The house wine, Taylor California cellars, is $1.50 a glass, $5.25 a full carafe. Desserts ($1.50 to $2.95) include mud pie, raspberry walnut torte and chocolate chip cookie sundae. The same menu is served downstairs in the evening at Webster's, with its walls of fieldstone and brick, and rust and green color scheme. Open daily, 11:30 to 9:30 or 10:30.

Quinton's, 7 Armory St., Northampton. (413) 586-6656. The most stylish restaurant in Northampton, which has more than its share, is this tiny place, opened in 1984 just off Pleasant Street by southern-born Quinton Baker. His hand-printed menu changes often but could include such goodies as, for first courses ($3 to $7.25), duck consomme with wild rice, fettuccine with lobster and tarragon or spinach salad with walnut truffle vinaigrette, and for entrees ($11.50 to $18), Louisiana shrimp Creole, Cajun blackened red fish or veal sweetbreads with lobster sauce. Desserts might be eclairs filled with hazelnut and amaretto pastry cream, hot buttered rum cake with ice cream and butter rum sauce or apple souffle. Wine and beer only are served; the house blanc de blanc is $2 a glass. A spotlit jungle of plants is over the front door; one white brick wall is decorated with hooked rugs in unusual shapes, and there are pretty stained-glass windows. Gray and burgundy linens, track lighting and gorgeous fresh flowers complete the decor. Next door is **The Lighter Side,** a cafe and takeout place, with three booths and a couple of tables. Several menu items from Quinton's are available here, plus soups, stews, interesting sandwiches, omelets, pasta primavera, spanikopita, moules mariniere and all the wonderful desserts. You also can get wine and beer, and candles glow at night. Hours are ll:30 to 3 for lunch; 6:30 to 11:30 for evening and after-theater fare. Quinton's is open from 5:30 to 10:30. Both are closed Sunday and Monday.

North Star, 8 Green St. at West Street, Northampton. (413) 586-9409. Front windows filled with sand and fake sea creatures (a glass lobster, for one) tell you this has got to be a seafood restaurant. Owner Ken Shapiro says his Chinese partner informs him that the Chinese god of the North Star is the god of higher education for women, a meaningful coincidence when you realize that Smith College is across the street. Enter through a room with a giant TV screen where homemade hot salsa and crisp tortilla chips line the handsome bar. One of the two dining rooms is oriental in feeling; both have pale blue cloths with navy overlays, a tulip in a white vase on each table, and comfortable cane and chrome chairs. The sushi here is outstanding; several kinds are available as a platter or a la carte. Otherwise, at lunch (sandwiches $2.95 to $3.50, entrees $4.95 to $8.25) you could choose something like clams carissi, haddock Mediterranean or fresh tuna salad. Dinner entrees, mostly under $12, embrace everything from bouillabaisse Marseilles to six shrimp concoctions, one Indonesian. A few vegetarian and meat dishes appeal to those who don't want seafood, and everyone loves the homemade sour cream apple pie and Bea's brownies. In season, you can dine on a pleasant rear patio where window boxes are filled with flowers and herbs are grown for the kitchen. North Star has an exceptional selection of beers and, of course, a good list of white wines. Lunch, 11:30 to 2:30; dinner, 5:30 to 10:30. Closed Monday.

Hot Tomato's, 12 Crafts Ave., Northampton. (413) 584-0010. This is a branch of a restaurant popular in our hometown, Hartford. Although the food is about the same, the ambiance is much more posh, since this one occupies the space of the former Andiamo, a suave establishment. The front of the restaurant is the Cafe Pomidoro, where you can order Sicilian pizza with many toppings, calzones, fried mozzarella, mussel soup, lasagna and desserts. In back, on two levels with wine-colored tablecloths, brass rails and some fascinating pictures and photographs of tomatoes is the main restaurant, with an extensive menu of pastas, cioppino, chicken and shrimp dishes, $6.50 to $12.95. Pasta pomidoro has artichoke hearts, broccoli and prosciutto in a dill cream sauce over tomato fettuccine. The wines are all Italian, with many choices one does not often see, starting at $8. We got some herb fettuccine ($2.50 a pound) and meat sauce ($2) from the takeout counter and enjoyed a late dinner at home. Open daily from 5 p.m., until 9 or 10 in dining room, 10 or 11 in cafe.

Paul & Elizabeth's, 150 Main St., Northampton. (413) 584-4832. Thorne's Marketplace, a warren of shops in a recycled department store, is the locale for this well-respected natural foods restaurant, basically vegetarian but offering fish as well. It's a large room with exposed pipes, Japanese-style paper globe lights and daisies on the tables, with a focal point of an old cast-iron stove. At lunch you could try a hummus or tabouli salad, an omelet, or vegetables tempura — nothing is more than $4.25. Whole grain noodles are the main ingredient in some of the evening dishes; with fried tofu, fish or vegetable tempura or pan fried with vegetable sauce. Deluxe tempura at $9.95 is by far the most expensive dinner item. Herb tea by the pot is 85 cents; wine and beer are available. Indian pudding, mocha custard and fresh fruit crunches are some of the desserts. Open noon to 9:30 or 10, closed Sunday.

Jialih's, 32 Pleasant St., Northampton. (413) 584-8242. Jialih Simeral, a pleasant Japanese woman who owns this new in 1984 restaurant with husband Wilfred, stands behind the counter and makes the sushi ($14.75 for a large platter). The long high-ceilinged room is handsomely plain with bleached wood walls and furniture, but with ornate crystal chandeliers. Noon dishes are $2.95 (vegetarian delight) to $4.25 (shish kabob); quiches, pork dumplings and udon (noodle) dishes are offered. Price-fixed dinners are $9.50 or $13.25; the latter include fuki plum duck, soft-shell crabs or bouillabaisse a la Japonaise. A la carte entrees are $6.95 to $9.25, except for sushi. Aperitifs, sake and some wines by the glass ($1.50 for Mondavi white) are listed, as is Suntory, a Japanese beer, $2. From 11:30 to 3 Sunday brunch is offered for $6.95.

Daytrip 4 _____

Thornton Burgess's house at Laughing Brook.

A Place for Peter Rabbit

Laughing Brook / Hampden, Mass.

Jimmy Skunk, Billy Possum, Prickly Porky Porcupine, Blacky Crow, Reddy Fox and Peter Rabbit — they're all here. And there couldn't be a better spot than the small outdoor zoo on the grounds of the late Thornton W. Burgess's home in Hampden, Mass. — the very place where the lovable author of nature stories brought the little animals of the woods to life in his books.

Besides visiting the small zoo, with its cages tucked into the woods near the brook for which the area is named, you can hike over several miles of marked trails, stop by the nature center, the live animal center or the new environmental center, and even view the studio where Burgess wrote. If you are here in the winter, you're welcome to cross-country ski. For the blind or visually handicapped, there is the Crooked Little Path, a "touch and see" trail with guide rope, signs in braille and animals along the way (owls, an eagle, white-tailed deer). It's not a bad lesson to have sighted children go through blindfolded.

Burgess was a Bay Stater by birth (born in Sandwich, Mass.), but it was at the little Cape Cod house on Hampden's Main Street that he wrote most of the 75 books that have become famous with generations of children. His column was syndicated nationwide in newspapers, including the old Herald-Tribune, for many years; adults may remember him from that contact.

He bought the 18th century house in 1928 as a summer home (he was living in nearby Springfield at the time) but soon moved out to Hampden year-round, finding the ambience of the woods and streams conducive to his writing.

Here in the quiet of the Massachusetts countryside, Burgess wrote the marvelous "Mother West Wind" stories which have become children's classics. Burgess's own life wasn't actually the easiest or most serene, but he managed to maintain the happy outlook and love of nature that characterize the thousands of stories he penned, and that made him a favorite of neighbors in Hampden. Although his father died when he was but a year old, he seems to have spent a happy childhood learning the secrets of nature on Cape Cod which would stand him in good stead in later life.

He didn't plan to write. But he was widowed early in his marriage and left with a young son whom he used to delight with a nature story every night at bedtime. When the youngster was sent to visit grandparents in the Midwest for a vacation, he became homesick for his father and the stories, so Burgess began to write a different story every day, which he then mailed to his son. That was the start of a lifetime dedication — and a new occupation.

Burgess died in 1965 at age 91 and there was some scrambling by his friends in town to prevent the house from being sold privately. The Lions Club paid $500 for an option on the property and was able to interest the Massachusetts Audubon Society into purchasing and maintaining the site. Since then, donations of acreage have enlarged the area to its present substantial size — 260 acres.

Building has continued as well. In 1980 a new Environmental Center with a solar greenhouse, which provides heat for one-third of the building, was dedicated. This center contains a resource library with more than 3,000 volumes on natural history and environmental topics, an art gallery featuring exhibits by local and regional natural history artists, a composting toilet and interpretive exhibit monitored by the Massachusetts Division of Water Pollution Control, and a natural history-oriented gift shop with a complete selection of natural history books, bird feeders, binoculars, field guides and fine gifts. There's also an auditorium for special programs; during December the gift shop takes over the auditorium and turns it into a very special place to shop for Christmas.

Finally, there is the Thornton Burgess house, and it should not be missed. It is open weekends and holidays during the winter from noon to 3 p.m. and daily June 15 through Oct. 15 from 11 a.m. to 3 p.m., but if you really want to visit the house, call ahead to make sure the schedule is as you expect.

The staff at Laughing Brook offers a number of special days throughout the year, ranging from Family Day in June to a Halloween family night in October. Every Sunday at 2 p.m. finds a particular activity scheduled; these may range from a nature film in the auditorium to a guided walk on one of the trails to a talk by a naturalist on birds or animals of the area. Admission to these Sunday programs is included with regular admission to Laughing Brook.

Walking around the sanctuary on one of the trails named after places in Burgess's books (Green Forest Trail, Striped Chipmunk Trail, Moccasin Trail) is a fun part of the visit.

A quote of Burgess's sums up the experience: "Nature was the first teacher...and is still the universal teacher. In the study of nature lies the key to the most successful mental, moral and spiritual development of the child."

Also in the Area

Norcross Wildlife Sanctuary, Peck Road, Wales. (413) 267-9654. This 3,000-acre wildlife sanctuary, established in 1939 by Arthur D. Norcross of the card company, is an extraordinary piece of real estate. The wooded hills, the lakes and streams are maintained by the Norcross Wildlife Foundation, an active group engaged in conservation for the benefit of the public. There is a particular abundance of wildflowers, many of unusual varieties, as well as ferns, including such rare varieties as the Scott's spleenwort. Fern enthusiasts have a whole Fern Area to

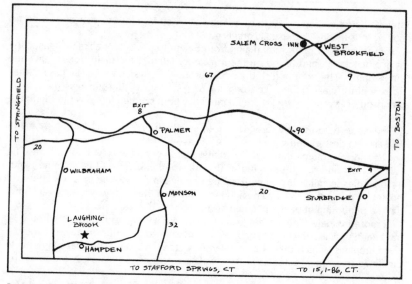

Location: 789 Main St., Hampden, Mass. Reached from Route 83 (west of Hampden) or Route 32 (east of Hampden). Via Massachusetts Turnpike take Exit 8, go south on Route 32, watch for signs for Hampden, which is about 6 1/2 miles west of Monson.

Open: Year-round, Tuesday-Sunday 10 to 5; closed Mondays.

Admission: Adults, $3; children under 16, $1.50; senior citizens, $1.50.

Telephone: (413) 566-8034.

visit, in fact. The Circle Garden, on an island formed by a brook, is another delight. There are two small museums on the site, hiking trails and picnic area, although no food is sold. A wide variety of courses is offered throughout the year. There is no charge to visit the museum or use the trails. The trails are essentially self-guiding and well-marked and the amount of time you spend here depends on how involved you want to get with the flora and fauna. At various times we have encountered deer, mourning doves, foxes and other wild animals. The sanctuary is open year-round, Monday-Saturday 8:30 to 5.

 **Dining 4**

Salem Cross Inn/West Brookfield, Mass.

"He goes not out of his way who journies to a fine inn."

This quote is on the cover of the Salem Cross Inn matchbooks and is particularly apropos. A bit off the beaten path in West Brookfield, Mass., this is a gem among old country inns. Its history, ambience and food combine to make it the essence of New England, popular with tourists and residents alike.

Listed on the National Register of Historic Places, the sprawling inn contains an attractive downstairs bar, several large rooms used for private parties, interesting planters and tables fashioned from massive tree trunks and enough memorabilia to warrant the offering of guided tours.

In an area historic in Indian wars, the main house was built around 1720. Interestingly, it has been restored and expanded by a family of Syrian brothers with the last name of Salem. Richard Salem, who first bought the structure to be his home, runs the inn and usually greets guests.

A crossed witch mark, emanating from Salem to protect inhabitants against the evils of witchcraft and found on the front door latch of the main house, gave the inn its name. The door, which the family proudly shows on tours, still has its small 18th century glass panes. The original King's Grant of the inn was made to a grandson of Peregrine White, the Pilgrim baby born on the Mayflower in Plymouth Harbor.

The cross, a handsome design, is used as a logo on the parchment-type menu and also on dessert and wine lists.

The spacious main dining room is rather typical of an old New England inn. The ceiling is low and rough-plastered, with dark wooden beams. On a summer night, fresh zinnias in miniature Mateus-shaped bottles and a candle in a wrought-iron holder brighten every table. The lighting is dim and the large windows reveal, until dark, a panorama of beautiful green lawns, trees and white fences.

A more intimate dining area goes off the main room into the original house. It has beautiful walls of wide plank boards, some horizontal and some vertical, and a huge fireplace, which makes it popular in winter. Two perfectly charming private dining rooms, their round tables set with pewter service plates, are also in the original house.

In season, cocktails and lunch (entrees, $4.95 to $5.95) are offered outside on a rear terrace. In summer, there are monthly outdoor drovers roasts, featuring cauldrons of chowder and 300-pound beef roasts skewered in a fieldstone pit. In late fall through spring, hearthside dinners on certain Friday evenings include a hay or sleigh ride, roasts cooked on the nation's only operating roasting jack and breads from a beehive oven.

At dinner, except for a Middle Eastern specialty, homus b'taheenie, the appetizers are fairly standard, ranging from 75 cents for California tomato juice to $4.95 for shrimp cocktail or Cotuit oysters on the half shell. The homus is a zesty mixture of chick peas, garlic, lemon juice and sesame seeds, topped with chopped onion and served with Syrian pita bread.

Before our cocktails arrived, we were served all kinds of food, including our appetizers. Crackers and butter came right away, then a basket of hot rolls and sticky buns, followed by a relish tray with cottage cheese and three kinds of spicy relishes.

For entrees, broiled scrod ($9.50) was fresh and moist, perfectly done, and served with lemon butter. The excellent baked stuffed scallops ($12.50) were served in a ramekin with plenty of butter and crumbs.

With these we had an herbed pilaf of Mediterranean rice, and a choice of steamed zucchini, peas, sliced tomatoes or boiled onions. Salad was a large bowl of crisp greens with the house dressing, a tart creamy Italian. A waitress went from table to table offering steaming hot ears of corn to anyone with room left to try.

Entrees range from $7.95 to $16.25 (filet mignon) and there are different specials every day. House specialties are sauteed pork tenderloin, calves liver and bacon, breast of chicken, baked stuffed filet of sole ambassador and fried scallops.

A small wine list on every table offers a few popular and reasonable wines, including the house Almaden, $1.95 a glass. By asking, you may see a larger list with upwards of 100 choices, including pricy vintage wines. We tried a featured special, an estate-bottled Chablis Vaillon for $10, delightfully dry and light.

Children have a choice of three dinners at $5.95, including soup or juice and dessert or, for those under 10, a child's portion of any other dinner for $1 less than the regular price. One of ours had seafood newburg, a special.

Special pie of the day was a mouth-watering Bavarian cream, and the nut roll with claret sauce, old-fashioned pecan bread pudding with fruited sauce, and baked Indian pudding with whipped or ice cream sound interesting.

With good big cups of coffee, we tried a small glass of the liqueur Strega, described on the dessert list as the Italian name for witch. As we headed back home, we felt that we had been well fed and for a short time protected from witchcraft.

Salem Cross Inn, Route 9, West Brookfield, Mass. (617) 867-2345. Two miles west of West Brookfield on Ware Road. Open in season, Tuesday-Friday noon to 9, Saturday 5 to 10, Sunday noon to 8. Closed Mondays except holidays. Major credit cards. Reservations recommended nights and weekends.

Also in the Area

The Whistling Swan, 502 Main St., Sturbridge. (617) 347-2321. This imposing white Greek Revival house built in 1855 has been restored by the Lofgren family, who added to it an old barn to which they gave wonderful fanlight windows, enhancing the facade. Three fairly formal dining rooms occupy the original house; the barn holds the Ugly Duckling Lounge upstairs. Outdoor dining on a brick patio under black and white umbrellas is offered in summer. The varied menu offers something for everyone; at lunch omelets, salads (one is marinated mussels and potatoes on spinach), sandwiches on various kinds of breads or croissants, stuffed potato skins and many daily specials. The lobster bisque was heartier than most; combined with an appetizer of four huge shrimp in beer batter, served with two sauces, it made a fine lunch. The pasta primavera salad (at $8.95 one of the most expensive things on the menu) was more than one person could handle, with shrimp, scallops, peas, broccoli, spinach and more, on top of a mound of fettuccine, with a large pitcher of delicious basil cream dressing. Hot fudge peanut butter parfait, macadamia nut⁺ pie, chocolate mousse loaf with creme anglaise, bread-pudding with whiskey sauce, chocolate almond pie and creme brulee are all home-made and good desserts. At night, when children have a choice of four entrees for $5.95 (with beverage and ice cream), grownup entrees range from $8.95 for calamari over linguini with marinara sauce to $17.95 for filet mignon choron. Medallions of veal in a three-mustard sauce, veal with garlic, pork normande and seafood bounty are appealing choices. The large wine list offers many bottles under $11. Open Tuesday-Sunday, lunch 11:30 to 2:30, dinner 5:30 to 9:30.

Crabapple's, Haynes Street, Sturbridge. (617) 347-9555. Located in the former Orchard Inn and opened in 1983 to accommodate the overflow from the historic Publick House, this is popular with families and singles. Apples are the theme (down to bright red cloths and green and white checked napkins), scores of baskets (some bushel) and even a bicycle hang from the ceiling, Tiffany-type lamps brighten the booths, and a small area has booths separated by chicken wire and is decorated to look like a chicken coop. A covered outdoor terrace offers lunch, snacks and cocktails in season. Steaks, swordfish and burgers are grilled with mesquite, dinner entrees range from $4.25 for pasta primavera to $10.50 for stuffed shrimp, with items like pork tenderloin picatta and seafood pie bargains for under $7. At lunch you'll find many of the same items plus croissants, omelets, salads and such. Wines are pleasantly priced, and cranberry apple wine is available by carafe or glass. Open daily from 11:30.

La Difference, 548 Main St., Hampden. (413) 566-5015. Innovative chef Pamela Yahn returned to home territory after six years' service on the Mississippi Delta Queen and opened an intimate restaurant in the former Picot's Place in late 1984. The Parisian-style decor continues, but Miss Yahn has spiffed up the front porch with thick gray carpeting and striking chrome and cane ladder back chairs. She also planned to enclose the courtyard entrance and refurbish other rooms. The most notable difference is the dinner fare: How about specials like pompano en papilotte, oyster crepes Lafitte topped with prawns or scallops with their roe from the Isle of Man, served with a julienne of leek, mushroom and truffle? The regular menu is no less ambitious, the more so since Miss Yahn is assisted only by a sous-chef. Soups and appetizers ($3 to $5.75) include Cajun gumbo, shrimp with cognac and gruyere cheese, pasta with red and black caviar and oysters Bienville. Among entrees ($12 to $19) are shrimp Creole, coho salmon, roast duckling cassis, tournedos with artichokes and Louisiana prawns, lamb chops Dijonnaise, and veal and lobster Pamela, a specialty served with watercress sauce. Desserts include strawberries Romanoff, New Orleans bread pudding with whiskey sauce, raspberry-poached pears with pistachios and chocolate mousse cheesecake. The wine list is as well chosen as the menu. Dinner, Wednesday-Saturday 5 to 9 or 10; Sunday, brunch 10 to 2, dinner 3:30 to 8.

L'Amitie, 674 Bliss Road, Longmeadow. (413) 567-3339. Susan and Forbes Dodge of Yesteryears on Cape Cod were persuaded by the founder of the Friendly Ice Cream chain to move to Longmeadow and open an elegant French restaurant to complement Friendly's at the other end of his Longmeadow Shops mall — hence the name, meaning "warm friendship." The setting is worthy of its numerous awards: upholstered Louis XVI chairs at well-spaced tables on two levels, fresh flowers and pink linens, mirrored walls with tiny lamps in sconces and portals filled with flowers. The menu is French-American nouvelle. Among appetizers is scotch smoked salmon with golden caviar and lemon-pepper vodka ($5.50). Entrees from $10.95 to $18.50 include duck breast with a wild mushroom timbale, braised bay scallops and oysters on spinach pasta with pernod cream sauce, pork provencale and steak Diane. An appealing earlybird menu for $9.95 is available from 5 to 6:30 daily and 3 to 6:30 Sunday. The wine list, heavy on imports, is one of the region's most extensive. Lunch entrees (4.95 to $8.95) include omelets with sauteed potatoes, exotic salads and broiled Norwegian salmon or chicken livers Madeira with spaetzle. Lunch, Monday-Saturday 11:30 to 2:30; dinner, 5 to 10; Sunday, brunch 11 to 3, dinner 3 to 9.

Valhalla at Quabog Country Club, Route 32, Monson. (413) 267-3800. The folks at Laughing Brook often refer inquirers to "the country club in Monson" for the $3.50 luncheon buffet. For good reason: The public can fill up from a tableful of salads, vegetables, and hot meat and fish entrees, plus dessert, with a view of the golf course outside. The regular menu is equally wallet-pleasing, $1.95 for a hamburger or BLT to $6.50 for broiled scallops. Lunch, Monday-Friday noon to 2; dinner, Thursday-Saturday.

Soup to Nuts, 559 Main St., Sturbridge. (617) 347-9771. In the Millyard Marketplace, a complex of antique and gift stores, is this cute little cafe and specialty food store seating 40 in a high-ceilinged, white-brick-walled room, part of which overlooks the promenade of shoppers. For a quick, inexpensive breakfast or lunch, this is a good place to know about. Hot Irish soda bread or homemade cinnamon toast are some choices at breakfast; homemade soups like spring lentil or creamy tomato rice are available at lunchtime, when pocket sandwiches are popular. Crab boat is the most expensive at $3.75. A cup of soup, quiche (made with aged Swiss cheese) and salad is $4.15. Domestic and imported beers are available and Taylor California Cellars wine is $1.25 a glass. You can take home a loaf of bread from the nuns of the Priory in Harvard, Mass., plus a jar of Trappist jam or a Ruffled Truffle dip. Breakfast daily from 8 a.m., lunch from 11:30 to 5:30.

Daytrip 5

Great Hall at Higgins Armory Museum.

For Knights: The Shining Armor

Higgins Armory Museum/Worcester, Mass.

If you've been enchanted by the idea of "knights in shining armor," you can at least see what the armor was like at the Higgins Armory Museum in Worcester. When you get through looking, you may decide that once he was dressed up in all that forged metal, it's a wonder a knight could even move.

More than 60 medieval suits of armor are displayed in this unusual museum, making it one of the largest collections of armor in the world. Add to that thousands of related objects — and even a suit of armor for a dog — and you can see why children, especially, have a good time here.

31

Museum founder John Woodman Higgins was a Worcester native who, on a schoolboy trip to Europe, rather precociously purchased his first suit of armor and brought it home with him. That was the beginning of a lifelong fascination with the art of the armorer, appropriate indeed when Higgins grew older and became president of the Worcester Pressed Steel Company. He became so involved with his hobby that right next door to his manufacturing plant he had a four-story museum building of steel and glass erected in 1931.

That's more than 50 years ago, and the Higgins Armory Museum has been in business ever since, still luring schoolboys (there were a few there on a Saturday morning when we visited) who peer at the intricate coats of mail, the suits themselves, and the weaponry, and imagine what it must have been like.

It must have been heavy and awkward to be dressed up in a suit that weighed 60 to 100 pounds and be expected to fight or joust in it. That's one impression we and our children carried home after an enthralling morning at the Higgins. Others were the subtle differences between one suit and another, the various styles and degrees of ornamentation, and some particularly unusual features such as face pieces that look like animals or a suit of Italian parade armor that had representations of faces on each shoulder.

The children with us were not only delighted by the dog's suit of armor (which was fashioned from a German breastplate by a staffer at the Metropolitan Museum of Art) but by the child-sized armor against which they could measure themselves.

The mood of the museum is enhanced by the interior architectural styling. While it's all glass and steel and looks like a modern industrial building on the outside, the Gothic Hall inside — modeled on the hall of the Hohenwerfen Castle outside Salzburg, Austria — evokes the proper mood. A full two floors in height, it has stained-glass windows and Gothic arches which add to the sense of authenticity.

The way to see the museum, the only one devoted exclusively to armor in this country, is to start on the fourth-floor balcony which overlooks the main hall. It includes exhibits on ancient armor and implements, such as projectile points of stone from as far back as the Stone Age, and Greek helmets dating from 600 B.C.

Possibly the best display on the floor is the Roman horse armor, made of iron scales and woven fabric, loaned to the museum by the Gallery of Fine Arts at Yale. The stained-glass exhibit was disappointing in that it was entirely reproductions of famous windows in cathedrals of Europe, often done in a smaller size, and displayed in a dark alcove where they could not be seen to best advantage.

It is downstairs in the Gothic Hall that the bulk of the collection is shown. This is a genuine treasure trove, displayed on mannequins up and down the length of the hall, without many ropes or glass cases to impede one's scrutiny. In fact, you can get very close to the armor here, which is one of the best parts about it. With a little care the visitor can examine it from all angles, slowly, and to his satisfaction.

The suits of armor are not all alike. We'd had some misgivings before our trip, wondering whether we and our children would feel that once we'd seen one suit of armor, we'd seen them all. That was definitely not the case.

Traveling in a counter clockwise direction about the great hall, which is roughly chronologically, we came quickly to the "touch table" where children (and adults) may finger mail, a helmet and breastplate. Above the table is a diagram of a full set of armor with each part identified in four languages. This is a helpful introduction to a new vocabulary (pauldrons, ventails, rondels, falds and the like) and takes the psychological pressure off by providing an opportunity to do what we all want to do: touch the stuff.

All of the armor except for one suit is authentic. Several are, however, composites. Full suits of medieval armor are relatively rare but there are some beautiful ones to be seen here. We remember the armor of Franz vonTeuffenbach (German,

Location: 100 Barber Ave., Worcester, Mass. Exit 19 from I-290.Take Burncoat Street to Randolph Road. Armory is at corner of Randolph and Barber.

Open: Tuesday-Friday 9 to 5; Saturday, Sunday and holidays noon to 5. Closed Mondays except in July and August, and New Year's Day, Thanksgiving and Christmas.

Special Events: Films shown Saturday and Sunday at 2:30 p.m.

Admission: Adults, $2.50; seniors, $1; children 5 to 16, $1.25.

Telephone: (617) 853-6015.

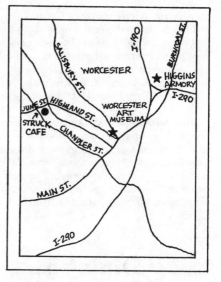

1554), a beautifully etched suit which probably took a few years to make.

The dog's armor, while recreated in modern times, would have been worn by an animal when on a wild boar hunt to protect the dog from the tusks of the quarry.

Maximilian armor, typically fluted in rows of three and so called because it was in vogue during the reign of Maximilian, was on display in a couple of different versions: A suit of French embossed parade armor from the 16th century was very elaborate, with the relief of famous battles displayed on the metal.

About midway in the hall, you can stop at the re-creation of an armorer's forge, showing the instruments which would have been used in the creation of the suits of armor.

In addition to the armor, you will want to examine shields, breastplates, lances, crossbows and one particularly gruesome weapon, the flail. Several oil paintings depict scenes of armorers preparing suits in their forges.

The gift shop at the Higgins is a find for parents, particularly those planning birthday parties for little boys and girls. Prices are still fairly low: post cards for 10 and 15 cents; dog-in-armor T-shirts and Knight-shirts; books on chivalry, heraldry, castles and the like.

The museum was handed over to the community of Worcester by the Higgins family in 1978 and a major fund drive was under way to expand the exhibition space and add an exhibit and banquet hall as well as an orientation theater.

Also in the Area

Worcester Art Museum, 55 Salisbury St., Worcester. (617) 799-4406. With a fine, well-rounded collection, New England's second largest museum, founded in 1896, has been attracting many out-of-towners lately. The original building has been expanded with five additions, the most recent the Frances L. Hiatt Wing in 1983. Particularly strong among the museum's European paintings is the 17th-century Dutch collection, with landscapes, still lifes, genre scenes and portraits by artists like Rembrandt and Ruisdael. The collection of early American art claims the finest examples of 17th-century American portraits in existence. Ten Roman mosaics excavated in the 1930s from Syria, dating from the Second Century, are displayed in the Renaissance Court. Classical sculpture, Eyptian, Persian, Indian and Far Eastern art also are exhibited, and a new gallery of American Decorative Arts opened in May 1985. This is a museum in the vanguard: The Norton Company's 1985 centennial exhibition, "John Frederick Kennett: An American Master," opened in Worcester before moving to the Los Angeles County Museum of Art and the Metropolitan in New York. Open year-round, Tuesday-Saturday 10 to 5, Sunday 1 to 5. Closed Mondays and major holidays. Free.

Worcester Science Center, Harrington Way, Worcester. (617) 791-9211. This is a "see and do" museum which kids love. Polar bears — including one born here — are always fun, and there are some nature trails and a three-kilometer railroad ride which tours the 60-acre site of the museum. Inside are exhibits (recently one of nature photographs), an optical illusion exhibit, and an "omnisphere" which is planetarium, oceanarium, etc., rolled into one with daily shows. Open year-round, Monday-Saturday 10 to 5, Sunday noon to 5. Adults, $3; children, $2.25.

 **Dining 5**

Struck Cafe/Worcester, Mass.

We've always been partial to restaurants that show the personality of the owners, quirks and all, and this small store front cafe has personality to burn. Formerly a vegetarian restaurant called the Struck of Loke, it was acquired in 1979 by Jeff and Barbara Cotter, she the self-trained chef, helped along by classes in Boston with some well-known chefs. "We didn't know much about cooking then," says gregarious Jeff, "but we gave it a shot."

After six years, Struck Cafe is considered one of the most innovative restaurants in the area. Its colorful rainbow sign over the facade of blue tiles and store windows filled with plants hints of an unconventional interior. The 45-seat cafe has chairs of every description, most obtained at tag sales as we suppose the mismatched and charming china was. The walls are covered with works of local artists, for sale. People pitch their coats onto a couple of free-standing coat racks (ours promptly fell over, which caused a momentary stir). The whole thing is finished off perfectly by a huge and colorful rainbow that climbs the side wall from the entrance, meanders over the ceiling and down the far wall at the rear.

Tables are nicely set with white cloths and purple napkins, a votive candle in a small glass dish, and fresh flowers in crystal vases. A glassed-in case backing up to the kitchen contains the elaborate desserts offered here.

Classical music plays softly, and two fans on the ceiling whir around — a bit off-putting to us but at least taking care of cigaret smoke. Service, when we had dinner, was slightly hectic, as two young servers had to take care of the entire place, but it was competent and cordial.

From the fairly priced and fairly extensive wine list (Struck has a beer and wine license only), we chose a Marten muscadet for $9.50. It was served in a tin ice bucket on the table. Fetzer chardonnay at $12.50 and Latour beaujolais villages at $11.50 also appealed among choices priced from $9 to $27.

The house salad exudes personality. It's a mixture of romaine and cabbage, all chopped up and topped with a good vinaigrette that includes grated cheese, and is served in a glass banana-split dish, one big leaf of romaine hanging over the side. Garnished on one end with a long slice of cucumber and on the other with a

Dining room at Struck Cafe.

diagonally sliced piece of carrot, it's a sight to behold. With this comes the bread tray; you may choose among excellent banana, lemon and carrot pineapple breads, which also are for sale. You may feel, as we do,that these are more appropriate for the tea hour, but there is no denying that they are delicious.

French onion soup is always on the menu, plus a soup of the day (mushroom bisque at our visit). Spinach balls rolled in sesame seeds and hummus are two of the limited selection of appetizers.

It's in the entrees where the creativity of the chef shines; every night provimi veal, filet mignon, breast of chicken and seafood of the season are served in varied ways, and then there are several other choices on a blackboard menu. Ranging in price from about $12.95 to $17.95 (for rack of lamb persilade), they could include one of the specialties of the house, veal frangelico, served with a sauce made of the liqueur and heavy cream, pistachios and almonds.

Veal might also be served with a three-mustard sauce, with fresh asparagus and mozzarella cheese, or with shrimp, julienned zucchini, summer squash and onion and seven Cajun spices. Filet mignon duxelle, with cucumber sauce, bigarade, Diane and chausseur are some of the steak choices. The chicken breast dishes are myriad: Diamant is stuffed with chicken mousse and vegetables and topped with Madeira sauce; en croute is covered with herbed watercress sauce and cream cheese and wrapped in puff pastry. Sometimes the chicken is topped with asparagus mousse and parmesan cheese; sometimes it is "in the pink" with a tomato-cream sauce that includes four cheeses and served over fresh pasta. The "chicken Stony Creek" ($12.95) we had was stuffed with a chevre, herb and chive mixture and was very nice.

Even better was the shrimp angelica ($14.95), eight or nine succulent shrimp in a coquille shell with a memorable crabmeat and artichoke cream sauce.

Both entrees were served with long crisp green beans topped with herb butter. The shrimp also had a mound of sauteed and heavily herbed potatoes; the chicken, half a baked potato, stuffed with cheese and goodness knows what else. Other blackboard entrees at our visit were sole with shiitake mushrooms, halibut Nicoise and lamb provence. Entrees are always garnished with fruit; ours were a large piece of watermelon, slice of orange and wedge of pineapple.

We really didn't need dessert, but one serving of amaretto mousse was left and we weakened. It was lovely, served in a flaky pastry shell and garnished with a big strawberry. All the desserts (which change daily) are $3 and look super — from the dark chocolate mousse pie with an oreo crust to a rhubarb torte to a flourless gateau St. Jacques heavily flavored with almond. A proper accompaniment is the strong coffee served in thick white mugs.

At lunch, there are soups, a couple of appetizers and several more salads ($2.50 to $3.95) including the orange blossom, which is romaine, spinach, orange and apple, topped with carrots, raisins, yogurt and coconut. Quiches and sandwiches, three good-sounding crepes and eggplant parmigiana round out the menu, and then there are several blackboard specials like a chicken pasta salad or picnic platter of sliced meats, Swiss cheese, potato salad and fruits, both $4.95. Desserts are the same as at night, and you can get herbal teas, lemonade and espresso or cappuccino, among other non-alcoholic drinks.

You'll probably be struck and conclude, as we did, that Struck is a fine place for an inexpensive lunch or an enjoyable, innovative and moderately priced dinner.

Struck Cafe, 415 Chandler St., Worcester, Mass. (617) 798-8985. Several miles west of downtown on Route 122 at June Street. Lunch, Tuesday-Friday 11:30 to 3; dinner, 5 to 9, to 10 Friday and Saturday. Closed Sunday and Monday. Major credit cards. Reservations advised at night.

Also in the Area

Hannah's, 595 Mill St. (at Tatnuck Square), Worcester. (617) 792-5660. Hannah's is named for owner Sandy Rosen's great-great-grandmother, but there is nothing old-fashioned about the complex of restaurant, cafe, food shop (Fabulous Foods Unlimited) and catering service that she and her husband Jonathan opened in 1984. The restaurant, with dark gray walls accented with framed posters, off-white cloths, burgundy napkins and comfortable cane and chrome chairs, exudes sophistication. The American regional and nouvelle menu is seasonal, with appetizers from $2.50 for Mediterranean fish soup to $5.95 for lobster ravioli with herbed cream sauce. Entrees ($7.95 to $14.95) could be marinated breast of duck with parsnips, carrots and celery, or sauteed medallions of breast of turkey with a cranberry vinaigrette. The dessert cart holds some incredible pastries, like a fresh strawberry and kiwi tart with an almond crust and apricot glaze, and a strawberry butter cream torte. The varied wine list offers many by the glass. Hannah's was serving dinner only when we visited, but planned lunch soon. You can have lunch (or coffee and croissant or whatever) from 10 a.m. on in the cafe, also very handsome with burgundy-topped blond wood tables, and choose from a blackboard menu which is exceedingly reasonable. Imagine fettuccine primavera for $5.95, old Montreal barbeque chicken for $6.95, shrimp and scallops Savannah for $7.50 and a Scandinavian plate of smoked fish, etc., for $6.95 — including salad and vegetables. On Fridays and Saturdays a complete prime rib dinner is $8.95. Sandwiches are New York deli-style with a quarter pound of meat; the corned beef comes from Brooklyn. The salads are too numerous to recount, but all look delicious. The desserts, salads and much more are available for takeout, and the store is well-stocked with Silver Palate products, Joyce Chen sauces, Nejaime's lavasch and all those goodies that gourmets depend upon. Hannah's, dinner from 5 to 10, to 11 Friday and Saturday, closed Monday. Cafe and Fabulous Foods open from 10 a.m.

36

El Morocco, 100 Wall St., Worcester. (617) 756-7117. "If you cook with love, you can't miss," the late Helen Aboody used to say, and the Aboody family has been cooking with love since 1945, first in a tiny place with two tables and two booths and, since 1977,in a sprawling palace-like structure poised on the hillside across the street. Helen and Paul Aboody were active until their deaths, leaving their eight grown children a hugely successful operation that serves up to 700 people on a Saturday night in a luxurious two-level dining room overlooking the city. You might think that to look over Worcester would not be an advantage, but you'd be surprised! The Aboodys lavish as much attention on their Lebanese and American food as they do their customers, at prices so low as to be unbelievable. The traditional shish kabob is $8.95 as is broiled haddock, seven Lebanese dishes including lamb stew are $6.50 to $6.95, the "variety platter" is $9.25; prime rib and filet top the dinner prices at $13.95. Start with lamb soup and finish with baklava and you can dine in style for $10 to $15. The extensive wine list is unusually reasonable as well. The small lunch menu has Lebanese specialties among its sandwiches, salads and entrees from $3.25 to $5.50. An outdoor terrace is popular in season, and the sunsets as dusk settles over the city are spectacular any time of year. Open daily except major holidays, 11:30 to 10.

Legal Sea Foods, 1 Exchange Place, Worcester. (617) 792-1600. The nicest, to our minds, of the expanding Boston chain is this smart-looking, two-story establishment fashioned from the former police garage across from the Centrum. Downstairs is informal, with a blue and white tiled floor, blue and white tiles on the walls, blue checked tablecloths and seating at the bar. Upstairs is quite elegant and sedate, with whitewashed brick walls and mahogany paneling, mirrors, beige oil cloths with blue napkins and striking flowers on every table — orange day lilies on the April day we visited. The huge menu offers the freshest seafood (delivered twice daily) — the normal fare plus more exotic items like king salmon, shad roe, mako shark, soft-shell crabs, red snapper and such. The problem is in making a choice. Entrees are $7.95 to $14.95, except for cioppino ($17.95) and lobster (priced by the pound and enumerated every half pound up to seven pounds ($56.95) — "over seven pounds ask staff for availability," the menu suggests. Lunch specials are $4.95 (fried squid) to $8.95 (shrimp kabob, two skewers). Desserts are limited to ice creams and grapenut custard pudding, but who cares? The ever-changing computerized wine list is amazing. In season, the outdoor courtyard the Legal shares with neighboring restaurants is packed for cocktails, appetizers and raw bar. Serving Monday-Saturday 11 to 10, Sunday 12:30 to 9.

Firehouse Cafe, 1 Exchange Place, Worcester. (617) 753-7899. The old firehouse was turned into a popular pub in 1984, but much fire memorabilia remains. The hostess station is in a fire truck cab, the large bar evolves out of the rear of a fire engine, the phone is in a red call box and a fake dalmatian is perched atop a piano. The main dining room looks out onto a courtyard, where the full menu is served in season. The drink list is far more elaborate than the menu, which lists appetizers, sandwiches and salads plus nine dinner entrees ($5.95 to $9.95), including two veal, two chicken, two steak and three seafood dishes. The green-board specials may have a few surprises like escarole soup and haddock pizzaiola. Open weekdays from 11:30, Sunday from 5.

Maxwell Silverman's Toolhouse, 25 Union St., Worcester. (617) 755-1200. The first Worcester restaurant in a restored building, Robert Giordano's award-winner emerged in 1976 from the screw machine department of an old factory. Some of the machines could not be moved, so the dining room was built around them, and very nicely, too. More luxurious than most of its ilk, this has comfortable chairs at generally well spaced tables, pink cloths with burgundy napkins, hurricane lamps and fresh flowers in old beer bottles. A tool and die box contains the menu, which is Yankee-continental (fried clams and prime rib, duckling bigarade and-chicken cordon bleu, $7.45 to $14.75). The salad bar is fairly standard. The lunch menu is more extensive, everything from croissants and salads to steak teriyaki ($2.65 to $9.45). The beer and wine lists are impressive, and there's entertainment after dinner. Lunch, 11:30 to 2:30, dinner 5 to 9:30, Sunday 4 to 9:30.

Cafe Pomodoro, Worcester Art Museum, Worcester. "Without doubt, this is is one of the finest places in town to eat," says a spokesman for the museum. "It's al fresco dining at its best." Open only in summer on nice days, it has wrought-iron tables topped with umbrellas and surrounded by sculpture and art works in an outdoor courtyard. The menu, described as French nouvelle at moderate prices ($3 to $7), offers soups, sandwiches and salad creations and such desserts as chunks of fruit dipped in chocolate and a French silk pie in a walnut crust. The cafe substitutes in summer for the museum's Victorian restaurant, Across the Street, whose future was uncertain when we last visited. Cafe, Tuesday-Saturday 11:45 to 2:45, July 5 through Labor Day. No reservations.

Country Inn at Princeton, 30 Mountain Road, Princeton. (617) 464-2030. Commanding a hilltop location with a view of Boston 45 miles away (the sunset gleaming off the downtown skyscrapers is quite a sight), this refurbished 1890 mansion also commands the highest prices around — from its $115 overnight rooms to dinner entrees averaging in the mid-$20s. Everything is tasteful and elegant in the Victorian parlor in which cocktails are served or the three dining rooms, the formal Washburn Room overlooking the gardens and countryside toward Boston, the tiny Library with plush carpet and wall of mirrors reflecting two modest bookcases and perhaps three tables, and the cheery Garden Room used only on weekends. Floral arrangements are everywhere but on the maroon and lace covered tables, which may have a dish of ceramic fruits in the Garden Room, ceramic flowers in the Washburn Room. The menu reminds the cognoscenti of Boston's top-rated L'Espalier; it's more than coincidence that chef Frank McClelland came from there in 1984. Dinner might start with Cajun spiced Louisiana shrimp or pate and terrine ensemble; second courses are seafood chowder or a changing salad (all range from $6 to $10). The six entrees, spelled out in great detail, might be a trilogy of freshwater fish with crayfish, corncob grilled sirloin steak with popover stuffed with rare mushrooms, or duck breast and leg stuffed with prunes and fois gras. Desserts, "the pride of our creative kitchen," according to new innkeepers Don and Maxine Plumridge, are priced from $4. The excellent, unusual wine list runs from $13 to $90. Interesting Sunday brunches range from $14 to $21, depending upon price of entree. And if you're really into a creative experience, a reservation-only "private gourmet-dinner party" is available every other month or so at $95 per person. Because this is a destination in itself, travelers or sightseers often come as early as 4 to sip cocktails on the outdoor veranda before dinner, which is served Wednesday-Saturday from 6, Sunday from 5. Sunday brunch, 11 to 2.

18th Century farmhouse at Fruitlands.

Utopia Was Here

Fruitlands Museums/Harvard, Mass.

People who visit Fruitlands are interested in one or more of the four museums on the open hillside site, each of which celebrates an interest of the founder, the late Clara Endicott Sears. The best-known of the four was also the first, the house that gives the site its name and where an unusual experiment in communal living was conducted before the Civil War.

When you think about communal living today, a certain image comes to mind: a run-down farmhouse peopled by long-haired men and women who survive on bean sprouts and wheat germ and prefer peace to prosperity. They wear plain, loose-fitting clothes, live off their own land, and do their own thing. Meanwhile, their neighbors, living lives of ordered conformity, regard them with suspicion, if not horror.

Actually, that's not too much different from the way it was in 1843 when Bronson Alcott, educator (and father of Louisa May), and Charles Lane, an English reformer and mystic, led a group of New England Transcendentalists (including Alcott's whole family) into the rural countryside at Harvard to start their experiment in the communal life. They called themselves a Con-Sociate Family, moved into the old red farmhouse on Prospect Hill, and tried to bring about a New Eden. They called it Fruitlands, and that is how Louisa May Alcott, author of *Little Women*, referred to it years later in a humorous piece about the venture called "Transcendental Wild Oats" (you can buy a copy at the museum store).

The group, shunning animal products because they believed in freedom for animals as well as people, ate only fruit (mainly apples) and vegetables. The diet was meager and water was the only beverage.

Nor was diet the only hardship. The Transcendentalists carried the ban on animals to extremes — refusing to use them for labor, to use manure to grow crops, even to wear woolen clothes. Then, because slaves were used to pick cotton, they banned cotton clothing as well. They garbed themselves in linen tunics (designed by Alcott) which were okay in June, when the experiment began, but less so when the chill winds of autumn and winter began to blow. By January 1844, the venture had ended.

Fruitlands wasn't quite as well known as that other Transcendental attempt at communal life, Brook Farm, which lasted for five years. But it continues today to interest, intrigue, even inspire those who visit the house where Louisa May Alcott, at 10, giggled with her sisters in their attic bedroom; where her mother faithfully, if not fervently, made meals for an assorted and changing cast of characters of which she was usually the only woman; and from which her father periodically went off to proselytize about the new religion. (Possibly too frequently; supplies and enthusiasm dwindled on the home front during his and Charles Lane's frequent absences.)

The wild-eyed utopians (who believed in knowledge received intuitively and the power to "transcend" one's senses) were usually no more than 12 in number. Others visited, like Alcott's friend and former neighbor from nearby Concord, Ralph Waldo Emerson. Wrote Emerson prophetically after one of these visits: "I will not prejudge them successful. They look well in July. We shall see them in December."

Because of the Transcendentalists' brief occupation of the red farmhouse on Prospect Hill (barely seven months) and its establishment as a museum so long thereafter (1914), there is little furniture from the Alcott period. But it is furnished as it might have been when the Transcendentalists were there, including the attic bedroom for the Alcott girls. Visitors get to smell spices in the Colonial kitchen, view drying herbs and an early toy collection, and even see framed locks of Louisa's hair.

An exhibit in the old granary wing of the house introduces the visitor to the Transcendental movement in general, in which, says director Richard S. Reed, "interest continues to grow." Theology and philosophy students are among the visitors. Some come just to see the historic spot, some to do scholarly research in the fine library (which is open year-round by appointment) and some because of an interest in the Shakers.

That brings us to our second museum. Going from the Transcendentalists to the Shakers might seem an abrupt jump, but at Fruitlands there is a connection, and an appropriate one. For one thing, at the same time the Con-Sociate Family was doing its thing, the United Society of Believers, as the Shakers were officially known, had a village of their own just across town. Charles Lane even lived with the Shakers for a while after the Fruitlands experiment fizzled.

But the real reason the Shakers have a place at Fruitlands is because of Clara Sears. Miss Sears, member of a distinguished and well-to-do New England family, arrived in Harvard in 1910 to build a summer place and stayed to build a museum. She first became interested in the Transcendentalists' farmhouse down the road from her own house, bought it, restored it and opened it to the public.

Next she turned her attention to the Shakers, even compiling a book about them, *Gleanings from Old Shaker Journals,* published in 1916 and credited with some of this century's interest in the sect. One thing led to another; specifically Miss Sears bought one of the Shaker buildings from the then-defunct Harvard group, had it moved across town, filled it with Shaker furniture and crafts, and opened it in 1922. The collection of Shaker objects at Fruitlands is considered quite fine.

At that point Fruitlands was (and still is) of particular interest to students of religious movements. But Miss Sears's interests could not be so confined. She delved next into the history of the American Indian and (you guessed it) an Indian museum appeared on the property in 1930. It is filled with dioramas, artifacts, baskets and other crafts of Indians north of Mexico.

Finally, another of Miss Sears's personal enthusiasms, art, came to have its place. A collector of primitive portraits by early American artists, and of works of the Hudson River School painters, she opened the Picture Gallery in 1940. Its collection is outstanding and still being added to.

You should visit Fruitlands for any or all of these four major reasons, but also for the ambience of the whole, for it is a special place. The approach up Prospect Hill Road is memorable for the view that comes almost as a shock: a magnificent panorama of the Nashua River Valley with Mount Monadnock and Mount Wachusett in the distance. Many visitors like to linger on the terrace of Prospect House,

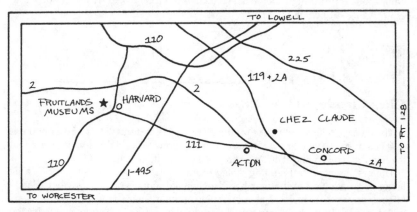

Location: Prospect Hill Road, Harvard, Mass. Two miles south of center of Harvard via Routes 110-111. (The town is not near the university, which makes for confusion. It is actually closer to Worcester.)

Open: May 30 to Columbus Day, Tuesday-Sunday 1 to 5. Closed Mondays except when a holiday.

Admission: Adults, $3; children, 50 cents.

Telephone: (617) 456-3924.

where there is a newly expanded tea room with light luncheon menu. It is a lovely place to rest and gaze out across the valley on a summer's afternoon.

Allow at least two hours in good walking shoes to climb up and down the hillside where the buildings are clustered (they are not far apart but the incline is appreciable). You will probably not be crowded because Fruitlands does very little advertising.

Picnicking is not permitted, but the luncheon tea room staves off hunger. The museum shop has expanded considerably in the past few years; it sells postcards, books, kit furniture, reproductions of Shaker baskets, educational materials and absolutely no gimcracks. The museum shop and tearoom are also open between Thanksgiving and Christmas when, according to director Reed, "the place takes on a whole new inspiration."

Also in the Area

Orchard House, Lexington Road, Concord. (617) 369-4118. About 15 miles east of Harvard is the home of the Alcott family from 1858-77, with much Louisa May Alcott memorabilia, including her famous "sausage pillow" by which she indicated her moods. This is the house where she wrote *Little Women* in 1868. The tour is most interesting and visitors also get to view the barn out back which housed Alcott's and Emerson's "School of Philosophy." Guided tours of house and school are given daily April-November 10 to 4:30, Sunday 1 to 4:30. Adults, $2; children, $1.

Emerson House, Cambridge Turnpike, Concord. (617) 369-2236. This great white house was Ralph Waldo Emerson's home from 1835 to 1882 and contains a wealth of family memorabilia. The study is a replica since the genuine articles are across the street at the Antiquarian Museum, but there's plenty of authenticity here. Open mid-April through October, Thursday-Saturday 10 to 4:30; Sunday 2 to 4:30. Adults, $2; children, $1.

 **Dining 6**_____

Chez Claude/Acton, Mass.

The charming little red house up the hillside just off Route 2A is 150 or perhaps 200 years old, no one knows for sure. But everyone around the area knows about the fine French Provincial cuisine and good value offered there.

The restaurant with three tiny dining rooms in the original house and one a bit larger in an addition at the rear has not changed much since chef-owner Claude Miquel moved there in 1977 after operating another Chez Claude for several years in Acton. He's from Paris, and his wife Trudy, who serves as hostess and tends the service bar, is French-Canadian.

One of the glories of Chez Claude is its unassuming durability. "Only the curtains have changed," Trudy said of the decor, in the period between our first visit in 1978 and our most recent in 1985. Only the prices have changed on the menu, which still offers a country French fare that is refreshing in an era of nouvelle conceits.

And the prices haven't changed all that much, which is one good reason for Chez

Chef-owner Claude Miquel at Chez Claude.

Claude's popularity. Dinner entrees range from $10 for filet of sole meuniere to $16 for pepper steak flamed with brandy or tournedos bearnaise, and include potatoes, vegetable of the day, salad and coffee — quite a bargain for the Boston area.

Another reason is the informal and friendly atmosphere — we spotted many gentlemen in somewhat casual attire on a snowy Saturday night. White paper placemats protect the white tablecloths and vacant tables may not be reset if things get busy. Even Claude in his chef's outfit may leave his kitchen to help clear a table or serve the wine, pausing to chat with patrons, many of whom are obviously regulars.

The decor is what you might expect of a restaurant in the French countryside. In the small dining room in which we dined at one of four tables one night, floors were bare wood, but softly draped flowered Austrian-style curtains and a creamy caramel color on the walls softened the feeling. Rough beams from the original structure are exposed and copper pans glow on what looks to be an original brick wall. An adjacent room in which we more recently had lunch has puffy rose curtains, large lanterns over the fireplace and a few old prints on the walls. The new and larger dining room has carpeting, floral wallpaper, brass chandeliers and white curtains with rose trim.

The wine list is extensive and primarily French. A 1976 Chateau Latour Pauillac for $64 is the most expensive. Beaujolais Villages is $12, Graves and Cotes du Rhones $9.50, and a Cuvee St. Pierre burgundy for $7 was fine with lunch. A number of half bottles are offered as well. The house wine is, surprisingly, Carlo Rossi, $1.25 a glass and $6.50 a liter.

At dinner, pate du chef for $3.25 (an artful combination of pork and chicken livers) was a thick slab atop a bed of bibb lettuce. Strongly seasoned with thyme and baked with a bayleaf on top, it was marvelous with the crusty French bread served with sweet butter.

The French onion soup with grated cheese ($2.25 for a good-sized cup and $3 for a bowl) was lukewarm and lacked that oniony zip, but had a thick layer of mild and melting cheese on top.

Other appetizers include tomato juice (!) for $1.25, lobster bisque for $3.25 and shrimp cocktail or escargots de Bourgogne, $4.50.

The salad is simple and classic — bibb lettuce, tossed masterfully with a delicious vinaigrette dressing.

Two special veal dishes were offered the night we dined. One was veal Normande, done with apple slices, cream and the calvados (apple brandy) of Normandy. The other, which we tried, was an excellent veal marengo, in a casserole with white wine, mushrooms, cream and tomato, faintly peppery and very flavorful.

We also tried a Chez Claude specialty, roast duck with orange sauce, $14. It was outstanding, the duck roasted for a longer time as requested so the skin would be extra-crisp, with a zesty orange sauce and orange segments.

All entrees were served with potatoes Anna (buttery potato cakes), and a vegetable of the season. Ours were carrots, slightly undercooked so they were crunchy, with parsley and onions.

One of the best sounding entrees is another house specialty, rack of lamb with mustard and garlic coating, a 30-minute wait and $30 for two. Chateaubriand bouquetiere is $33 for two. Other entrees include trout amandine and coq au vin (both $11), frogs legs in garlic butter ($12) and crepe maison with shrimp, scallops, lobster and crabmeat ($14).

Desserts are fairly standard (chocolate mousse, creme caramel, pear Belle Helene and vanilla ice cream, $1.75 to $2.50). We tried the special of the night, an extraordinary almond pie with apricots and a crumb crust with the texture of a pecan pie. Coffee is a good strong French blend.

For luncheon, served only Wednesday through Friday, entrees are $6.75 to $7.75 and include several items on the dinner menu plus choice of omelet or quiche. One devotee who thinks Chez Claude is the best place for lunch in the area raves about the omelets. We certainly could vouch for the special of the day, rabbit stew in a lovely cream sauce, served with sauteed sliced potatoes and carrots and, strangely, an iceberg lettuce salad but again with that nice vinaigrette.

Chez Claude is one of those places that gives off good vibes and lives up to its reputation. And the prices for such an experience area pleasant surprise.

Chez Claude, 5 Strawberry Hill Road, Acton, Mass. (617) 263-3325. Just off Route 2A on the north side, east of Route 27 and two miles west of the Concord traffic rotary. Lunch, Wednesday-Friday noon to 2; dinner, Monday-Saturday 6 to 9:30. Reservations recommended. Major credit cards.

Also in the Area

Ciao, 452 Great Road (Route 2A), Acton. (617) 363-6161. A small, crowded, cozy and rather grotto-like northern Italian restaurant at the rear of the small Collage Mall, Ciao is acclaimed both for its regular menu and its "molto speciale" blackboard offerings of the day. One example is the torta rustica, a country pie of layered eggplant, three cheeses, two kinds of sausage and five herbs and spices. The onion soup is served inside a loaf of bread, there are three kinds of antipasti, the garlic bread is extra good, and the pasta dishes always interesting. Noon specials are $5 to $7; at night, pasta dishes are in the $7.50 range; veal, beef and fish, $11.95 to $14.95. The decor is made special by the stained-glass windows, taken from churches being dismantled, and especially by a large one that owner Jim Bailey had copied from the famous Tiffany wisteria window at the Metropolitan Museum — but with grapes instead of wisteria. Villa Banfi ($1.50 a glass) is the house wine; the wine list is all Italian. Lunch, Monday-Friday 11:30 to 2:30; dinner, Monday-Saturday 6 to 9:30, Sunday 5:30 to 8, Sunday brunch, 10 to 2.

The Rusty Scupper, Nagog Square, Great Road, Acton. (617) 263-8327. At the edge of a shopping center in a contemporary gray wood building with angled roofs and skylights, this exemplar of the chain commands a view of a manmade pond and, across Route 2A, the Concord reservoir. The view is particularly appealing from the upstairs cocktail lounge, with comfy low sofas made from thick wood planks and topped with colorful cushions. On the main floor, cushioned captain's chairs are at inlaid wood-topped tables. Presented on a wooden paddle, the limited menu is notable at lunch for salads and omelets (crab and shrimp, $4.50), and a "shrimply sensational" sandwich; prices are $3.75 (salad bar only) to $6.50 for steak sandwich. At night, seafood, beef and a number of teriyaki entrees start at $9.95 and only a few go much higher; they come with soup, salad bar, bread and rice pilaf or red skin potatoes. Lunch, Monday-Saturday 11:30 to 2:30, dinner 5:30 to 10 or 11, Sunday 3 to 9.

A Different Drummer, 86 Thoreau St., Concord. (617) 369-8700. A menu so extensive that some wonder how they can do it from so small a kitchen is offered upstairs in the Concord Depot building. Good-looking dried flowers decorate the walls of the two dining rooms. Popular at lunch are any of the nine salads ($4.50 to $6.50) served in large glass bowls. We liked our choices of spinach with egg, bacon and mushrooms and a sweet and sour dressing, and a tuna, egg and olive with creamy Italian. You can also mix and match a cheese sandwich, choosing one or more toppings from walnuts to mandarin oranges. Baked filet of sole Florentine is the most costly entree at $6.75. At night, upwards of three dozen entrees run from $5.25 (spinach salad) to $15.25 (baked stuffed shrimp and sirloin); most are around $10. Light meals are served in season on an outdoor patio. Lunch, Tuesday-Saturday 11:30 to 3; dinner 5 to 9 or 10; Sunday brunch, 11:30 to 3, dinner 4 to 8; closed Sunday in summer.

The Nickel Inn Cafe, 19 Summer St., Maynard. (617) 897-9512. This colorful little cafe next to the Fine Arts Theater is at its best when the crowd spills out from an enclosed foyer onto a canopied sidewalk patio. Inside, the white stucco walls are accented with barnwood beams and shutters; blue-linened cafe tables seat 24 on white wooden chairs. Votive candles floating with two carnations in a wine glass are on each table. The menu is strictly cafe: soups, salads, sandwiches, sweets and sodas, plus an entree of the day. The specialties are "jaffles" ($4), sandwiches sealed and grilled in a European toasting iron — choices like shrimp and cream cheese, ham and avocado, crab or vegetarian the day we visited. A cherry amaretto sorbet and mocha cooler (both $2) are among the sweets and sodas; many people enjoy herbal teas or coffees with pastries before or after the theater. Hours vary with the theater; generally, lunch Tuesday-Friday 11:30 to 2; dinner Tuesday-Sunday 5:30 to 10:30; closed Monday.

45

 **Daytrip 7**_____

The Oldest Museum

Peabody Museum / Salem, Mass.

It started with an elephant's tooth, a battak pipe and a few shells. The benefactor was Capt. Jonathan Carnes, who'd returned from a voyage at sea with some trinkets from Sumatra. But what a collection he started in Salem!

To get an idea of its worth, consider this: When the National Gallery in Washington, D.C., organized an exhibit of art of the Pacific Islands, it borrowed 17 pieces from the Peabody Museum, including "Kukuilimoku," the wooden carving of a Hawaiian war god. On that trip, Kukuilimoku alone was insured for $4 million.

The Peabody Museum has such extraordinary collections that several of them are unparalleled in the world. One example is the Japanese collection of household arts and crafts, considered better than that to be found anywhere else — including Japan. The Polynesian collection is just as good and possibly better than any similar one in this country. Famed anthropologist Margaret Mead visited several times to do research.

And now there is the collection of the former China Trade Museum in Milton, Mass. In 1984 the Peabody and the China Trade merged to form the largest and most representative collection of Asian Export Art in the Western Hemisphere and one of the finest such collections in the world. A new wing to house it will be completed by late 1987.

Founded in 1799, the Peabody is the oldest continuously operated museum in the country. While oldest isn't necessarily best, because the Peabody got a jump on everybody else in the matter of collecting, it had a chance to get some pretty good stuff.

The East India Marine Society, a group of sea captains from Salem, were the founding fathers. It was an appropriate group to start a museum, for the captains, busy in the lucrative China trade, had a rare opportunity to pick up some unusual pieces while on their travels.

Wealthy families and big names were associated with the museum from the start. The Crowninshields and the Derbys, the Ropeses and the Silsbees, all first families in the Massachusetts coastal city, contributed items. After 25 years, they raised enough money to build a meeting hall and museum.

The 1824 building with its columned facade faces East India Square, downtown Salem's pedestrian mall with a shopping area that is often bustling. A relatively new addition soars in contemporary splendor next to it, and the new Asiatic wing promises an extraordinary complex.

The museum is still a surprise to many visitors, who wander in on trips to Salem in search of witches. Says museum public relations director Bryn Evans, "People associate Salem with witches or the House of the Seven Gables. The trade which made the city what it is is less known."

But the Peabody — whose major benefactor was the same George Peabody who funded museums at Harvard and Yale and the famous music conservatory in Baltimore — is reason enough for a visit to this seaside spot. A visit can take an entire day if you want to linger and look; allow at least three hours.

Three major areas form the strength of the collection: the ethnology of non-European peoples, worldwide maritime history and the natural history of Essex County, Mass. The first two are most impressive to the visitor.

Peabody Photo/Sexton

Peabody Museum of Salem from East India Square.

Salem's trade with the South Pacific in the early 19th century was extensive and in many cases Salem shipmasters were the first Westerners to be seen by island natives. The cultural purity of their artifacts was incredible, and the sailors picked up early specimens which are, today, very important. Since the early Polynesian material was collected before white traders and missionaries landed on the islands, it forms the only sizable residue of such material in the continental United States.

The wooden idol of Kukuilimoku is an example. All but a few of these once numerous figures were destroyed by the Hawaiians when they became Christians in about 1817. The Peabody's wooden idol is one of three surviving in the world.

In the Polynesian collection visitors will also see outrigger canoes, Hawaiian tattooing implements, shark-tooth weapons, fish hooks, fans and wooden bowls.

The museum's Fiji collection is also important. The rarest specimen of all is a model of two-towered native temple which for many years after its arrival in Salem was used as a birdhouse. As far as museum officials know, it is the only one of its kind in existence; all other models have just one tower. It's a grand thing to see.

And now there is the entire collection of the China Trade Museum to consider. That collection, when on display, will enchant visitors with such items as intricate carved ivory fans, porcelain, elegant fabrics, furniture and Chinese tableware.

In fact there is such a wealth of things to see that you must pull yourself together and forge ahead in order to make it through, and that may not be the best way to do it. A return trip, to see the things you've missed, might allow you to bite off manageable chunks.

The marine collection at the Peabody should not be overlooked. It includes paintings by some of the best marine artists in the world. When we were there, those by the Roux family of Versailles were being given a special exhibit. We also looked at pictures of Gloucester fishermen out on the deep, of Chesapeake Bay and of the Pacific off the coast of San Francisco.

The men in our party could barely be dragged away from the beautifully displayed collection of nautical instruments, including many which had been owned and used by Nathaniel Bowditch, a wealthy Salem merchant. Contemporary examples of nearly every major type of navigating instrument are shown and we pored over backstaffs and quadrants, sextants and chronometers, compasses, sounders and log lines with fascination.

47

While whaling never played as important a role in Salem's maritime history as it did in other coastal New England cities, a portion of the collection here is of scrimshaw, whaling gear, harpoons and related objects — all on display in the whaling gallery.

Then there are the ship's models. A Dutch admiralty yacht, two 1:48 scale models of the Cunard steamships, the Queen Elizabeth and the Queen Mary, and possibly the most fascinating, a model of the first oceangoing pleasure yacht in the world, "Cleopatra's Barge," are among the group. The original Cleopatra's Barge was owned by the wealthy Salem merchant, George Crowninshield Jr., and cruised to the Mediterranean in the early 19th century.

The reconstructed main cabin from Cleopatra's Barge is enough to convince you that it must have fostered the concept of boating in the style of an Aristotle Onassis.

The museum store is as outstanding as you'd expect and you can buy Oriental notepaper, kimonos, dragon kites, parasols, chopsticks, maritime books, Chinese doll furniture and Takatori porcelain.

Also in the Area

House of the Seven Gables, 54 Turner St., Salem. (617) 744-0991. Salem's single most popular attraction was built in 1668 by John Turner, a Salem sea captain. It was gradually added onto by succeeding inhabitants until it gained its famous seven gables, about which New England author Nathaniel Hawthorne wrote in his novel by the same name. Hawthorne was the cousin of Susan Ingersoll, who lived here. He visited many times, learning the history of the old place, and eventually becoming inspired to write about it. Six rooms and the secret stairway are on the tour. You also get to visit Hawthorne's birthplace, a 1750 house on the same site. Open year-round 10 to 4:30; July to Labor Day 9:30 to 5:30. Adults, $3.50; children 6-17, $1.50.

The Essex Institute, 132 Essex St., Salem. (617) 744-3390. Seven architectural masterpieces are combined in this museum complex, the main building of which is right across the street from the Peabody. You can see a good slide show on Salem's era of witchcraft, historic rooms and special exhibits. There are lovely antique furniture and an especially fine collection of dolls and dollhouses. The institute also owns and operates several historic homes, including the Gardner-Pingree House next door to the main building. Summer hours for the museum are Monday-Saturday 9 to 6; Sundays and holidays 1 to 6; rest of year, Tuesday-Saturday 10 to 4, Sunday 1 to 4. Admission to the main museum building is $2,

Location: 161 Essex St., Salem, Mass. Exit 25 from Route 128 North. Follow Route 114 east into Salem.

Open: Year-round, Monday-Saturday 9 to 5, Sunday 1 to 5.

Admission: Adults, $2; senior citizens, $1.50; children, $1.

Telephone: (617) 745-1876.

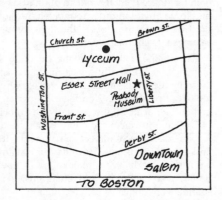

adults; $1, children. A combination ticket to the complex (museum and three houses) is $5, adults; $2.50, children.

Salem Maritime Museum, Derby Wharf, Salem. (617) 744-4323.The National Park Service operates a site including the Derby Wharf, Central Wharf, the Custom House, the Scale House, the Bonded Warehouse, the Hawkes House and the Derby House — the oldest brick building in Salem. The Custom House, which serves as headquarters for the site, is open from 8:30 to 6 daily in summer, 8:30 to 5 daily the rest of the year. Nathaniel Hawthorne worked in the Custom House at one time, which adds to its interest. From this building, where a 10-minute slide presentation provides an overview of Salem, tours of the other sites are given on a somewhat irregular basis. Try to visit the Derby House and the Bonded Warehouse at least. Free.

 **Dining 7**

Indoor patio at the Lyceum.

The Lyceum / Salem, Mass.

In a building just about as full of history as any in Salem is a restoration that made history of its own. When it opened in 1972, it was the first business to be supervised by the Salem Redevelopment Authority.

Many new restaurants have come and gone in Salem since, but we still consider the Lyceum the one to visit if you have time for only one meal. It's equally appealing for lunch, dinner or Sunday brunch, and you can order anything from the massive menu all day (except for certain lunch items weekend evenings in the dining room), so you can snack, or dine elegantly, at any time.

The Lyceum's hours are especially appealing to the daytripper; it's open every day from 11 a.m. to at least 10 p.m. and until 1 a.m. in the pub (where your meal is apt to be accompanied by noise from a large television screen).

With its arched windows, brick facade and colorful banners attached to the upper story and flying in the breeze, the Lyceum is appealing from the outside. Inside, you'll dine in a building that drips with culture, although the restoration is so complete that you might not know it. The Salem Lyceum, founded in 1830, hosted some formidable Americans, including Daniel Webster, John Quincy Adams, Frederick Douglass and Henry David Thoreau. History was made here in 1877 when Alexander Graham Bell demonstrated the first telephone, talking to his assistant, Thomas Watson, 18 miles away in Boston.

The main dining room is handsome, but we prefer the indoor patio, which is especially nice for lunch or Sunday brunch.

The patio's "country" feeling is enhanced by brick floors and exposed brick walls. Fresh flowers and pretty, quilted oval mats with a tiny floral print grace the bare wooden tables. Light streams in through large windows and ceiling skylights The lighting is more theatrical at night, with the kind of bulbs you see around an actor's makeup mirror.

The extensive menu has many innovative dishes along with old favorites, plus blackboard specials that take advantage of seasonal produce (apple cheddar quiche and apple vegetable soup, for example, in November).

For appetizers, fresh mushrooms are sauteed four ways: with scallops and white wine, with snails and tomatoes in garlic butter, with artichoke hearts or with red wine and seasonings. There's a bit of creativity! Duckling gallantine with a Cumberland sauce and oysters Rockefeller also sound worth a try. Two or more can try an assortment of hors d'oeuvre (rumaki, spanakopita, baked mussels, oysters Rockefeller and baked stuffed mushroom caps) for $6.95, plus a variety of other items ranging from crudites, cheeses and marinated mushrooms to cheese nachos.

Along with the usual baked onion soup and clam chowder, there's a chilled soup of the day.

The house French bread, a dense wholewheat type and extremely good, comes with all meals.

The mixed green salad has tiny homemade croutons; the Greek salad has loads of feta cheese, black olives and red onions, and the orange almond salad tastes as good as it looks. Of five homemade dressings, the sweet and sour poppyseed seems to be the most popular (and the recipe for it has been reprinted on the menu), but the feta cheese and caviar dressings sound great, too.

Five kinds of crepes, omelets (one has bacon, mushrooms and Swiss cheese) and frittatas are good luncheon choices. So are the hamburgers, made with feta cheese and bacon, or melted cheese and sauteed mushrooms. Sandwiches come on toasted rolls, whole wheat rolls or croissants.

Interesting lunch platters, all under $5, could include shrimp with tomato wedges sauteed in garlic butter and served in a baked potato, ratatouille Nicoise au gratin with rice pilaf, chicken liver schinoise, or a couple of delicious salad plates we've tried: Nicoise, with the usual ingredients, or savory salad, which is topped with steamed mussels, along with green beans, potatoes, feta cheese and artichoke hearts. Interesting sounding hot salads are spinach with breast of duck, and wilted lettuce with scallops, scrod and shrimp, both with hot bacon dressing.

The menu lists two pages of entrees, many of them under $10. You can be in a dilemma choosing among shrimp Rockefeller, seafood casserole, soft-shelled crab, sole prepared in three different ways, duckling flambe a la Montmorency, veal and shrimp Lyceum, beef Wellington or rack of lamb. There are five meatless entrees, including Nicoise vegetables pot pie and chickpeas in tomato sauce over orzo, and seven "calorie-counted entrees" served with mixed green salad, baked potato with yogurt and melba toast.

Desserts here are irresistible. We've tried the cherries royal crepes — topped with ice cream, whole black brandied cherries, chantilly cream and toasted almonds — and the crepes Dobosch with apricot preserves, chantilly cream, chocolate sauce and almonds. Both are heaven and big enough to serve two gluttons; the waitress will gladly bring an extra plate and fork for sharing. There's a "small and sweet selection" including chocolate-covered ice cream petits fours and Salem's own harbor sweets, plus a glorious array in the pastry case near the entrance.

Wines are served in the large globes we like; the choice is reasonable if limited. You can get a bottle of Graves for $7 or vouvray for $8.50, and a Liberty Napa cabernet sauvignon is $11. The house wine is Coastal Valley, $1.25 a glass and $5.50 a carafe.

Pleasant service and appealing music complete a picture that ought to put anyone into a good mood. And if you can feel the march of history or the ghostlike presence of some of those illustrious American men of letters, why, that's a bonus.

The Lyceum, 43 Church St., Salem, Mass. (617) 745-7665. Lunch and dinner daily from 11 a.m. to 10 p.m., to 11 on weekends. Credit cards. Reservations accepted.

Also in the Area

Victoria Station, Pickering Wharf, Salem. (617) 745-3400. Part of the chain, always quite amusingly decorated with British Railways memorabilia, this particular one — strikingly modern on the outside — has the best location in Salem, right on the water. In season, you can eat or drink outdoors on a spacious deck if you're lucky enough to get a table. Victoria Station specializes in prime rib and steaks, although there are seafood and chicken entrees as well, and has a big salad bar (unlimited, $4.95). For lunch, you can get fresh catch of the day (grilled swordfish, $7.95, when we were last there), prime rib from $11.95 or "saloon favorites" like fettuccine Alfredo, nachos grande, quiche or chicken teriyaki in the $4 to $6 range. Many of the same items, slightly more expensive, are offered at night. Try a special drink, the Wharf Rat, if you dare. The small but serviceable wine list includes a San Martin chardonnay for $11.95. House wines are $1.95 a glass. Decor includes a red telephone booth from London and a plant-laden rowboat, suspended from the ceiling near the huge black fireplace in the tree-filled lounge. Open daily from 11:30 for lunch and dinner; Sunday brunch, noon to 3.

Topsides Seafood Grill, Pickering Wharf, Salem. (617) 744-8588. Owned and operated by the Hampshire House of Boston, this attractive second-story restaurant with canopied outdoor deck offers Salem's best view of the waterfront — a clear shot down the harbor. The seafood menu is fairly standard and of the fish and chips variety, as are the salads, sandwiches and burgers. The fishermen's platter is $10.95 for lunch, $14.95 for dinner. French fries and cole slaw come with entrees; house salad, vegetable or baked potato are extra. Downstairs is the Bull & Finch pub, with a plainer menu and decor. Open daily for lunch and dinner.

Tammany Hall, 206 Derby St., Salem. (617) 745-8755. A small cafe with exposed brick walls, mismatched kitchen chairs and old oak booths with chintz cushions, Tammany Hall is quite charming, with an entertaining menu and posters ("re-elect Herbert Hoover") and Presidential memorabilia on the walls. The same menu is served at lunch and dinner, plus daily specials like baked scrod au gratin with duchess potatoes and peas and mushrooms ($3.95 for lunch) or crock of lamb stew, salad and garlic bread ($3.50). Soups and breads are listed under "Stocks and Buns," salads under "Grass Roots" and sandwiches under "The Bread Line" — among them are the Warren Burger, Jerry's Fjord and the If Reuben Askew; the Tricky Dick ("wait until you break into this one") has lean pastrami and provolone on a sesame seed roll. The fettuccine is great here. For "The Last Hurrah"(dessert, you must have figured out), try the impeached melba. A popular Sunday brunch has an assortment of eggs and entrees, $2.25 to $5.95. Open daily from 11 a.m. to 11 p.m., Sunday brunch 10 to 3.

Soup du Jour, 7 Central St., Salem. (617) 744-9608. Creative soups, quiches, breads and specials are the fare at this rather spare, informal spot with hanging plants and brick walls. Patrons in two dining rooms can make their own salads, sample special soups like French onion, German mushroom, potato cheddar or New England clam chowder or a luncheon special, something like fresh vegetable lasagna with soup for $5.25. Interesting wines and beers are available; liquor seasonally, April-January. Classical music plays in the background, and dinner is by candlelight. Open from 11a.m. daily to 9 or later; closed Sunday.

As You Like It, 203 Essex St., Salem. Breakfast and lunch only are served at what one afficionado called "this treasure of a place" missed by most tourists on the downtown pedestrian mall. Salads, sandwiches and 16 creative entrees are on the menu, supplemented by specials like sole Florentine, beef forestiere and veal chasseur — all under $5. How about quiche for breakfast? You may have to wait for a table at this chef-owned establishment, which has a beer and wine license. Open Tuesday-Saturday 8:30 to 4.

The Barnacle, Front Street, Marblehead. (617) 631-4236.The best water view in historic Marblehead — a town seemingly surrounded by the sea and full of small restaurants — is at this crowded, no-nonsense restaurant on the harbor. In fact, you can sit at a narrow counter running the width of the restaurant smack dab against the windows at the rear and feast on the view as you eat. The old-style typewritten menu lists New England seafood basics, from $6.50 for haddock to $10.95 for scallops, "jumbo shrimp scampi" and such for dinner. All entrees are served with cole slaw, French fries and rolls — "no substitutes." No credit cards or checks are accepted either. The tables are almost on top of each other, the nondescript decor is vaguely nautical and the small bar in front also has a good view. A sign at the entrance warns to make sure your car is parked legally. Lunch and dinner daily.

Rosalie's, 10 Sewall St., Marblehead. (617) 631-9888. Other Marblehead restaurants come and go, but Rosalie's has been catering to local gourmets since 1973. Housed in an 1890 box factory, the restaurant on three floors is a family operation — Rosalie Harrington, her husband and four children — and reflects the eclectic personality of its namesake, who also teaches cooking classes upstairs. The main-floor dining room is notable for its three cozy canopied booths in the bar area, a dogwood tree lit with white lights and striking balloon curtains on the windows. The menu is Italian, with nine entrees like fettuccine with scampi and veal scaloppine Sorrentino from $5.75 to $8.50. One day's specials were spinach salad, pasta with clam sauce and mushroom and cheese quiche ($3.95 to $5.50). Oysters Danielle, baked with garlic butter and prosciutto, is a popular appetizer at lunch and dinner, as is the antipasta ($4.95), served for two or sufficient as lunch for one. Dinner entrees are $9.95 to $14.95 and include salad, linquini and mixed vegetables. Cappuccino or espresso makes a fine ending to what locals consider the area's fanciest meals. Lunch, daily 11:45 to 2:30, dinner 5:45 to 10, Sunday brunch.

Gardner Museum Photo

Gardner Museum courtyard from north cloister.

Art in a Many Splendored Place

Isabella Stewart Gardner Museum/Boston, Mass.

Changes occur infrequently at Boston's Gardner Museum, but one change is welcome. There's now a lovely little ground-floor restaurant/cafe with a glass wall which overlooks the outdoor gardens. In nice weather the terrace is open for al fresco dining.

The cafe is a good idea, because the Gardner Museum is one of those places you hate to leave. Here you can sit amid the treasures, sipping sherry or lunching on sandwiches, salad or quiche, and extending the pleasure of your visit.

53

There are also the flowers in the gorgeous arched and statuary-filled courtyard, the breathtaking central focal point of this unusual museum. They change with the seasons, cared for by gardeners who work in the greenhouses nearby and whose sole purpose is to provide flowers for the museum. We've been to the museum at Easter time when the courtyard was bedecked with lilies and spring blooms, and in the fall when banks of chrysanthemums are used. At Christmas time, there are often poinsettias.

People visit the Gardner Museum again and again despite the fact that the collection itself does not change — nor is it moved. It remains exactly where it was at the time of its founder's death in 1924. Not a painting may be added or subtracted.

Isabella Stewart Gardner was a transplanted New Yorker, married to a Bostonian, John Lowell Gardner, but never truly accepted into Boston's staid society. Maybe she was too flamboyant. Perhaps, a bit too independent. Music, art and flowers were her passions and she indulged them all despite any criticism she incurred (we're told there was a lot).

Mrs. Gardner's life was not without its tragedies, the greatest being the death of an adored only son when he was but two years old. This led to a deep depression and illness which lasted for more than two years. Her husband, in an attempt to divert her from her mourning, took her on an extended trip to Europe.

If Boston had not been a proper stage for the high-spirited Isabella, Europe proved to be. Quite simply, she adored it. Especially enthralling was Venice, where she and her husband spent quite a long period — and then revisited on several subsequent trips.

The Gardner Museum in Boston was styled after a Venetian palazzo and designed by the Boston architect John Sears. It fulfilled a dream of both Isabella and her husband, but Jack Gardner died before its completion, sending his indomitable widow into a frenzy of activity to see that it was completed as they both had envisioned.

On New Year's Eve, 1903, the museum was officially opened — lighted for the occasion with strings of lanterns and flickering tapers. It became the talk of the town for months to come. The strong-willed Mrs. Gardner had even imported Italian builders to do the work, men who spoke no English and who could, therefore, not reveal the treasure and the surprise she had in store.

Visitors to the museum today are just as surprised and overwhelmed as were the Bostonians in 1903 who danced at Isabella's New Year's Eve party. The museum is filled with all sorts of extraordinary items, including paintings, sculpture, furniture, textiles, ceramic, glass, manuscripts and rare books. The impression is of great ornateness and effusion: dark woods and gold gilt (on frames, on dishes, on frescoes), deep red brocades and intricate carvings. There is the feeling of a cathedral, a castle and a manor hall all rolled into one.

The architectural elements of the Gardner Museum are exceptional. Modeled after a palazzo of the 15th century, its central courtyard rises the full four floors of the building to a skylighted roof. There are mosaics, arches, railings, murals and frescoes all collected in Europe and brought to Boston especially for the building. Huge fireplaces and magnificent arches and statuary are among the architectural and artistic treasures.

There is even a small chapel in the building, a perfect jewel of a room on the third floor, where annually on April 14 an Anglican High Mass is said to commemorate Mrs. Gardner's birthday. (Friends of the Museum attend and breakfast afterward.)

Tapestry Hall, with its polished mosaic floor and fine acoustics, is the site of some very special musical events throughout the year. The Gardner Museum is well

Location: 280 The Fenway, Boston. Public transportation: from Park Street Station, take the Arborway or Huntington subway car and get off at Louis Prang Street.

Open: Year-round, Tuesday noon to 9, Wednesday-Sunday noon to 5. Closed Mondays, national holidays and the Sunday before Labor Day.

Admission: A suggested donation is $2.

Special Events: Musical concerts are offered free three times weekly: Sunday at 3 p.m.; Tuesday at 6 p.m., and Thursday at 12:15 p.m. during lunchtime in the Tapestry Room on the second floor. Program information is available at the beginning of the month for the entire month.

Telephone: (617) 566-1401. For information on concerts call (617)734-1359.

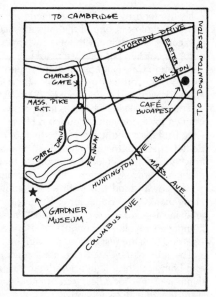

known for these concerts, and guest soloists from the neighboring Boston Symphony, chamber groups or music students from Boston's wealth of colleges have appeared. You can just walk in and sit down (first come, first seated) for concerts on Sunday afternoons, Tuesday evenings and Thursday noon.

Among the items in the museum collection are fine American paintings by John Singer Sargent, who was a personal friend of Mrs. Gardner's. In fact, his full-length portrait of the museum's benefactor and founder shows how pretty and diminutive a woman she was.

Other paintings are by many European masters: Vermeer, Titian, Rubens, Rembrandt (his only known seascape, for example), and there's a collection of letters and manuscripts from famous poets. Musical instruments, Japanese screens, even toilet articles in a guest room on the first floor are among the visitor's treats. Eclectic to be sure, but the more you see, the more you'll marvel.

The Gardner Museum is not a place to rush through. A slower pace is demanded if one is to catch the spirit, and not to miss the wonders that are here. And then, on the upper floors there are the marvelous Gothic arched windows through which you'll want to get new views of the flower-filled courtyard below. Allow at least two hours.

The motto of the Gardner Museum — *c'est mon plaisir* ("it is my pleasure") — reflects Isabella Gardner's attitude perfectly. Once you visit, it's likely it will be your pleasure, too.

 **Dining 8**

Cafe Budapest/Boston, Mass.

For years considered by many to be Boston's best restaurant, the elegant and terribly Old World romantic Cafe Budapest is situated in a rather unlikely place, the basement of the Copley Square Hotel, not one of the city's best.

It's the kind of lavish place where you'd expect to see Zsa Zsa Gabor dallying with an admirer in one of the intimate alcoves off the lounge, sipping champagne and eating something with lots of whipped cream on top. Actually, she has dined here, on chicken paprika, we're told.

Although Cafe Budapest is in the expensive category at night (entrees are $16.50 to $24.50), you can get a table d'hote lunch including soup of the day, salad, entree, pastry and coffee for $12.50 to $14.50.

You're not likely to have as inexpensive a lunch as we once enjoyed, however. In town for a convention during a blizzard, we staggered through the drifts to the Cafe Budapest about 1 p.m. At the foot of the stairs, the captain informed us that Edith Ban, the autocratic Hungarian who owns the restaurant and is always dressed in white (fetching culottes and blouse that wintry day), had decreed that the first patrons to brave the storm were to have lunch as her guests. And we were they!

We slowly dried out from all the snow, sipping from a bottle of the delicate Hungarian wine, Badacsonyi Keknyelu, listening to gypsy music on tape and enjoying the splendor of our own "private" dining room and staff. We felt like Hungarian royalty, although Mrs. Ban, a practical businesswoman, admonished us, "don't tell the rest of your convention that lunch is on the house!"

The soup of the day, a peasant soup combining pinto beans, Hungarian sausage and ham in a thick liquid, was hearty enough for a blizzard and, topped with the thinnest of fried noodles, was truly outstanding. Crusty, sesame-studded hot rolls were served with sweet butter.

The baked paprikas chicken pancakes were actually crepes, exquisitely thin and wrapped around tender pieces of chicken in a wonderfully rich sauce, dusted with the true Hungarian paprika, rosy and piquant. A small salad of cucumber — marinated, sliced razor-thin, very crisp and also anointed with paprika — accompanied this fine dish.

Gypsy baron rice pilaf proved to be a melange of beef and lamb cubes in a flavorful rice pilaf laced with peas, and served with lightly marinated and shredded red cabbage. It was a most satisfying meal.

Our Hungarian strudel, with the flakiest melt-in-your-mouth pastry, was thick with apples and accompanied by fragrant Viennese coffee, served in glass cups (the beans are ground fresh every hour). Hungarians claim their pastry is better than Vienna's and, judging from the strudel, they may be right.

At other meals here we've had the stuffed mushroom crepes, the mushrooms being stuffed with delicate minced turkey breast and served with a cranberry and cinnamon relish. We've also tried the authentic beef goulash, which an Austrian friend, who is manager of a fine hotel, thinks is the best in the world.

At night, the menu takes on a bit of French accent, so you have such curiously named dishes as "stuffed cabbage a la Hongroise" and "steak a l'Americaine."

Most of the entrees are middle European, although chateaubriand for one person, filet of fresh lemon sole and tournedos with goose liver and truffles do appear. The last is the most expensive single entree at $25; the potpourri full-course dinner for two and mixed grill a la Hongroise for two are $65 and $68 respectively.

If you are really in the mood for splurging, imported Beluga caviar is available by the ounce (unpriced, about $30) and goose liver with truffles is $9. Hungarian geese are force-fed on corn soaked in milk to fatten their livers, which are highly prized.

Desserts are $4 to $8.50 (crepes suzettes). The champagne torte and a chocolate, raspberry and walnut cake are specialties. The Gundel pancake for $5 with almond-orange cream filling, raspberry souffle topping and chocolate sauce sounds enticing.

56

All kinds of teas ($1.50) and coffees ($1.50 to $3) are available to round off the meal; cafe royale flambee is $7. The bottles of unusual dinner wines on the Hungarian wine list are priced in the mid-teens. If you have any romance in your soul, you'll love the decor at Cafe Budapest. From the main dining room, all in red and white and dark woods, with old Hungarian flasks, walking sticks, wine jugs and decorated plates on the walls, to the small blue dining room used at night, with handsome stenciling done by a Provincetown artist and glazed ceramic della robbia all around the arched entry, to the dining room off the lounge all in pink except for some green chairs (pink is so flattering to a lady's complexion), it's almost too pretty for words.

A pianist and violinist in the lounge provide more romantic atmosphere, and here, ensconced in French Louis XV-style gilt and brocade chairs, you may have crepes flambeed at tableside.

Some things never change, and the menu rarely changes at Cafe Budapest. Restaurants and fads may come and go, but Edith Ban's formula for romance and fine dining still casts its wondrous spell.

Cafe Budapest, 90 Exeter St., Boston. (617) 734-3388. Lunch, noon to 3; dinner, 5 to 10:30, to midnight Friday and Saturday, Sunday 1 to 10:30. Major credit cards. Reservations required at night.

Also in the Area

Arne's at Copley Place, 100 Huntington Ave., Boston. (617) 267-4900. Best of the new seafood restaurants springing up in and around Copley Place is this contemporary, airy spot with blue tiled walls, pale wood tables and Windsor chairs, tweed banquettes and dining on several levels, some opening onto the interior food court at Copley Place and others looking through a greenhouse affair out over the street. Two small loaves of crusty bread with sweet butter are preliminaries to some exceptional luncheon fare like the two fancy tomatoes stuffed with shrimp and crab salad and garnished with eggs, scallions, carved carrots, cucumber and pineapple ($7.95) or the mesquite-grilled salmon steak ($6.50). The ambitious dinner menu entices with entrees ($8.95 to $18.95) like broiled wolf fish, tuna peppercorn steak, cioppino, lotte francaise, shrimp saganaki, blackened redfish and baked squid provencale. Lunch, daily 11 to 3, dinner 5 to 11, raw bar from 11 to midnight.

Turner Fisheries, 10 Huntington Ave., Boston. (617) 262-9600. The Boston seafood house of the same name supplies all the fish to the new Westin Hotel's large restaurant with its many-boothed dining room, bar, greenhouse dining area and several raw bars. Paintings of underwater marine life dominate the dining room walls, fans whir overhead and brass hooks between the booths are for hanging coats on. Prices are the same all day, making it a bit expensive for lunch, but you can get a large bucket of mussels for $8.95, oysters or clams for 75 cents each (with a garlicky mignonette sauce if you want) or clam chowder ($2.10 a cup). Only what is fresh that day is served; we had monkfish ($9.50) broiled to perfection, served with crisp carrots, cauliflower, broccoli and red skinned potatoes. Bouillabaisse ($13.50) is a house specialty, and a seafood salad special of the day was an interesting mixture of green and white pastas with salmon, shrimp, mussels and scallops. All the 15 wines are available by the glass and fairly priced. For dessert, you can choose from the many pastries and cakes of the day; we had a commendable almond slice pastry, and the mile-high ice cream pie ($2.95) is a Boston tradition borrowed from the old Statler Hotel. Open daily, 11 a.m. to 11:30 p.m.

Back Bay Bistro, 565 Boylston St., Boston. (617) 536-4477. True to its name, this intimate new bistro across from Copley Place offers something for everyone with cheese and fruit platters, five salads (Nicoise and oriental chicken are $5.95), interesting sandwiches and a handful of entrees from poached bluefish in a fresh dill and orange beurre blanc to grilled pork tenderloin ($5.95 to $9.95 at lunch. $9.95 to $15.95 at night). There are surprises like carrot ginger soup, warm chicken liver salad, loup de mer (breaded and baked with a sauce of roasted red pepper and pernod) and poached trout stuffed with fish mousse and served with watercress beurre blanc. The high-ceilinged room with hanging brass lamps, pink linen and pictures of grapes on the wall provides a congenial setting. Lunch, Monday-Friday 11:30 to 2:30, dinner 5:30 to 10:30 or 11 on weekends; Sunday brunch 11:30 to 3.

The Zodiac, Neiman-Marcus Co., Copley Place, Boston. (617) 536-3660. Just as unique as you might expect from the Dallas-based department store is its maroon and white mezzanine restaurant overlooking the Epicure Shop and an assortment of delicious attractions. Lunch is served, the lounge stays open until 6:30 and a violin and flute duo begin playing at 3. The menu has things like the Zodiac sampler (finger sandwiches with assorted fillings, soup of the day and salad, $5.95), an orange souffle ring filled with chicken salad, avocado stuffed with shrimp, chicken Georgia and souffled omelets ($5.50 to $9.95). Neiman-Marcus wines are $2.95 a glass, $11.50 a bottle. Regular desserts include caramel souffle, cappuccino ice cream pie and toasted pecan ball with praline sauce. Lunch weekdays, 11 to 5.

St. Botolph Restaurant, 99 St. Botolph St., Boston. (617) 266-3030. The corner turret with tables at its curved windows adds a distinctive touch to this fashionable South End neighborhood spot, which set the pace for restored brownstone restaurants in 1975 with a stylish red-brick interior and track lighting. Located a few blocks southwest of Copley Place (roughly behind the Colonnade Hotel), it's worth finding, especially if you get a window table. The salad of sliced breast of duck with raspberry vinaigrette ($7.50) is typical of the nouvelle American menu. Dinner entrees ($13.50 to $19.50) include things like rainbow trout stuffed with salmon mousse and wrapped in pastry, poached salmon with camembert and chive sauce and prime lamb chops with pommery and chevre. We recall fondly the desserts ($2.50 to $4.25), especially the hot walnut pie and a chocolate cappuccino torte. Open daily, lunch, Monday-Friday noon to 2:30; dinner 6 to 10:30, to midnight on weekends.

Singleton's, Marriott Hotel, Copley Place, Boston. (617) 236-5806. The mid-priced dining room at Boston's newest Marriott serves breakfast, lunch and dinner next to Gourmeli's, the open gourmet deli. The floral tablecloths are striking in this predominantly burgundy room with colorful floral paintings, and upholstered chairs at nicely spaced tables. Burgers are $6.25, salads about $7.95 and a limited selection of entrees ranges from $6.95 for fettuccine Alfredo to $10.25 for broiled swordfish. Desserts include Boston cream and peanut butter pies. Lunch daily, 11:30 to 2:30; dinner 5 to 11.

Early computers in SAGE control room at Computer Museum.

For Big and Little Kids

The Computer Museum and the Boston Children's Museum / Boston, Mass.

The newest museum in Boston — at least at the time of this writing — is one devoted to technology's love affair with the computer.

Housed on two floors of the restored brick waterfront warehouse which is also home to the popular Boston Children's Museum, The Computer Museum attracts big kids: 25-year-old computer junkies, Dads, and the teenagers in the group who really don't want to play with water or explore the Japanese House at the Children's Museum one more time.

This is fine and makes for a good combination. Big kids can go off and play with the computers; little kids will be happy for hours in the wonderful world created just for them.

The Computer Museum had its beginning back in the early 1970s when Ken Olsen, president of Digital Equipment Corp., and Bob Everett, founder of Mitre Corp., discovered that the Whirlwind Computer which they had helped design and build 25 years earlier at the Massachusetts Institute of Technology was about to be scrapped.

They thought the first vacuum tube computer with core memory — which took more than five years to build and occupied an entire building at M.I.T. — deserved a better fate. The computer memorabilia they owned, and some other items owned by friends, became a growing collection. For a while it was displayed at one of DEC's buildings but eventually needed a home of its own. In November 1984, to everyone's delight, The Computer Museum took over the upper two floors of the building at Museum Wharf.

Getting there is some of the fun. A large glass elevator on the building's face overlooks Fort Point Channel and the Boston financial district, a view almost worth the price of admission on a clear day. This view is continually recreated inside the museum by a pen plotter Hewlett-Packard computer.

Organized chronologically, the museum takes visitors through the relatively recent history of the computer (35 years) with well-exhibited displays. First we meet TV newsman Edward R. Murrow, in a replay from his "See It Now" program of 1952, "interviewing" the Whirlwind Computer. What is apparent in Murrow's attitude — and that of newscasters Walter Cronkite and Charles Collingwood as they report on the Eisenhower-Stevenson election (the first to be reported by computer) — is their amazement that a machine can "think."

Audiences at The Computer Museum chuckle to themselves as they listen to these men and note their unconcealed surprise. We've come farther than we believe.

The early displays allow visitors to walk through a re-creation of the AN/FSQ-7 computer, at 175 tons the largest ever built, and past the SAGE (Semi-Automatic Ground Environment) Blue Room in which the Air Force kept track of positions of aircraft flying over the U.S. until as late as 1983. There is also a small recreation of the Whirlwind, the first vacuum tube, real-time computer with an operational core memory.

Downstairs is UNIVAC I, the first commercial computer in the United States, which was first installed in the Census Bureau in 1951.

Then we're on to Gallery 2 (of four in all) with transistorized office computers including key-punch machines where visitors can punch their own names. Because insurance companies, with their reams of data, were among the first to computerize their operations, there is a full-scale re-creation of a Travelers Insurance Cos. data processor's office, complete with empty Coke bottles and a red Travelers umbrella.

Vintage films from 1920 to 1981 are fun to watch in a small theater in this area.

But now we're getting to the good part. Gallery 3 — "The Integrated Circuit Era" with a usable display on personal computers — and Gallery 4 — "The Computer and the Image" — take most of the visitor's time since he gets to sit down and play at a host of computers.

You can watch a computer draw your picture, hear a computer say what you've written, color a picture with a variety of shades, simulate lighting on an artificial stage set or draw ellipses or circles by means of "fractal graphics."

"This is really the fun stuff," proclaimed the 14-year-old in our party, and we had trouble dragging him away.

Next door to The Computer Museum, occupying four floors most creatively, is the **Boston Children's Museum,** certainly the best children's museum we've ever visited.

There is just so much to do here — and all ages find something to enchant. Little ones love the Waterplay area where they can shoot streams of water at plexiglass water wheels, or float brightly colored balls on more streams of water and watch where they go.

Grandparents will love to share memories with their grandchildren in Grandparents' House, a Victorian structure filled with the utensils and furniture used at the turn of the century.

The Japanese House — an authentic two-story artisan's house from Kyoto with adjoining garden and street — is especially popular and symbolic of the long involvement the Children's Museum has had in teaching its young visitors about other cultures. Special exhibits and events — such as celebrations of the Japanese

Museum Wharf in Boston.

New Year, for example — mean that something is going on all the time here and repeat trips are far from ho-hum.

Teachers love the Children's Museum, which maintains a special, warm relationship with the education profession. Not only are school trips welcomed, but teachers' seminars are held, elaborate kits on a variety of topics are lent out for classroom use, and a Resource Center is maintained with a large inventory of appropriate books.

"Recycle" is a shop that kids and teachers alike love. Pay $1.25 for a small bag or $3.75 for a large one (supermarket size) and fill it with all sorts of neat stuff ranging from the ends of paint rolls to empty plastic bottles to strips of foam in crazy shapes. Both teachers and children will know what to do with these inspirational items and parents will be glad to foot the bill when they can imagine the hours of happy play ahead.

The Museum Shop is a good one. On one side is the room with educational and lovely toys; these are adult purchases since they're not particularly cheap but are the kinds of things that parents who care will find it easy to invest in. Another, smaller room, has kid purchases: stickers, crayons, finger paints, bubble blowers, inexpensive kites, erasers in the shapes of fruits and vegetables — all the goodies that are fun to take home.

Also in the Area

John F. Kennedy Library, Morrissey Boulevard, Dorchester.(617) 929-4567. Boston's museum and library honoring the nation's late President is a great attraction to young people. Designed by I.M. Pei and opened in 1979, the museum features audio-visual presentations beginning with a 30-minute film and including continuous clips on TV monitors and screens throughout the exhibition area. The exhibit is primarily chronological and includes endearing mementoes such as journals kept by J.F.K. when a student at the Choate School, his naval uniform and, ensconced in glass, his Presidential desk and rocking chair. The introductory film is

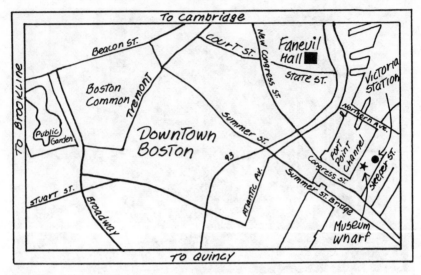

Location: Museum Wharf, 300 Congress St., Boston, Mass.

Open: The Computer Museum is open Wednesday, Saturday and Sunday from 11 to 6, Thursday and Friday 11 to 9. Closed Mondays (except holidays) and Tuesdays as well as New Year's Day, Thanksgiving and Christmas. The Children's Museum is open Tuesday-Sunday 10 to 5, Friday to 9. Closed New Year's Day, Thanksgiving and Christmas.

Admission: The Computer Museum charges $4 to adults; $2 to students and senior citizens. Admission is free after 6 p.m. on Fridays. The Children's Museum costs $4 for adults; $3 for children (2 to 15) and senior citizens. Friday evening is also free.

Telephone: Computer Museum, (617) 426-2800. Children's Museum (617) 426-6500.

stirring and the assassination is not emphasized. A certain stark grandeur is provided by the building's setting on the waterfront of the University of Massachusetts Boston campus. Open daily 9 to 5. Adults, $1.50; under 16, free.

 **Dining 9**_____

A Family Potpourri/Boston, Mass.

The waterfront or Faneuil Hall? A casual spot or a place to celebrate a special occasion? The possibilities for dining in the square-mile area between the Freedom Trail in downtown Boston and the Northern Avenue fish piers are as endless as they are varied. In the Faneuil Hall Marketplace alone there are approximately 20 restaurants and 30 snackeries or food stalls from which to choose.

To start, three choices outside the Faneuil Hall Marketplace that are particularly good for families:

Victoria Station, 64 Sleeper St., Boston. (617) 542-7771. A McDonald's is around the corner, but for a treat you could bring the kids here — it's right on Museum Wharf and from large windows on the west side, there's a close-up view of the Boston docks and skyline. For lunch, children can get a cheeseburger ($3.50) or smaller portions of a couple of the day's specials — grilled monkfish or baked scrod ($5.95 and $4.75, respectively), the last time we were there. As steakhouses go, this one is done up pretty nicely with many booths for two or four (a railroad lantern over each), British Railways signs all over and a pleasantly rough-hewn feeling. The place goes on endlessly, with several salad bars and room after room. Happy hour is well populated, cheese and crackers are there for the taking and wines are offered by the glass. The menu concentrates on steak, of course, but the beef ribs ($3.95 at lunch, $8.95 at dinner) are renowned. Entrees are $3.50 to $7.45 at lunch, $7.95 to $13.95 at dinner. Nachos, deep-fried zucchini sticks and fried potato skins are among the appetizers; desserts include cheesecake, carrot cake and chocolate mousse Victoria. Open daily for lunch and dinner, except Sunday when it opens at 4.

No Name Restaurant, 15 1/2 Fish Pier, Boston. (617) 338-7530. Not only is there no name but no sign or identifying reference other than a makeshift winter storm entrance. You have to know where this is, halfway down Fish Pier, not far past the Super Snooty Seafood Co., but almost any Bostonian could tell you. Fish (broiled or fried) is impeccably fresh if rather unseasoned; the price ($4.75 to $5.75 at lunch, $5.15 to $6.95 at night) is right. Specials of the day's catch (salmon, bluefish, mussels with garlic) are offered daily, and the seafood chowder has many fans. The pies are also good — 90 cents a piece. No Name is very plain, the tables are topped with a knife and fork on a paper napkin, a ketchup bottle and blue plastic cups, and you'll probably have to wait in line unless you go at an off hour. Try to sit in the rear, where there's a water view. The place was expanding in 1985 and was expecting a liquor license; before that you could bring your own. Open Monday-Saturday from 11 to 10.

Anthony's Pier 4, 140 Northern Ave., Boston. (617) 423-6363. Many famous people have dined here (Richard Burton and Elizabeth Taylor, to name two). You can see them all in the hundreds of pictures on the walls of the largest of Anthony Athanas's restaurants beside Boston Harbor, where 600 diners can be seated at a time. Extravagance is his byword, with lots of seafood, lots of dining rooms, lots of plants and ferns, lots of nautical mementoes — in fact, lots of everything, including food and value. It's all a bit overwhelming but fun, and the views of the Boston skyline, the planes landing and taking off at nearby Logan Airport and the passing ships add even more color to this vibrant establishment. The outdoor patio is good for cocktails and, for the first lucky 75, dinner. Entrees at lunch start at $6.95, dinner at $9.95; the clambake special at $21.95 and baked lobster Savannah at $29.95 are available all day. Open from 11:30 a.m. to 11p.m., Saturday from noon, Sunday from 12:30.

And now to Faneuil Hall.

You can eat very well and get just about anything imaginable from the various food stalls in Quincy Market, from breakfast right through to midnight snack.

Mexican or Chinese, barbecue, seafood, Greek or pizza — just buy what you want and take it to the seating area under the dome, where you'll be lucky to find a seat, or outside onto the benches. Here is the ultimate cafeteria for the American family.

For less hectic dining, try any of the sit-down restaurants in the complex (but, on busy days, get there early or expect to wait). Even that can be pleasant — just stop at the bar or sidewalk cafe and sip a drink as you watch the world pass by.

Among the choices:

Durgin-Park, North Market, Faneuil Hall Marketplace. (617) 227-2038. What can you say about an institution that's been around, in one form or another, since

1742 and is as well-known as the Freedom Trail? But for a new facade and a downstairs oyster bar when it was incorporated into Faneuil Hall's North Market, Durgin-Park remains its own solid self amid the trendy marketplace and every family ought to eat here at least once. Yes, the decor is plainer than plain — the ceiling is tin, the light bulbs are bare and you often share tables with strangers after waiting in line. But the line moves fast, you may luck out and get a table of your own, the reputedly snippy waitresses can be delightfully funny, and the prices and portions are right. Entrees start at $3.95 for franks and beans (these beans are proper Bostonians; those who love them may purchase a pint or two in Quincy Market). Prices rise to $18.95 for three one-pound boiled lobsters; the prime rib, a huge rare slab that spills off your plate, is $13. Nearly half the 47 entrees are under $6.95, including broiled salmon and roast turkey. For dessert, most folks choose Indian pudding or fresh strawberry shortcake. Open daily from 11:30 to 10, Sunday noon to 9. No credit cards and no reservations.

The Romagnoli's Table, Lower Level, North Market. (617) 367-9114. The main Romagnoli restaurant is exceptionally good-looking, all modern blond wood amid brick floors and walls of brick and beam, with wine bottles in shadow boxes creating dividers between tables. Facing the open kitchen is a long counter table where you can watch the chefs make fettuccine, linguini and tortellini (all pastas are made from unbleached wheat flour). Try one of the many Italian vermouths as an aperitif or order from what is said to be the nation's most extensive Italian wine list. Pastas, of course, are what most order here; they run from $6.25 to $7.95, a dollar less for "lighter portions" with dinner. The paglia e fieno primavera with fresh vegetables and a creamy sauce is great; our pasta with tomato and basil sauce could have used more basil. All appetizers are $4.25; the carpaccio, razor-thin sliced raw beef doused in virgin olive oil, capers, herbs, mushrooms and lemon juice, is remarkable. Dinner entrees with vegetable range from $10.95 for chicken breast stuffed with prosciutto and mozzarella to $12.95 for filetto Marco Polo (beef marinated in wine and brandy with fresh ginger). Lunch entrees are fewer but priced about the same. Desserts include zuppa Inglese, meringues and bomba mocha (all $3.25). A cup of espresso is a worthy and less caloric substitute. Open daily for lunch and dinner.

Serendipity, South Market, Faneuil Hall Marketplace. (617) 523-2339. The branch of Manhattan's popular Upper East Side restaurant and general store opened in 1984 on three floors of the former Bookstore Cafe. A tiled spiral staircase leads to a second floor that is all Victoriana, with mismatched marble-top tables, cushioned chairs, hanging silk lamps and more, a good deal of it for sale. A section in the rear with tiny hanging lamps is darker and more intimate. You can get everything from foot-long hot dogs ($3.25) and shepherds pie to Zen hash and Louisiana fried shrimp ($10.95). Ice cream and sweets are a large part of the appeal, and the frozen hot chocolate ($3) is a specialty non-sequitur. Open daily for lunch, dinner, coffee and ice cream.

The Landmark Inn, North Market, (617) 227-9660, has three restaurants and a pleasant wine bar, the **Bunch of Grapes.**

In the basement is **Thompson's Chowder House,** with an appropriate ancient basement decor of stone walls and a raw bar. An international tureen is served daily for $15.50: Mediterranean bouillabaisse, Italian cioppino, Belgian waterzooi or Russian solianka (lobster, crab, mussels, shrimp, clams and whitefish in a dill, cucumber, pickle, olive and caper broth — whew!) are some. Entrees start at $8.50 for Boston scrod and include such seldom-seen items as butterfly skate wings piquant, Atlantic cod cheeks, baked giant grouper and Florida pompano.

The **Landmark Cafe** on the ground floor has a large area for outdoor dining in summer, plus a glass-enclosed room that is pleasant in all seasons. There are pots of flowers, tiny twinkling colored lights, a Spanish tile floor and ropes of garlic and salamis hanging over the bar. The limited all-day menu has burgers, nachos, lamb stew and a Parisienne picnic of pate, cheeses, French bread and fruit, the most expensive item at $6.95.

The **Wild Goose Grill & Rotisserie** upstairs is a luxurious restaurant of pink, purple and burgundy hues, where you can have spit-roasted young goose or leg of lamb with goat cheese, ragout of rabbit with apricots or mesquite-grilled swordfish ($11.50 to $16.50). Fettuccine carbonara with duck and goose sounds interesting for lunch ($7.95 to $12). Lunch weekdays, dinner nightly.

Four Faneuil Hall standbys are Lily's, Crickets, Cityside and its spinoff, Seaside.

Lily's Cafe, under the south canopy with a bar under the north canopy, is one of the under-glass people-watching places, and there are usually lines waiting for a table. The all-day menu goes from soup and salad for $4.25 to $8.95 for sirloin steak. Louisiana-style redfish was the day's special for $7.95 when we last visited.

Cityside is also in the south canopy, even more in the thick of things, and also has a casual menu. Specials are filled in daily: when we stopped the quiche of the day was broccoli, the crepe ratatouille, the salad seafood and the entree scallops ($3.95 to $7.50).

Seaside is at the far east end of the South Market Building and has a handsome street-level bar that pulls in the crowds. The attractive main dining room is upstairs, with arched windows looking onto the marketplace. Dinner entrees are $8.95 to $14.95 for bouillabaisse and $16.95 for sirloin steak; the sole Caprice has a delicious topping of almonds and bananas and the scallops are topped with a sauce of crabmeat and shrimp. The sidewalk cafe is popular for lunch and snacks.

Crickets, at the other end of the South Market, has a prime corner location for its glass-enclosed Palm Court, a good place for Sunday brunch. Three pretty dining rooms are upstairs. The all-day menu is fairly standard and expensive (hamburger, $6.25); the specials are interesting with dishes like broiled yellowtail snapper with cilantro butter ($10.95 at lunch, $14.50 at dinner).

Guadala Harry's, 20 Clinton St., Boston. (617) 720-1190. Somewhat away from the hubbub of Faneuil Hall across the street is this large, colorful Mexican restaurant, with upholstered bentwood chairs, green or orange napkins and a decor of plants, roosters, wheels and such. Spicy but not too hot salsa with unsalted tortilla chips accompanied our margarita and a Dos Equis beer garnished with a lime. Little John's wild tostada salad ($6.75) came in a shell a foot high and could have made a meal for two; Harry's sampler plate ($5.75) is a good way to try a variety of Mexican food. Open from 11:30 daily, Sunday from 11 for a $6.50 brunch.

Seasons, Bostonian Hotel, North Street, Boston. (617) 523-3600. Across from Faneuil Hall Marketplace and with a fine view of it all from its curved-windowed fourth-floor dining room is this inspired restaurant, where the American menu changes with the seasons. The several levels are a stunning mix of stainless steel and glass, upholstered armchairs and extravagant floral arrangements. Spring dinner might begin with carpaccio of young lamb with grilled fennel and capers, move on to steamed spiced scallops with lemon, leeks and white peppercorns or rack of lamb with spring vegetables in roasted eggplant skins, and end with pecan cheesecake with raspberries. The enormous, all-domestic wine list is a joy. Dinner prices are high (appetizers, $7.50 to $13.50; entrees, $21.50 to $29), and even the garlic peasant soup with crouton is hardly for peasants at $6. Prices at lunch aren't much cheaper, but the food and experience are worth it for serious diners. Breakfast, lunch and dinner daily, Saturday and Sunday brunch.

Daytrip 10

Down to the Sea in Ships
The Whaling Museum/New Bedford, Mass.

The tale of the whale is best told in New Bedford, and why not?
The world's largest collection of log books from whaling ships is housed in the New Bedford Whaling Museum on Johnny Cake Hill. And it's not inappropriate: New Bedford was, at one time, the most active whaling port in the country.

New Bedford is also next door to the town from which Herman Melville shipped out to sea on a whaler on Jan. 3, 1841 (Fairhaven, across the river), a voyage that would result in his writing the greatest whale story of all time, *Moby Dick*.

"Whales are pretty popular critters right now," agreed one of the guides at the museum, although she said the site has so far steered clear of making a formal statement about the conservation of the sea mammals. Informally, there's no doubt where it stands.

From the moment you step into this spot atop cobblestoned Johnny Cake Hill and are greeted by the "Welcome Aboard" carved onto a quarter board, you know you're on the right turf. Probably our strongest recollection from a busy Saturday morning's visit at the museum is the graciousness of the staff, unfazed by the flurry caused by a couple of Scout troops and two busloads of senior citizens.

The building is in seven sections, although inside it seems like, and is treated as, one. The Old Dartmouth Historical Society, the parent organization, was founded in 1903. By 1915 the museum was a reality. Its newest addition, opened in 1981, is a beautiful climate-controlled library to house the valuable collection of log books as well as a great assortment of seascapes and other sea-related books and art. It claims the largest collection of printed material on the history of American whaling in existence and welcomes researchers.

The best mood setter for a visit to the museum might come from viewing portions of the film, "Down to the Sea in Ships," filmed in New Bedford and at sea in 1922, and recounting one of the last whaling voyages to have gone out from that port. It is a silent movie, but one of the exceptionally well-trained docents explains the story as it unrolls in the beautiful amphitheater. The film is exciting; knowing it is a real voyage that you're seeing adds to the thrill of the scene which depicts a "Nantucket sleigh ride."

The museum's specialization allows it to be well-focused; its scrimshaw collection, for example, is one of its splendors. We saw finely-executed hatpin boxes, rolling pin handles, jagging wheels or pie crimpers, and cane handles accompanied by this notation from a whaleship log: "nothing to do but make canes to support our dignity when we are home." There are even a scrimshaw bird cage and a child's sled. Those days on whaling ships could be filled with tedium.

The collection also includes old paintings of whaling voyages and, when we were there, a photographic display of sea vistas — one of the frequently changing exhibits. Ships' flags hang in the stairwell of the museum and there's a small model of a whaler.

But the ship model that attracts the most attention is that of the bark Lagoda. This was the whaleship captained by Jonathan Bourne, whose family donated the building and the model in his memory. A half-scale replica of the original whaler,

The ship model, Lagoda, at New Bedford Whaling Museum.

the Lagoda is plenty large enough to climb aboard, and children particularly love the chance to do so.

Built in 1916 to copy the original 1826 ship, the Lagoda has all the necessary elements of a whaleship, including the try works where the whale blubber was melted to oil while the ship was at sea. Stand at the wheel, study a harpoon, peek into the small whaleboats that chased the angry whale, and feel part of the great history of this once active seaport.

All around the room where the Lagoda is displayed are galleries filled with ropes and pulleys, figureheads, and the jaw of a sperm whale. In an adjoining area, displays depict the supporting industries of whaling: a chandlery, a tin and copper shop, a cooperage, a counting house. Also included in the exhibits are a doll collection, fans and export china from the East Indies.

The Panorama Room is considered important. Two sections of the 19th century Russell-Purrington panorama are immense and specially displayed so that the visitor can follow a worldwide whaling voyage. The panorama measures eight feet in height and about a quarter of a mile in length. Scenes show the sightings, chase, capture, blubber-stripping, disasters and successes of a whaling voyage. A portion of one section is a depiction of Tahiti as remembered by the whaling men who called there for provisions and fresh water.

One of our favorite items in this museum is the crew list of the Acushnet, the ship on which Melville sailed, giving his age as 21 and his height as 5 feet, 9½ inches when he set out to sea. One other name on the list, Tobias Greene, is underlined; it is said he was the model for the character Toby in Melville's first book, *Typee*.

Melville's relationship with the city of New Bedford was actually a bit fleeting. He supposedly came into port on Dec. 27, 1840, to await the sailing of the ship onto which he had signed himself and which he would say later "was my Harvard and my Yale."

Melville was in New Bedford when the river was frozen over, the ground snowy and the air far from salubrious. He didn't return again until 1858 and then it wasn't under much better conditions. By that time, the gifted writer who had churned out 10 books in 11 years had given up writing, primarily because of the lukewarm reviews received for *Moby Dick*, and he was trying to make a little money on the lecture circuit, talking about ancient Rome.

Rumor has it that Melville's sister, Catherine, and her husband resided briefly in New Bedford and the author may have visited again. But there's no doubt that it was this man's writing about whaling that provides the richest depiction in American literature of the period in the country's seafaring history.

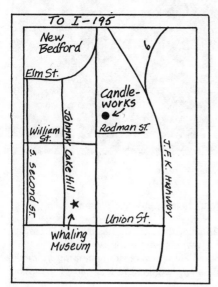

Location: 18 Johnny Cake Hill, New Bedford, Mass.

Open: Year-round, Monday-Saturday 9 to 5, Sunday 1 to 5.

Special Events: Walking tours of the historic district around the museum are given in the summer months.

Admission: Adults, $2.50; children 6 to 14, $1.50; under 6, free.

Telephone: (617) 997-0046.

Other log books can be perused at The Whaling Museum, too; they are the strongest link we have to the lives of these brave seamen. Be sure to stop at the attractive gift shop, where the emphasis in on whaling and seafaring books and small mementoes having to to with a life at sea.

Also in the Area

Seamen's Bethel, Johnny Cake Hill, New Bedford. Directly across the street from the whaling museum is the little non-denominational chapel with its pulpit in the shape of a ship's prow which was immortalized in *Moby Dick*. The author, we're told, sat in one of these pews before he shipped out to sea. It is part of the romance of the sea that the life is fraught with danger and the cenotaphs along the walls are reminder enough. One dated Feb. 15, 1981, remembers "the men of the fish vessel, 'Irene and Hilda,' Captain William Rebello and five crew members." Below is enscribed, "Oh God Thy sea is so great and my boat so small." Among the more poignant services still held in the 152-year-old chapel are memorial services to men who have been lost at sea. After such a service the flowers are given to the charge of the captain of the next ship to leave port; he will see that they are tossed into the sea somewhere near the spot where the men are believed to have lost their lives. But on the spring day when we tiptoed into the small gray building and climbed the stairs that Melville did, we were cheered by the service in progress: the baptism of a handsome young boy in a white christening suit. Later in the day the pulpit was draped with flowers for a wedding. Downstairs in the community room is a little organ that used to be wheeled to the docks for a ship's departure service. Next door is the Mariner's Home for transient seamen. Both are run by the New Bedford Port Society. A vesper service in the bethel is sometimes presented on a Sunday afternoon.

The Millicent Library, 45 Centre St., Fairhaven. Cross the bridge over the Acushnet River separating New Bedford from Fairhaven to see this gift of Henry Huttleston Rogers, one of Fairhaven's fairest sons. The library, in Italian Renaissance style, is soft pink stone with turrets and is named for a beloved daughter of the donor who died at the age of 17. Mark Twain was a close friend of Rogers; many of his manuscripts are here. So is a valuable collection of signatures of all the U.S. Presidents.

Drive along **County Street** in New Bedford to see the mansions built by whaling and seafaring money when the city was at its height.

 **Dining 10**_____

The Candleworks/New Bedford, Mass.

Maurice Jospe, the courtly Belgian owner of the Candleworks, is yet another corporate dropout who decided he preferred the world of restaurateuring to that of stock brokering. The restaurant over which he presides is a grand — and successful — addition to the once-tatty New Bedford downtown.

"It took six years to make it in New Bedford," M. Jospe told us in his charming accent. "But now we're on the map and people come from all over."

Owner Maurice Jospe on enclosed terrace at Candleworks.

At the edge of the Historic District, the handsomely restored gray stone building that formerly housed the Rodman Candleworks, dating from 1810, is now occupied upstairs by a New Bedford bank and, around the side and down a few stairs, by Candleworks.

The interior dining room has the original gray stone walls and beams. A large square bar with leather chairs centers the room, comfortable wing chairs around small tables make up La Bar, and the effect is a cross between a cozy tavern and clubby lounge.

For a more open feeling, an enclosed terrace has been added to the side of the building. With its blue-and-white striped canvas ceiling, abundance of plants and large windows, it is also a choice spot in which to dine, especially in summer when you may get a glimpse of a small outdoor garden.

Flowers in Perrier bottles, crisp napkins in the glasses, blue and white woven mats and gentle classical music add to the rather European feeling of Candleworks. So does the menu, which is mostly French, while taking advantage of the fresh seafood supplied daily by the large New Bedford fishing fleet.

Drinks are a decent size and the extensive wine list — the fancy kind with labels pasted in — has some real finds, like a Beringer chardonnay for $8.25 or a La Cour Pavillon bordeaux for $10.50. The house wine is Cuvee Saint Pierre, $2.25 a glass and $9.25 a bottle.

A part from the well-rounded dinner menu which changes seasonally (eight seafood, five veal or beef and three poultry entrees), a few specials are chalked up on the blackboard.

Of the 20 appetizers ($2.50 to $5.95), we liked the chicken livers in port and the marinated mushrooms. Mussels mariniere, clams Portuguese, calamara Romana, smoked salmon pate and carpaccio are worth ordering, too. The house salad has a good and sharp vinaigrette dressing.

Pecan chicken breast, roast duckling with apricot and cranberry sauce, poached halibut with Mornay sauce (we tried this and it was a lovely dish), gumbo Mercier and scallops Matiche (the recipe is named for and comes from M. Jospe's mother in Brussels and includes carrots and mushrooms sauteed with white wine and cream) are good bets, as are the veal and mussels in a marsala sauce and choucroute au riesling.

The prize is a spicy bouillabaisse, a bowl of wonderfully saffrony broth filed with lobster, scallops, shrimp and other regional fish, served with garlic toast — quite a bargain at $15.95. Entrees priced from $9.95 to $15.95 include potato, rice pilaf or pasta, vegetable of the day and fresh French rolls.

Desserts like pear raisin mousse or strawberry custard puffs may be accompanied by espresso, cappuccino or international coffees, and with cordials in La Bar they top off a memorable meal.

People who aren't up to a full dinner can sample "the Hors D'oeuvrerie," 20 hot and cold appetizers followed by dessert or coffee. M. Jospe is particularly proud of his "grazing" menu, which he pioneered in the New Bedford area, plus his changing selection of fine wines by the glass. For vegetarians, there is always an interesting vegetable casserole and a pasta like fettuccine Alfredo.

At lunch time, you can get croissants, quiches and crepes of the day, salads (the pasta and mussel and the house chicken salad with curry are super), plus some hot entrees, mostly seafood. Prices are in the $4 to $7 range.

Sunday brunchers can enjoy a host of interesting dishes, from eggs Purgatorio (poached with a spicy tomato sauce served on pasta) or a medley of seafood in puff pastry to French toast with almonds, cheese blintzes with strawberry sauce or Belgian waffles ($2.50 to $6.95).

So it's not only the building that is what one architectural critic called "a milestone in the amazing revival" of a forlorn downtown. The creative food served with Belgian flair reaches a new height for the New Bedford area.

The Candleworks Cafe Restaurant, 72 N. Water St., New Bedford, Mass. (617) 992-1635. Lunch, Monday-Saturday 11:30 to 2:30; dinner, Monday-Saturday 5:30 to 10, Sunday 4 to 9; Sunday brunch. 11 to 2:30. Major credit cards. Reservations advised for dinner.

Also in the Area

Freestone's, 41 William St., New Bedford. (617) 993-7477. A brass monkey from Pavo Real Gallery hangs over the crowded bar at Freestone's, a "casual dining and socializing" spot in the Citizen's National Bank Building, built in 1883 and part of the renovation of New Bedford's historic district. It's almost impossible to get in on a Friday night since this is a popular gathering place for singles. The front rooms are fairly noisy; a quieter room is tucked away in back. The all-day menu includes chowders, appetizers like chicken wings, stuffed potato skins and Syrian nachos, as well as salads and sandwiches in the $3.50 to $4.50 range (one sandwich is a taco pocket). Entrees ($6.25 to $9.95) include baked vegetable casserole, grilled scallops, sole with scallop dressing, chicken teriyaki and barbecued ribs. Wines are served by the glass, carafe or bottle, and there's an eight-page list of fanciful drinks. Open daily from 11 a.m. to 11 p.m.

New at the rear of Freestone's in the old Bourne Warehouse and Auction Room at 47 N. Second St. is **Croissant,** a cafe/bakery serving breakfast and lunch from 7 to 5:30. Beside it is a small seafood counter where you can get clam chowder and the like, and more counters are planned. Bentwood chairs at small high tables, polished black and white tile floors and carafes filled with flowers provide the setting for interesting, reasonably priced items like pasta salad, oriental crab, tuna twist and tuna baguette.

Bridge Street Cafe, 10 Bridge St., South Dartmouth. (617) 994-7200. Greg and Sally Morton have turned a former coffee shop into a larger, sparkling restaurant with a rooftop deck which gives a glimpse of the harbor in the picturesque village of Padanarum, the center of South Dartmouth. The regular menu is supplemented by printed menus that change daily and give Greg Morton a chance to experiment. The pasta primavera salad is a specialty served all day for $5.95. Although lighter offerings are available at dinner, changing entrees are pricier ($13.95 to $16.95) for seafood jambalaya, veal marsala, mesquite-grilled shrimp en brochette, pepper steak or pasta Angelique with smoked salmon. Sally Morton says she's been told her key lime pie is better than the real thing from Florida. Nautical photos from the family scrapbook adorn the rather spartan, tile-and-slate-floored main dining room; the open kitchen takes up about half the space in the adjacent bar room. On warm days and nights, snacking or dining on the canopied roof is popular. Lunch and dinner daily except Tuesday.

Call Me Ishmael, 226 Union St., New Bedford. (617) 997-6637. Run by the Coury family for several years in a small location on Johnny Cake Hill, this establishment moved uptown early in 1985 to large, funky quarters with brick walls, bentwood chairs, tables with red or white cloths and an assortment of hanging kites. Advertising homemade pastries and the largest muffins in town, Theresa Coury offers things like crabmeat quiche, tabouleh and hummus, Lebanese pizza, chowders, salads and sandwiches, plus an abundant breakfast and desserts like baklava. Prices are downright cheap, and there's a deli in the rear for takeout. Open Monday-Saturday, 7:30 to 5.

Yesterday's, 1 Merrills Wharf, New Bedford. (617) 992-2700. The attraction here is the view, for Yesterday's occupies the 1847 granite-block Bourne Counting House, from which whaling master Jonathan Bourne amassed part of his fortune. The huge wrap-around windows make the most of the busy wharves and harbor. A large square bar is centered in the middle of a large square dining room and is raised one step so everyone gets a view. Lunch and dinner items are fairly standard, with an emphasis on seafood. Dinner prices go from $6.50 for fish and chips to $12.95 for beef and reef (steak and shrimp). On the main floor is the boisterous, masculine **Cafe Estoril,** where the fishermen go to eat, drink and be merry after coming in from sea. A replica of a cafe as seafarers would have found it in the 18th century, the cafe serves three meals daily from a menu written in Portuguese. The proprietors were planning to open **Cafe Lisboa-Acores** on the other side of the ground floor to serve fancier Portuguese fare in a setting that would appeal more to tourists.

Muldoon's Saloon, 17 Mechanic's Lane, New Bedford. (617) 999-1010. A green and white color scheme and Irish flavor prevail year-round at this bar and dining room with full-length windows opening onto Pleasant Street downtown (there's a suburban Muldoon's at 1309 Phillips Road, Exit 5 off Route 140). The menu is heavy on nibbles, soups, salads and sandwiches, plus a French meat pie, Irish quiche of the day and a few entrees like steak, chicken, barbecued ribs and three fish items. The wine selection is mediocre at best, but there's a special children's menu leading off with linguica sandwich. The decor is ladderback chairs, butcher block tables, hanging plants and fans. Open from 11 a.m. daily.

Bringing in the harvest at Sakonnet Vineyards.

Vineyard with a View

Sakonnet Vineyards/Little Compton, R.I.

They are wine lovers and sailors and their interests are combined in Little Compton, R.I., where Jim and Lolly Mitchell produce wines with names like America's Cup White, Spinnaker White and Compass Rose, all within a short drive of the ocean.

A rooster standing on a bunch of grapes is their symbol (Rhode Island Red is another of their wines) and the vineyard's name was written in calligraphy for their tasteful bottle labels. The Sakonnets were the Indians who originally farmed the land.

Much of the Mitchells' past experience — he was a researcher with Arthur D. Little and she was a publicist for an architectural firm — is combined in their venture. His fervor, her flair.

Sakonnet Vineyards, New England's third winery, was established in 1975. The Mitchells were living and working in Boston at the time and one Thanksgiving weekend were discussing what they'd *really* like to do in life. They say it was too cold for tennis and too warm for skiing and when Jim said he'd be happiest growing grapes, Lolly promised "if you can make it, I can sell it." He has been making it and she has been selling it ever since. They now produce 30,000 gallons a year with 45 acres of a former potato farm in production and another 15 acres rented from a neighbor.

The Mitchells chose the site carefully. Little Compton is an exceptionally pretty, quite toney community, but it was the weather that mattered to these future vintners. According to Jim, his study of weather maps for a 20-year period convinced him that the climate of Little Compton, which is washed by the salt waters of the broad Sakonnet River on one side, was similar to that of the great wine-growing regions of France. The winters were milder than most places in New England. Summers on their hilltop site could be hot and dry.

They trekked down from Boston to the newly purchased site over a 16-day period — their two weeks' vacation — to plant 16 acres of grapes the first year. "The books said you could plant an acre an hour," recalls Lolly, laughing at their rate of production the first year. "We managed an acre a day."

The Mitchells crushed 9,000 gallons in 1976, doubled that figure by 1978, and have reached their goal of 30,000 gallons annually. More important, the wines they produce are often award-winners. Beginning with their 1976 Vidal which won the Maitres de Taste vins Honorable Mention Award in 1977, the wines have received seven gold medals, six silvers and 17 bronzes.

The Mitchells grow both viniferas and American hybrids and truck in a few grapes grown at other vineyards within the recently established Southeastern New England viticultural area. They label some of their wines "estate bottled" because they are entirely produced at the Rhode Island site.

Visiting Sakonnet Vineyards is a pleasant summer excursion. The area all around is quite lovely, and the winery, residence and vineyards are laid out attractively. The buildings seem almost Scandinavian in their contemporary simplicity; the vineyards stretch between and you can get a nice view of part of a reservoir which touches their land.

What does one see, walking through a vineyard? Well, it depends on the time of year. In July, when we visited Sakonnet, the grapes were still quite green and hard, but more than 200 specimen day lilies at the end of rows add color. Start and end the tour at the winery, which contains the reception area, office and production space all under one roof. Here Lolly and one or two employees will provide a pretty and colorful map, which plots the course for an easy walk around the property.

Because we visited on a hot day and had elderly people in our party, we opted for a short walk around the vinifera vineyard closest to the winery. Even on this route, the visitor gets a good look at the grape vines, well-marked as to variety, and a nice view of the Mitchell residence, which is stunning in its contemporary simplicity. At the far end of these rows are rose bushes; red for red grapes, white for white ones.

But the roses do more than mark the varieties of grapes, Lolly explained later. "Roses are barometer plants," she said, something she and her husband discovered after they'd planted them. If there are diseases on the grapes, they tend to show up first on the roses, which may give them enough time to take preventive measures.

Summer is a time for watching the grapes to see that they are brought to the peak of perfection before they are picked. In spring the Mitchells and their staff spend six weeks tying the vines; in the fall, six weeks picking the grapes. Bottling the previous season's crop starts in May.

In the East, explained Lolly, grapes are lower in sugar and higher in acid than they are on the West Coast, so Eastern vineyards have the opportunity to produce drier wines, which is the way we like them.

Sakonnet Vineyards grapes are fermented with liquid yeast. Blair Tatman, a former chef turned winemaker who trained at the University of California at Davis, is responsible for the wine.

The Mitchells have more than 100 oak barrels, both French and American, in which they age some of their wines. Others are put into large stainless steel tanks.

Altogether the vineyard produces eight commercial varieties of wines, but exper-

Wine casks and fermentation tanks at Sakonnet Vineyards.

imentation is always taking place. Because of the relatively small size of the production, Sakonnet wines are available in Rhode Island retail outlets but not in many other places. They can, of course, be purchased at the vineyard, and if you'd like to crack one open, you may use one of the picnic tables on the grounds.

While all of their wines have fans, their chardonnay may be the Mitchells' best revenue producer in more ways than one. That's also the name of their beautiful pedigreed female golden retriever, who, says Lolly, is really "the cash crop." At this writing she'd produced 50 gorgeous pups.

Also in the Area

Wilbor House and Barn, West Main Road, Little Compton. This complex, run by the Little Compton Historical Society and located a short drive south of Sakonnet Vineyards, is most attractive. The land on which the house stands was part of a purchase from the Sakonnet Indians, dating back to 1673. The original house was built by Samuel Wilbore in the early 1680s had just two rooms, one above the other, a cramped stairway and attic. These two rooms are restored to their original form with high, small casement windows (in case of Indian attack). The north ell of the house dates from 1850 and has not been altered; on the site of what was once a porch is a wing built in 1967 to serve as a reception room and museum. The furnishings are not original but they are old and some are quite fine. The huge barn out back is filled with old tools and implements, carriages and sleighs. It's fun to wander around here. Open end of June to mid-September, daily except Sundays and Mondays 2 to 5. Adults, $1.50; children, 50 cents.

Blithewold, Route 114, Bristol. (401) 253-2707. The mansion and gardens which belonged to Marjorie VanWickle Lyon were willed to the Heritage Foundation of Rhode Island in 1976 and opened as a public museum in 1978. The gardens are perhaps more famous than the early 1900s seaside home and visitors may wander about the grounds without visiting the mansion if they want to. A Japanese-

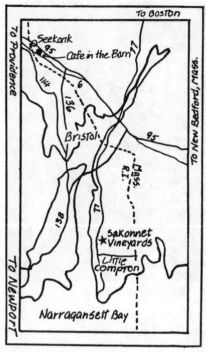

Location: West Main Road (Route 77), Little Compton, R.I.

Open: For tours, May 30 to Oct. 30, Wednesdays and Saturdays 10 to 4. Wine tasting room is open daily.

Admission: Free.-

Telephone: (401) 635-4356.

style water garden, a rock garden, a formal cutting garden, a fountain garden and a bosquet are of great interest to horticulturists. The mansion is furnished as it was at the time of its benefactor's death and is "as if the owner just went out the door," according to a guide. Open daily except Monday, 10 to 4. Tickets for mansion and grounds, $2.50; grounds only, $1.50.

Dining 11

Cafe in the Barn/Seekonk, Mass.

The front part of the barn dates from 1864 and has survived hurricanes, fires, floods, neglect and the honky-tonk of Route 6. You would hardly expect it to contain so sophisticated a restaurant, pleasantly attractive by day and positively enchanting by night.

The greenhouse out front supplies many of the plants that hang all over the restaurant in huge woven baskets. The gorgeous flower arrangements in grapevine baskets (there's even one in the ladies' room) are done by one of the waiters.

The entry full of potted flowers leads on the far side to a small and choice charcuterie, where you can find everything from Texas champagne (hot pepper sauce) to Australian golden preserved ginger and Hawaiian Plantations pineapple syrup. Specialties like smoked bluefish mousse and raspberry squares are available to go.

On the near side of the foyer is the airy, windowed cocktail lounge, unusually inviting with large sofas and brown director's chairs. Some interesting appetizers, light entrees and desserts are served here after 10 on Friday and Saturday nights.

Ahead through the foyer is the barn — but a barn unlike any you ever saw — which serves as the dining room. Assorted baskets, garlic ropes, stuffed chickens and the like perch on a high ledge, but it is the plants and flowers that dominate. A huge tree in the middle is festooned with tiny white lights and surrounded by pink and rose azaleas (this in mid-winter). Azaleas are in silver bowls on each white-clothed table and, at night, two small votive candles in clear glass holders flicker on each table. Classical music plays and it couldn't be more romantic.

A basket of raw vegetables — carrots, cauliflower and broccoli with a very garlicky mayonnaise — accompanies generous drinks. They tide you over as you make your selections from the small but most creative menu.

We started with buffalo pate (which had intrigued us earlier in the charcuterie), studded with macadamia nuts and served with an orange cranberry relish, and a California chevre custard tart with scallions and apple; both were nicely presented on clear glass plates. Other appetizer choices ($3.50 to $6) might be grilled mussels with pistachios and garlic butter one night, baked mussels in a garlic, rosemary and Maine crabmeat butter another; pasta wheels prepared with lobster, shrimp, scallops, pesto, artichokes and tomatoes, vegetable calzone with Monterey (Mass.) goat cheese or lobster fettuccine with smoked trout, four-herb pesto and cream.

Small, choice salads on glass plates contain olives, cherry tomatoes, green pepper, cauliflower and blue cheese and are topped with a zippy vinaigrette.

Our poached sole was three rolled-up filets bathed in a crayfish sauce topped with golden caviar. The dish of Louisiana shrimp was a triumph, stuffed with a mixture of spinach, feta cheese and pine nuts and wrapped in triangles of phyllo dough. Although it was February, crisp snow peas and fresh asparagus accompanied.

Other entrees ($13 to $18) included sauteed bay scallops in a Sakonnet riesling creme fraiche sauce with broccoli, peppers and cucumbers, grilled medallions of veal with a raspberry vinaigrette, grilled beef tenderloin with a Chicama zinfandel herb cheese sauce and diamonds of sauteed chicken breast served with a sauce of lemon, bourbon and hazelnut butter.

Charcuterie off foyer at Cafe in the Barn.

Another night, the chicken was poached and stuffed with asparagus and red pepper mousse, sliced and served with salsa. Cold poached baby coho salmon came with marinated carrots and artichokes with a watercress cream.

The wine list is small but select, with interesting regional varietals like Prudence Island and Hargrave chardonnays, Sakonnet compass rose and Chicama zinfandel. Most bottles are priced in the single digits or low teens. Our French Macon-Chardonnay Talmard ($9.50) was served in an attractive stoneware ice bucket, which also contained a fresh white freesia blossom.

We had to try one of the splendid desserts, which change daily and cost about $3. Our shared lemon and cassis charlotte was great. Others might include praline cheesecake, chocolate truffle cake, raspberry trifle, walnut raisin pie, frozen lemon souffle or strawberry mousse. We recall fondly blueberries Romanoff from a previous visit.

Lunch and Sunday brunch menus are equally inventive. Lunch items ($3.75 to $8.50) might be golden caviar and sour cream omelet, spinach rotelle and smoked shrimp with a fennel cream sauce, breast of turkey schnitzel, vegetables steamed with herbs and wrapped in puff pastry with mixed cheeses or seafood salad sandwich. For brunch, how about poached eggs in spinach timbales, buttermilk pancakes with macadamia nuts and passion fruit syrup or currant and apple open-face omelet with calavados?

Even the late-night menu in the bar intrigues with things like phyllo stuffed with feta cheese, broccoli and smoked turkey, or a fish plate with sliced Pacific salmon, bluefish mousse and marinated mussel salad.

It all makes one wonder what cafe owner Guy Abelson and chef John Elkhay will dream up next!

Cafe in the Barn, Route 6, Seekonk, Mass. (617) 336-6330. Lunch, Monday-Saturday noon to 3; dinner, Wednesday-Saturday 6 to 10; Sunday brunch, 11 to 3. Major credit cards. Reservations advised.

Also in the Area

Arboretum, 39 Warren Ave., East Providence. (401) 438-3686. Owner Roxy Nathanson's collection of Haitian art made the move with her in 1984 from the old Arboretum in the garage up the street to the handsome brick bank building at No. 39, but that's about the only thing recognizable. Large lanterns in niches flank the black and white canopy over the front door; inside, massive brass chandeliers hang from the high ceilings, a blue and rose carpet covers the floor, and sections of the dining room are divided by settees in a deep blue tapestry. On the bar side, with its upholstered bar stools and black and white tile floor, a small band plays mellow jazz on Friday and Saturday nights for dancing; other nights there's a pianist. Arboretum serves Saturday brunch (for those of us who never on Sunday, says the owner) with entrees from $2.95 for two eggs to $9.95 for steak and eggs. The mixed grill at $8.95 is popular. At lunch, a much-ordered special is sole margarita, done in lime juice and tequilla and topped with avocado. Rumaki, curried chicken salad plate, a fruit, cheese and pate plate, quiches and crepes with salad, a stew of the day and croissant sandwiches (one had ham, ricotta cheese and pesto at our visit) are in the $3 to $6.95 range; mixed grill or petit filet mignon are $8.95. At night, when appetizers are from $2.95 for spiedini alla Romano and include baked brie with mango chutney, seviche and fettuccini Alfredo, entrees are $12.50 to $17.95. The former price is for sauteed Provimi calves liver; the latter for rack of lamb persillade or bouillabaisse that includes half a lobster. Among desserts are a Viennese apricot pie, a coffee cheesecake with walnuts, frozen lime pie, Irish coffee pie and creme caramel. Several wines are available by the glass; the house, at $2 a glass, is Grand Yvecourt red or white bordeaux. Lunch, 11:30 to 3, dinner, 5:30 to 10 or 11, closed Sunday.

Eliza's, 1 State St., Bristol. (401) 253-2777. Since Eliza (Beth Gerrior) departed from her namesake restaurant after 10 years, the place hasn't been the same in terms of creative cuisine, though the pubby atmosphere and basic menu remain much the same. A sign, "All drinks are free tomorrow," hangs over the tiny bar which separates two small main-floor dining rooms with exposed brick or green stucco walls and bare wooden tables topped with mats at lunchtime, with a single tulip in a tiny vase. For our latest lunch there, soup of the day was plain onion (not even French), which sounded boring but people at the next table pronounced it fine. The seafood crepe was nearly ruined by the dressing and overflow from a green salad served on the same plate. When, starving, we asked for rolls, we couldn't get any, but then a bunch were served with the entree. The scrod with blue cheese special was exactly that, plus rice and crisp yellow squash. If the food was mediocre, the price was right (nothing over $5 except a steak sandwich). The dinner menu is more interesting (scrod India, seafood in puff pastry and steak au poivre, $7.95 to $12.95). Last time we were there, Eliza's famed pastry cart had been replaced by a salad bar. Lunch, Monday-Saturday 11:30 to 2:30; dinner, Wednesday-Saturday 5 to 9 or 10.

Bullock's, 50 Miller St., Warren. (401) 245-6502. Owner Paul Bullock, a native Rhode Islander, tries to feature wines from Sakonnet, beer from a brewery in Cranston and seafood, of course, from Narragansett Bay — a chauvinistic idea that works. His is a pert, modern place with good-looking pale wooden chairs, blue cloths and rondelles created by a professor at Rhode Island School of Design. In winter, a potbelly stove takes the chill out of the air; in summer, a small outdoor dining area with striped canvas deck chairs faces a Water Street scene that can be busy. The all-day menu leans to light fare like steamed mussels, seafood salad roll and seafood antipasto. Among appetizers are conch salad and clam zuppa. The seven entrees range from spinach lasagna with no noodles for $5.25 to scallop and lobster casserole for $10.50. The chili here is good, as is the seafood chowder, and prices are gentle. Lunch and dinner daily except Monday, from 4 p.m. Sunday.

Provender, 3883 Main Road (Route 77), Tiverton Four Corners. (401) 624-8084. Right on the way to Sakonnet Vineyards, this is a special (and expensive) food shop and bakery which could have been lifted straight out of New York City. It also has a handful of small tables at which you can sample the most interesting salads and sandwiches, exotic cheeses, pates, the most divine breads (we always take home a loaf of whole wheat French), coffees and cookies. It's a popular spot for snacking or picking up the makings for a picnic to gladden the heart of a gourmet.

Abraham Manchester Restaurant and Tavern, Adamsville. (401) 635-2700. In the center of tiny Adamsville (home of our favorite Stone Bridge Dishes store and a funky general store where we buy aged cheddar, called, simply, Adamsville cheese), is this rather large place with a cheerfully rustic atmosphere, a bright yellow garden room and a large Italian and seafood menu. Although the place and the prices are straight out of the past, the eight-page menu has something for everyone; appetizers vary from tomato juice and fruit cup to chicken wings and clams casino. Broiled fish is a bargain $4.95 (with Creole sauce, $5.25) and a broiled seafood platter is $9.75. You can get a hot roast turkey plate for $5.50 or a filet mignon with garden salad for $10.75. The special sandwich is steak with melted cheese, fried onions or mushrooms, served on an Italian roll with French fries for $4.50. Mud pie is a dessert specialty. Open daily from 11:30 to 10, Sunday from noon.

79

Daytrip 12_____

Slater Mill complex viewed across river.

Just Milling Around
Slater Mill Historic Site/Pawtucket, R.I.

A spool of thread seems like a fairly ordinary item until you visit a place like the Old Slater Mill in Pawtucket. After that, it's a sure bet you'll have more respect for thread.

For instance, suppose you had to make your own? That's how it was done in the early homes in America and the first stop on a tour of the Slater Mill Historic Site is the 18th century Sylvanus Brown house, where the story of hand-weaving is told.

In all there are three main buildings, all impeccably restored, at this riverside site in Pawtucket; a fourth (to house a steam engine already owned by the Old Slater Mill Association) is in the works. For now, in addition to the Brown House, visitors tour the old stone Wilkinson Mill, which houses an authentic 19th century machine shop, and the big wooden Slater Mill itself, which was the first cotton mill in the country and where visitors follow the whole process from bale to bolt in the production of cotton thread and cloth.

Because Pawtucket is such an industrial city and the mill site so old, we had expected the neighborhood to be like one of those dreary New England mill towns of the 19th century. Not so: This part of downtown Pawtucket has been spruced up and is a pleasure to visit. The vista from the mill site across the river, or across the river to the site, is lovely. And the deep red of the Brown house, the solid gray stone of the Wilkinson and the pale yellow of the Slater Mill building make a most aesthetically pleasing group.

The Slater Mill is an "educational" site in the full sense of the word and we think

11-year-olds who are studying the Industrial Revolution for the first time, or mechanical engineers interested in early machines, would love the place. But almost anyone should come away with a new sense of how it was when mass production wasn't a household world.

Our guide to the site was an ebullient young man in denim overalls and work shirt, whose enthusiasm for machinery and mills made the 90-minute tour perfectly enjoyable. And while he wasn't quite as much at home with the spinning wheel as he was later in the machine shop, he did a creditable job in the 1758 Brown house, explaining the process of spinning wool from the natural product or working with flax after the plant itself was pounded to reveal the tough inner fiber.

What many people don't realize is the high value of textiles prior to their industrialization. Sylvanus Brown, a millwright and pattern maker in Pawtucket, left an inventory of his belongings, which at the time of his death were worth $97. Of that, fully $40 was for bed linens, tablecloths and other textiles. A tablecloth, our guide told us, might easily cost three times the price of a table, reflecting the greater amount of time required to produce it.

The struggle to produce cloth becomes abundantly clear in the large L-shaped kitchen beneath the house, where a "flax break," spinning wheel and hand loom are on display and demonstrated. At most, two to three yards of cloth could be woven by a housewife in one day. Modern day weavers will agree that it's not speedy work.

Stepping from the Sylvanus Brown house, then, to the great stone Wilkinson Mill is like going from one chapter to the next in one of those old fifth-grade social studies texts. And the interior of the Wilkinson, with its outstandingly recreated machine shop of the mid-1800s, is like stepping into a photograph in that text.

This is where mechanical engineers tend to go a bit crazy. In fact, their professional organization, the American Society of Mechanical Engineers, has designated the Wilkinson Mill a National Historic Mechanical Engineering Landmark.

But even non-mechanical types find the Wilkinson Mill a fascinating place. We visited on a gray day in November, but were not treated to any indoor lighting because machinists in the mid-19th century would not have had any, even in gray November. That lends even more authenticity to the spot.

With a flip of the switch, our guide had the entire place humming (all machines powered centrally by the main source). Since 1982, the source has been a 16,000-pound water wheel in the mill's basement, which was reconstructed to its 1826 version by the purists who run this site. The mid-breast wheel is operated by a series of bevel gears and shafting, which transmits the power to the floor above. Water comes to the wheel from the river through a head race which travels under the Slater Mill, through the trash rack, to the gate right in front of the wheel. The weight of the water and gravity are what turn the wheel.

In the mill, as we walked from machine to machine, the guide pulled a wooden handle to activate the particular one under consideration, and told of the dangers as well as the delights in the swiftly turning parts. In particular, the fly planer is potentially so dangerous that guides are not allowed to operate it. The machines, all in working order, include a rare wooden lathe which makes wooden bobbins, old iron cutting lathes, an early jig saw, table saw, and that Daniels fly planer which revolutionized the American building industry by standardizing lumber sizes.

Last stop on the tour is the Slater Mill itself, a pretty building with bell tower on top, from which the call to work was issued each day.

The mill was named for Samuel Slater, who came in 1789 from England to America as a 21-year-old, fresh from a seven-year apprenticeship in a large textile mill. What he knew about mill operations was vital to men like Moses Brown, a Pawtucket businessman who was trying to operate a small textile mill on the banks of the Blackstone River. Slater and Brown joined forces, and the Slater Mill rose to the fore in a city that led the nation industrially from 1780 to 1820.

The mill is such an authentic replica of those days that CBS and the BBC, among others, have done on-site specials on the Industrial Revolution from the Slater. Inside, the visitor follows the process of cotton weaving from the weighing of a bale of cotton (it should weigh 500 pounds; the scale was to keep the suppliers honest) to weaving cloth via the first fully automated power loom. The precision with which such patterns as herringbone were created on those early looms is impressive. Industrialists from as far away as England and Japan have traveled to Rhode Island to visit this mill.

A slide theater completed in June 1985 shows a 12-minute, multi-image slide show on the history of Pawtucket and is included in the price of the tour or can be seen separately for a nominal fee.

The site is not all history, either. Regularly, a group of textile artists meets here for lectures and workshops and to produce exhibits of their members' work. Other exhibits are mounted throughout the year on the floor above the machine shop in the Wilkinson Gallery.

The area around the buildings is pleasant, and you can walk up the river for a short way to look at the dam, which is the last before the Blackstone eventually empties into Narragansett Bay.

When you've finished, stop at the small but fine museum shop. Rhode Island craftsmen sell their wares here and weaving supplies are also available.

After the mill, or before, there is all of Providence just down the pike with Brown University, the Rhode Island School of Design, shops and historic homes to satisfy a variety of tastes.

Also in the Area

Museum of Art, Rhode Island School of Design, 224 Benefit St., Providence. (401) 331-3511. One of the nation's outstanding small art museums, that at RISD is a find. From mosaics and other treasures of ancient Greece and Rome to a fine collection of Oriental art to an outstanding selection of works by French artists

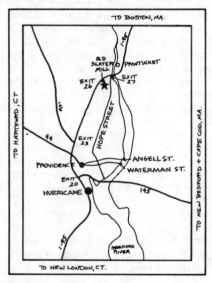

Location: Roosevelt Avenue, Pawtucket. Center of downtown area, reached via Route I-95 north from Providence, Exit 28 (School Street). Turn left, cross river and take your first right. Heading south, it's Exit 29.

Open: June 1 to Sept. 5, Monday-Saturday 10 to 5, Sunday 1 to 5. March 1-May 31 and Sept. 6 to Dec. 22, Saturday and Sunday 1 to 5.

Admission: Adults, $2.50; children 6 to 14, $1.

Telephone:: (401) 725-8638.

(Monet, Degas, Manet, Cezanne, among others), there is a bit of everything here. You can check the changing exhibitions, as well. The famous bronze of Balzac by Rodin is a prized possession of this museum. The adjoining **Pendleton House** has early American furniture and decorative arts and is the earliest example of an American wing in an American museum. Open Tuesday-Saturday 10:30 to 5, Thursday 1 to 9, Sundays and holidays 2 to 5. Mid-June through August, Wednesday-Saturday 11 to 4. Closed Mondays. Adults, $1. Free on Saturdays.

Roger Williams Park, 950 Elmwood Ave., off I-95, Providence. (401) 785-9450. This famous 430-acre public park has waterways, drives, rose, Japanese and Hartman outdoor gardens, park museum and planetarium and paddleboats in summer.

 Dining 12

Dining room and alcoves at Hurricane.

Hurricane/Providence, R.I.

The perfect example of a restaurant as a theatrical set, Hurricane was opened in late 1984 by Grace Kohn, a former co-owner of Rue de L' Espoir. Snappy and sophisticated, and almost too trendy for words, it is more New York style than Providence.

A little off the beaten track, Hurricane is located in a nondescript brick building protected from, we're told, hurricanes by a high stone barrier. Franklin Square is just past Providence's new and nice shopping complex, Davol Square.

Like a good stage set, Hurricane does not reveal all its secrets at first glance. One enters from a foyer into a striking, large square room backed by a large mural; the ceiling is covered with small pink and white track lights. Beyond and to the right past a display counter of some of the wares are a long narrow room with many private alcoves, and yet another dining area at the back.

The color scheme could not be more coordinated; everything is black, gray and white, with the exception of the bright blue seats on the black chairs, and a small vase holding a sprig of lilac on each table. Designed by a RISD graduate who also studied architecture at Princeton, the decor is post-modern and the walls provide space for changing art exhibits. The works on paper of Stephen Brigidi were gracing them at our visit. All serving staff are in black and white, and we even saw a couple of model-like women in outfits of black and royal blue to go with the room.

The menu, which changes four times a year, is also up-to-the-minute, with many choices for the "grazer" along with the hearty eater. The wine list offers infinite choices, with eighteen whites and twelve reds available by bottle, glass or tasting. Tastes are $1 to $2.25; glasses $2 to $7.50 (for Heitz Cellars Fay Vineyard cabernet sauvignon 1978) and bottles $9 to $30. House wines are Yvecourt blanc de blanc or Robert Mondavi rose or red, $14 a magnum and $2.25 a glass.

We loved the sound of almost everything on the luncheon menu — which is unusual for us — and had a hard time choosing from things like goat cheese and onion tart, seafood terrine, smoked marlin pate, salmon cheesecake and carpaccio. But the poor man's bouillabaisse, with bluefish and mussels and only $1.50 a cup, couldn't be passed up. It was just spicy enough, tomatoey and filled with large pieces of bluefish and two big mussels. A wonderful rabbit and pork pate came with Bremner wafers, real cornichons and a nippy mustard. A basket of corn bread and crumbly herb biscuits and herb butter was enjoyed with these goodies.

The four salads come in small or large versions: Chinese vegetables with tamari or ginger dressing, arugula with hearts of palm, mandarin oranges and red onion and the Hurricane salad (greens with Stilton cheese, walnuts, bacon, radish sprouts and croutons) are $3.75 to $4.25, small, and $5.50 to $6.25, large. We sampled the aioli platter, a nice mix of cauliflower, broccoli, chick peas, artichoke hearts, tender little red potatoes and hard-boiled egg, with a very garlicky mayonnaise. A salad of the day, lamb with lentils, was also unusual and good.

Other lunch entrees ($5.25 to $7.25) include smokey chicken pot pie, farmer's veal stew, grilled knockwurst and bratwurst, and T.J.'s barbecued pork.

Some might think the best thing here is the desserts, most on display in the case and available for takeout (as are many of the pates, soups, salads and the like). Sacher torte, chocolate praline truffle cake, frangipane pear tart, banana kiwi tart and chocolate raspberry rum torte are some, priced from $2.75 to $3.50. The linzer torte we tried had a wonderfully buttery crust and an intense raspberry filling. Chocolate chip cookies are 75 cents, and ice cream comes in two flavors, vanilla and (!) grapefruit. The strong and delicious coffee is Graffeo, shipped from San Francisco.

Many of the salads, soups and appetizers are available (and priced the same) at dinner as at lunch. Some winter dinner entrees at our visit included hassenpfeffer, a traditional German rabbit stew; grilled pork tenderloin with cranberries, apples and grand marnier; skewered seafood, and boneless breast of chicken stuffed with sweet potatoes and Italian sausage, $9.50 to $14.50. Sliced leg of lamb marinated in mint, vinegar and garlic, Cajun barbequed shrimp and grilled steak are some entrees on the regular menu; all grilled items are done over a special blend of hardwoods.

Excellent service, great food and wine, fairly moderate prices and a chance to see some of Providence's beautiful people in an appropriate setting — what more could you ask?

Hurricane, 1 Franklin St., Providence. (401) 274-5560. Lunch, Tuesday-Friday 11:30 to 3; brunch, Saturday and Sunday 11:30 to 3; dinner, Tuesday-Sunday 6 to 10, weekends to 11. Reservations recommended. Major credit cards.

Also in the Area

Pot au Feu, 44 Custom House St., Providence. (401) 273-8953. This split-level restaurant (a bistro in the basement; a glamorous salon upstairs) has long been one of our favorites and we're happy to report it has retained its good name. In the Bistro, with its ancient stone and brick walls and zinc bar, you may order typical bistro food — omelets, onion soup, pate, escargots, quiche, fruit and cheese plates and salade Nicoise, all at reasonable prices. The hazelnut tart is not to be missed. Fourteen or fifteen dinner specials ($7.50 to $12.50) might include lotte amandine, poulet aux fine herbes and tournedos bearnaise. Upstairs, with crisp white linens, lacquered black chairs and wall panels with a striking peach, white and foam green print, you may order the same bistro items for lunch or choose again from daily specials, $5.75 to $8.25. Fettuccine with pecorino cheese, heavy cream and Nova Scotia smoked salmon sounds nice. But we'd rather save up to have dinner here; it is a special-occasion place with perfect lighting, service and classical music. Five-course dinners are $17.50 to $21, depending upon the entree ordered, or $11 to $14.50 for the entree alone. You could start with snails in garlic butter on mushroom caps, go on to a watercress salad with sieved egg, enjoy duckling flambed with whiskey and sauced with ginger and cashews, and end with lemon mousse or that divine tarte aux noisettes. Several wines are served by the glass; these change every week and are most reasonable. Upstairs, lunch 11:30 to 2, dinner 6 to 9 or 10, closed Sunday and Monday nights. Bistro, 11:30 to 3, 5 to 10 or 11 daily.

Raphael's, 207 Pine St., Providence. (401) 421-4646. In the old red brick Waite-Thresher Building, one of Providence's many jewelry factories, 27-year-old Raphael Conte has opened a wow of a restaurant in the boiler room. With the help of his mother, the pastry chef and business manager; his dad, the bartender, and his fiancee, a RISD graduate and jewelry designer, who acts as hostess and painted the colorful and joyous pictures on the walls, he is off to a roaring start since his February 1985 opening. Pizzas from his brick oven and salads are the rage at lunch; the latter include squid and shrimp ($6.25) and shredded beef vinaigrette ($3.95). Eighteen pizzas ($2.95 to $9.95 for assorted seafood) include capricciosa, with artichokes, ham, olives, mushrooms, egg, mozzarella and tomatoes and macedonian, with assorted garden vegetables. The dinner menu is extensive, with almost every classic Italian dish you could think of; for example, veal prepared ten ways. How about sweetbreads with macademia nuts, mushrooms, and a lemon-wine sauce? Prices are in the $7 to $14 range. Conte, a graduate of Johnson and Wales, right around the corner, has studied extensively in Italy with his uncle, a culinary professor. In the high-ceilinged room, exposed pipes are painted in soft pastels, pretty peach chintz covers the chairs, Italian jazz plays (his customers love it, says the chef), oil lamps float in little vases and the fancy desserts are displayed on a flower-bedecked stand. In the large bar/lounge is a raw bar and light snacks are served. In the works was outdoor dining on a brick-floored courtyard. Lunch, 11:30 to 2:30, dinner from 5:30, lounge only on Sunday.

City Lights, 4 Davol Square, Providence. (401) 421-9331. Aptly named, this very deco bar and restaurant in the upscale Davol Square shopping complex is all gray and black with pink accents, tile floors, brick walls and exposed ceiling pipes. Canopied windows look out onto the entrance court. A large all-day menu starts with a raw bar and tempura, adds salads, "whitefish and city fries (alias fish and chips)," grilled chicken breast or shrimp, sandwiches and eight entrees ($4.25 to $5.95 lunch, $7.25 to $9.95 dinner) and ends with desserts like mocha java fudge cake or hazelnut souffle torte. The regular entrees, things like bay scallops in a brandy cream sauce over a pastry shell or pasta with smoked chicken, artichoke hearts and pine nuts, are supplemented with daily specials — bluefish dijonnaise and grilled chicken topped with warm blueberry chutney were two when we visited. A weight watcher special of tuna and veggies is $4.95 and calories (397) and exchanges are listed. Open daily from 11:30.

Scotland Yard, The Arcade, 65 Weybosset St., Providence. (401) 351-6550. With its British flag, green color scheme and tartan carpet, skylight and windows onto the third level of the Arcade, this is a cheery place by day. At night, it turns "English formal" for four-course candlelight dinners priced by the entree, $9.95 to $14.95. Meals begin with choice of soups and tossed salad. Regular entrees are Dufftown steak with scotch and peppercorns, scrod and scallops Frederick, Welsh chicken with wine, plus specials like pork a l'orange, ocean perch Grenobloise and chicken francais. Lunch, Monday-Saturday 11:30 to 3:30; pub service in lounge, 3:30 to 10 or midnight; English dinners Wednesday-Saturday 5 to 10. Closed Sunday.

Rue de L'Espoir, 99 Hope St., Providence. (401) 751-8890. When it opened a decade ago, this Left Bank-style bistro was far and away the city's most interesting eatery. With the proliferation of restaurants of late, it has lost that claim, but remains an authentic cafe that could have been lifted from the streets of Paris. Tables of quarry tile, leather seats and booths, hanging pots, a wall of artistically arranged copper molds and cooking utensils, framed Toulouse-Lautrec posters, and two huge baskets laden with greenery hanging from the pressed-tin ceiling enhance the interior dining room on several levels. The limited menu concentrates on pates, soups, salads, crepes, quiche and a cheese board (served with choice of cheese, fruit, French bread, wafers and a house salad — "a meal in itself" for $5.25). The artichoke and mushroom salad ($4.95) has a nippy curry dressing and the croque monsieur with salad is popular. The charlotte malakoff is a masterful dessert for $2.50. Four lunch and dinner entrees change daily, and the adjacent bar offers an interesting selection of beers and wines. Lunch, dinner and Sunday brunch; closed Monday.

Al Forno, 7 Steeple St., Providence. (401) 273-9760. Since it opened a few years ago, this tiny and chic two-roomed restaurant, with black walls and ceiling, has become a mecca for those who love innovative Italian food. They love the pizzas with ever changing toppings, done over the open fire, they love the salads dressed with extra virgin olive oil and balsamic vinegar, they love the pastas ($12.95 and $13.95) and the grilled dishes (redfish in a spicy dry marinade and garlic butter is $13.95) done on the wood fire grill using fruitwoods and even grapevines from Sakonnet Vineyards and the roasted baby chickens (under 14 ounces — "we don't lose a bit of their juices," says the owner) specially raised for Al Forno. The blackboard menu changes nightly, the wine list is excellent, and there are desserts like Michael's sin, a dense chocolate cake with buttercream between the layers. Dinner only, 5:30 to 10, closed Sunday and Monday.

The Maharaja, 303 S. Main St., Providence. (401) 421-5970. Indian music, comfortable tweed-upholstered chairs and good prices are pluses for this new in 1985 restaurant serving northern Indian cuisine of the Punjab region. A large glass window at the back shows the tandoori chef at work by his clay ovens. An assortment of appetizers ($4.50) includes vegetable and chicken pakoras, samosas and kababs; six breads include paratha stuffed with potatoes and naan filled with minced beef ($1 to $2.25), and rice and vegetable dishes abound. Tandoori specialties run from $5.50 for chicken to $11.95 for shrimp; chicken korma is $6.50 as are the other five chicken dishes. Open daily, 11:30 to 2:30, 5:30 to 10:30.

Daytrip 13

Topiary garden at Green Animals.

Where Topiary Is Tops

Green Animals/Portsmouth, R.I.

The *flora* turns out to be the *fauna* (or vice-versa) at Green Animals in Portsmouth, R.I. And even though one may not think of camels, elephants, giraffes or lions as native to this climate, they were the original four residents of the unique topiary garden on a small country estate overlooking Narragansett Bay.

Formal gardens, in the Williamsburg tradition, are not unknown in this country. But the animal garden, like that in Portsmouth, combined with geometric figures (the spiral, for example) are less common, and the brochure printed for visitors proclaims Green Animals "the finest topiary in the country."

Allowing for a little poetic license, it is a splendid place. The art of fashioning living plants into the shapes of animals and geometric figures has been carried to the point where no fewer than 85 pieces of topiary are on view. Add to that the seasonal displays of annuals and perennials (when we visited in October, the chrysanthemums were especially profuse); throw in a vista of sea sparkling under a brilliant sun, and long manicured lawns extending down to the water's edge, and you have an idea of how lovely the place is.

Green Animals became a public garden in the fullest sense of the word after the death in 1972 of its owner, Alice Brayton. Miss Brayton, a member of The Preservation Society of Newport County, which manages a number of Newport's finest old homes as museums, willed the estate to the society. Prior to that, on her own impulse, she would open the gardens to visitors and friends so that Green Animals had gained something of a reputation around Newport before it was opened to the public.

The story of its creation is interesting. Alice Brayton's father, Thomas E. Brayton, who was an executive with a cotton manufacturing plant in Fall River, Mass., bought the estate (consisting of seven acres of land, a white clapboard summer residence and a few out buildings) in 1872. A few years later, noticing that one of the Portuguese employees at the cotton company was doing a creditable job of landscaping, he invited Joseph Carreiro to become his private gardener.

At that time the estate was little more than pasture land. But Carreiro, a native of the Azores and familiar with topiary gardens from Europe, began the creation of the formal garden after having been told "do what you want" on the Brayton estate.

Brayton's estate passed into the hands of his daughter in 1940 and she made it her permanent residence. A horticulturist in her own right, Alice Brayton devoted great interest to the garden, which by then was being managed by Carreiro's son-in-law, George A. Mendonca, who lives on the property and is now retired.

The affable Mendonca, whose garden has been featured in national magazines on more than one occasion, remembers how he got his job — and his wife. A native of nearby Middletown, R.I., and the son of a tree surgeon, Mendonca says "it got into my blood when I was only about 10 years old." Years later he landed a job on the Brayton estate and met and married the daughter of the boss.

Patience is required to create a true topiary — an average of 16 years before a full-sized animal is created. The animals, or geometric shapes, usually of privet, sometimes boxwood, are trained while they are growing, without the help of a frame. They are self-supporting and free-standing.

The four large animals — camel, giraffe, lion and elephant — at the corners of the original garden, are easily visible as soon as you enter. There's a story about why the giraffe has a short neck. Mendonca explains that during the hurricane of 1952, when Miss Brayton was 76 years old, the topiary garden was badly damaged. The giraffe, which was her favorite animal of all, lost its head in the high winds of the storm. According to the story, she said sadly to Mendonca, "I'm afraid I'll never live long enough to see a new head on my giraffe."

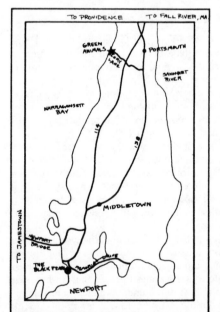

Location: Cory's Lane, off Route 114, Portsmouth, R.I.

Open: May-September, daily 10 to 5; October, weekends.

Admission: Adults, $4; children 6 to 15, $2.

Telephone: Newport Preservation Society (401) 847-1000.

Mendonca, in a flash of creativity, carved some of the giraffe's long neck into a head, there by shortening its neck. Meanwhile, Miss Brayton lived another 18 years.

Today, visitors wander through the garden on their own, assisted by a printed guide which they receive when they pay their admission. Among other shapes they view are a horse and rider, an ostrich, a rooster, a donkey, a bear, a mountain goat and some dogs.

But gardeners needn't think that all they'll see at Green Animals is topiary. There are seasonal displays and some unusual other plants, including an entire area devoted to dwarf fruit trees. We have a lasting impression of a hardy orange with thorny branches and miniature fruits, some of which were lying on the ground in October. We picked one up and took it with us and enjoyed the aroma for a longtime.

No, Green Animals won't take an entire day, but it can be the highlight. Allow an hour or two. Nearby Newport should be included in your itinerary, with its famed mansions along the Cliff Walk, the Touro Synagogue, the renovated waterfront area with marvelous restaurants and shops and even the Tennis Hall of Fame.

Also in the Area

Prescott Farm, 2009 W. Main Road (Route 114), Middletown. (401) 847-6230. This group of restored buildings includes an operating windmill which was originally located in Warwick, R.I., and which grinds cornmeal (on sale at the museum's Country Store). Also on the property is General Prescott's guardhouse, c. 1730. People are welcome to walk around and see the farm animals, including ducks, geese, goats and rabbits. If you want to visit the windmill, the charge is $2 per person. Open May-October, daily except Monday and Thursday 10 to 5.

The Mansions in Newport, also operated by the Newport Preservation Society, include the Marble House, Rosecliff, The Breakers, The Elms. Most are located on Bellevue Avenue and are open May-October, daily 10 to 5. The most palatial of all is The Breakers, built for Cornelius Vanderbilt by Richard Morris Hunt in 1893-95 and containing 72 rooms. We rather like Rosecliff, which was designed by Stanford White after the Grand Trianon at Versailles and which has a famous heart-shaped staircase. The restored kitchen of the Marble House is an attraction to many. The mansions are individually priced at $4 for adults; $2 for children 6-11 except The Breakers or the Marble House, which cost $4.50 per adult. For information call (401) 847-1000.

 **Dining 13**_____

The Black Pearl/Newport, R.I.

An astounding 1,500 meals a day are served in the summer from the tiny but organized kitchen at the Black Pearl. With its picturesque setting by the water on Bannister's Wharf and its colorful outdoor cafe tables shaded by Cinzano umbrellas, the Black Pearl is incredibly popular and, ever since it opened in 1972 as what manager Durbin Wells describes as the first of Newport's innovative restaurants, it has remained an "in" place on the bustling waterfront.

Yacht owners and their crews, the rich and not-so-rich, blue-jeaned youths and tourists of all ages mingle here, drawn, no doubt, by the informal milieu and good, solid and reasonably priced food of the Black Pearl Tavern (the fame of the clam chowder has spread beyond the borders of Rhode Island).

In the Black Pearl's other dining room, the formal Commodore's Room, the cuisine is French nouvelle and expensive, and even very young gentlemen are expected to wear jackets and ties for dinner.

The informal tavern is hectic, crowded, noisy, smoky and fun. Customers often are still lined up at 2:30 p.m. for late lunch. Ladies with a need for the one ladies' room line up five deep in the extremely narrow corridor (a 15-minute wait is not uncommon) while harried staff race back and forth to the kitchen, yelling "coming through" and brandishing heaping plates of food. It's a wonder there aren't more bowls of chowder on the floor than on the tables!

The chowder — creamy, chock full of clams and laced with dill — is served piping hot and with a huge soda cracker, for $1.75 or $3. Lobster and crabmeat bisque are often available, as is an onion soup gratinee, with lots of onions in a good strong stock, topped with an oversized cracker, instead of the usual crouton, heaped with cheese.

Omelets and other and egg dishes, starting at $3.95 and increasing by the price of fillings, are served from 11 to 2:30. A salmon, sour cream and dill omelet is $5.25; eggs benedict or florentine are $5.75. The crepe of New England shellfish, mushrooms and cream is $6.25.

Very popular with customers are the hamburgers ($3.95, with 50 cents added each for cheese, bacon, fried onions or lettuce and tomato), served on Syrian bread or onion roll. The Pearlburger ($4.50) adds a minty salad atop the hamburger and is especially delicious.

Hefty sandwiches like roast beef and Russian, tarragon chicken salad with bacon and corned beef reuben on rye are $4.25. The hot marinated mushroom and spinach salad ($2.50) is a healthy plateful with thinly sliced marinated onions, lots of fresh mushrooms and crisp bacon bits and a nippy hot dressing including mayonnaise, mustard, oil and herbs. You can get a tarragon chicken salad plate for $4.75 and an "assiette" of cold meats, cheese and apples for $6.50.

A special the day we dined was bouillabaisse, a huge bowl wtih large pieces of Dover sole, clams and mussels in a fantastic saffrony broth, delicious when sopped up with the tavern's good French bread. About five daily specials are written on a blackboard, ranging the last time we visited from $5.75 for seviche and aioli or crab Benedict to $13 for grilled salmon and tomato in a basil beurre blanc sauce.

Formal Commodore's Room at the Black Pearl.

Informal outdoor cafe on Bannister's Wharf at Black Pearl.

Also offered all day are a few entrees ($9.25 to $13.50) for Cape scallops with almonds, baked filet of sole marguery, calves liver, boneless breast of chicken and petite tenderloin bearnaise.

Desserts are limited to things like chocolate mousse, English trifle and chocolate chip cheesecake, in the $2.50 range. You can also get cafe au lait and cappuccino. The cappuccino Black Pearl ($3) is enhanced with courvoisier and kahlua.

For dinner in the fancy Commodore Room, very pretty with its view of the harbor through small paned windows, the fare is elegant indeed, with such appetizers as pate du chef, fried brie, escargots bourguignon, clams casino and lobster mousse with a saffron mayonnaise priced from $4.25 to $5.75. The clam chowder is $2.75 and a raddichio and tomato salad marinated with basil is $3.

Lobster and soft-shell crab (no fixed price), poached filet of sole, Cape scallops meuniere or amandine, and a dish of shrimp, scallops and lobster with pink peppercorns and cream are the seafood items among the entrees priced from $11.50 to $19. You also can have sauteed duckling with a Nicoise olive sauce, medallions of veal sauteed with wild mushrooms and a champagne sauce, pepper steak or sweetbreads sauteed with leeks, truffles and madeira. The wine list is extensive.

It's an ambitious menu, and we are impressed that it can be done from such a miniscule kitchen. Still, we prefer the tavern side, with its low-ceilings, dark beams, old charts on the walls and red and white tablecloths. Whether in the high season or decorated for Christmas in Newport, it's fun.

The Black Pearl, Bannister's Wharf, Newport. (401) 846-5264. Open from 11:30 a.m. to midnight (closed February). Reservations recommended in Commodore Room, 6 to 10:30 p.m. Major credit cards.

Also in the Area

Main Brace, 91 Long Wharf, Newport. (401) 849-4397. Since it opened in May 1984, this casual spot on the waterfront has done a land-office business in seafood. The long bar takes up half the downstairs, but upstairs is an informal, high-ceilinged dining room with blue and white linen, and candles in shaded hurricane lamps — about half the tables have a view of the harbor. Dinner entrees start at $9.95 and include things like grouper with lobster sauce, San Francisco cioppino, shrimp and scallops Portuguese and a pasta special with shrimp, mussels and scallops in virgin olive oil. The oyster bar special for $14.95 offered lobster, mussels, littlenecks and steamers. The oyster bar also has Rhode Island oysters (75 cents each), steamed mussels, seviche, and lobster and oyster stews or a combination thereof. Lunch and oyster bar daily from 11:30 to midnight, dinner from 6, from 4 on Sundays.

The Mooring, Sayer's Wharf, Newport. (401) 846-2260. Our favorite outdoor spot by the water is this casual place with dining on a brick patio under blue umbrellas or an upper deck covered by a green and blue canopy and brightened by colorful geraniums. The lines for meals can get long, naturally, but you can stop in off-hours for a strawberry daiquiri, a bowl of prize-winning clam chowder ($2.50) or cheesecake with strawberries. The all-day menu offers a mixed-bag of steamed mussels, cold shellfish medley, crabmeat salad and entrees up to $23.95 for baked lobster stuffed with scallops and crabmeat. The inside is blue and nautical (the building used to belong to the New York Yacht Club) and is warmed by a large fireplace in winter. Open daily from 11:30.

Le Bistro, Bowen's Wharf, Newport. (401) 849-7778. The second-floor dining room and third-floor lounge of this sprightly restaurant offer a view of the water. The dark green linen, colorful flowered wallpaper and Toulouse-Lautrec prints set a country contemporary air for French provincial food that is interesting and creative both at lunch and dinner. Lunch might be omelet piperade, salade Nicoise, hot sausage with hot potato salad or a classic bouillabaisse ($8.95). Dinner entrees, $14.50 to $19, could be coquilles St. Jacques, veal kidneys in mustard sauce or sirloin steak with mustard and garlic sauce. The lunch menu is served from 11:30 a.m. to 11 p.m., dinner from 6 to 10.

The Ark, 348 Thames St., Newport. (401) 849-3808. This restored 1898 structure houses a crowded indoor sidewalk cafe and raw bar on the main floor. Upstairs, it's a different world in the serene and unusual Victorian dining room, all gray and white except for the lighted ficus trees. Downstairs are snacks, sandwiches and pasta, $2.95 to $6.75. Upstairs you can get sole with white asparagus, shrimp and vegetable tempura, lobster fra diablo or veal with wild mushrooms ($5.50 to $16.50). Open daily from 11:30.

Frick's, 673 Thames St., Newport. (401) 846-5830. Some of Newport's finest dinners — at exceptional value — are served up by Austrian chef-owner Volker Frick in two elegant, quiet dining rooms in this small house. The French-Austrian-Hungarian menu is ambitious and extensive, with off-season prices from $6.75 to $10.75. A prix-fixe dinner in March 1985 included Irish cockle soup, house salad, schrod with mushroom and pepper, rice, vegetable, fried apple rings and coffee for $10.75. Dinner nightly from 6, Sunday brunch, lunch according to chef's whim.

Southern Cross, 514 Thames St., Newport. (401) 849-8888. A special edition of Sidney's Daily Mirror with the headline "Aussies Win Cup" is framed discretely but proudly at the side of the bar by Australian owner Peter DeCaux. Australian ports, New Zealand lamb and other specialties from Down Under are featured in the trendy pink and black dining room, its intimacy at once heightened and its size enlarged by walls of mirrors. Dinner appetizers $4.75 to $6.75, entrees $9.75 for fettuccine Alfredo to $19.75 for delmonico bordelaise. Dinner 6 to 10, Sunday brunch; lunch in season.

Adelma Grenier Simmons at Caprilands Herb Farm.

An Herbal Environment

Caprilands Herb Farm / Coventry, Conn.

"Caprilands is the realization of a dream...the recreation of a very old, worn-out farm, of neglected land turned into production. It is the transformation of an area, once a trash heap, that has now become a thing of beauty: our herb garden."

The description is straight from the heart of Adelma Grenier Simmons, who wrote it in the preface to one of her many books about Caprilands Herb Farm in eastern Connecticut. Today it is not easy to remember the trash heap; it's much easier to see the treasure.

Mrs. Simmons, who presides over her creation in high-spirited fashion, who breathes life and love into the endeavor, and who never seems to tire of the throngs who come to see what she has wrought, describes herself as an herbalist. That she is conversant with herbs is no exaggeration. One suspects she must converse with them. She says quite earnestly that "borage makes you feel very, very happy" and crowns her statement with a smile. In another vein, she recommends rue to keep the witches away.

Caprilands is a place of celebration and Adelma Grenier Simmons celebrates everything: liturgical festivals, pagan feasts, the cycles of nature. She knows about them all and uses the knowledge in her famed luncheon lectures, which draw garden clubbers and other visitors five days a week for three-fourths of the year. There is also "high tea" on Sunday.

She dresses for the occasion. Her outfits are designed by and made especially for her. Once a buyer in a department store, Mrs. Simmons has this theory about fashion: "I came to believe that in a way fashion is for the birds. You should really dress in your own style."

The fashion is her own: easy to work in but more than faintly reminiscent of liturgical garb. It is certainly appropriate when she is leading a tour through the Saints' Garden, one of 31 individual gardens on the property that also includes greenhouses, shops, barns, and the lovely old brown 18th century house where the luncheons are served. What she usually wears are full jumpers over turtleneck tops with matching capes and little circular head caps that remind you of Cardinals' garb in the Roman Catholic Church.

They are eminently suitable for her work as she clambers over the grounds with hordes of disciples in tow, stopping to break off a piece of lovage here, a few basil leaves there, and offering them to guests to smell or touch or taste.

Caprilands is a total herbal experience. All of the gardens contain "useful" plants — Mrs. Simmons's definition of an herb — even when they seem not to be. Zinnias and marigolds, for example, are included because they were used as dyes.

While the herb gardens are open every day of the year but Thanksgiving and Christmas, the most satisfying way to visit is to reserve a space for the noontime lecture and luncheon. You should plan in advance because the secret is out and places are booked far ahead.

The popularity of Adelma Simmons stems directly from the magic of the herbalist herself. The experience is theatrical and she is unquestionably the star. For this reason, ask when you reserve if Mrs. Simmons is expected to be in residence (she's infrequently away on trips). She revels in the role of leading her minions and says she can cheerfully address 80 people daily without tiring.

Visitors gather for the lecture at 12:30 p.m. and can plan on spending 45 minutes to an hour on the garden tour before trooping into the house for luncheon. Have snacks before you come, advises the hostess, recalling that on a few occasions people have become almost faint with hunger.

The focus changes with the time of year. Our first visit to Caprilands was in May, and our most recent in October, and it's hard to say which is better although spring is somehow special. Each season has its legends and its beauty, and Mrs. Simmons weaves a seasonal spell as she leads you through the gardens.

The woman is not, by the way, an herbal freak who drinks and eats nothing else. While she enjoys a good cup of herbal tea, she also confesses to a hankering for other foods and something stronger than herb tea to drink.

The lecture, whether outdoors in the gardens, or inside the aromatic and pleasant old barn, is spirited, informative and quite funny.

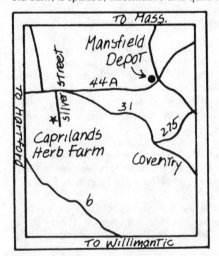

Location: Silver Street, Coventry, Conn., off Route 44A.

Open: Grounds and shop open daily except Thanksgiving and Christmas 9 to 5. Herbal luncheon programs are conducted from April through Dec. 22.

Admission: Gardens are free. The herbal lecture and luncheon is priced at $11.

Telephone: (203) 742-7244.

Afterward, guests are drawn to the 200-year-old house by the aroma of herbal foods. Inside, three rooms — including the original keeping room with its large fireplace — are set up with a comfortable melange of furniture including antique chairs and tables, sofas, a candelabra, and everywhere swags and bunches and arrangements of dried herbs.

Although the menu changes frequently, there is a pattern. First a punch: in May and June a delectable May wine, often afloat with Johnny-jump-ups or violets; in autumn, a sherried cider. While guests sip their cups of punch, a variety of herbal canapes is passed, and guests are allowed to nibble a few before the ingredients are revealed.

Soup is next, possibly a curried corn chowder or a sorrel soup, two favorites. The meal consists of a meat or fish dish, a vegetable casserole, a garden salad, and dessert. Herbs are used in all of the dishes but are combined so artfully that you won't feel as if your senses have been assaulted.

As the luncheon progresses, and it is a leisurely affair, Mrs. Simmons goes from room to room, explaining the courses and telling more stories about the herbs used in that day's food. After lunch, visitors are welcome to wander about the property on their own. Many are drawn to the book and gift shop where Adelma Simmons may be on hand to autograph her books (five in hardcover plus a slew of paper-covered booklets). She will also discuss in greater detail the care and use of herbs. She is quite accessible, a reason for her popularity.

Visitors also like to head for the greenhouses: the geranium greenhouse specializing in scented geraniums, and the new greenhouse gallery with flower and herb seeds, herb plants and perennials. A bouquet and basket shop is adjacent.

The property was bought by Mrs. Simmons and her parents in 1929. The herb farm grew gradually out of a strong, abiding interest in the earth and equally out of her own gift for marketing and selling a concept.

Adelma Simmons is a consumate salesman, but she is a great believer in the product. And if you've never had an herb garden before, don't be surprised if a visit here prompts you to start one.

Also in the Area

Nathan Hale Homestead, South Street, Coventry. (203) 742-6917. Not far from Caprilands is the rambling red house built in 1776 by the patriot's father and home of the Hale family until 1832. Deacon Richard Hale held court here when he served as a justice of the peace. The 10 rooms are furnished as the Hales might have had them with a few items of family memorabilia. An outstanding antiques show is held on a Saturday in late July every year. Open May 15 to Oct. 15 daily 1 to 5. Adults, $1; senior citizens, 75 cents; children, 25 cents.

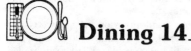 **Dining 14**

Mansfield Depot/Mansfield, Conn.

You might think it curious that a restaurant in which patrons hang their hats on racks strategically placed near the tables in the dining room offers a sophisticated wine list.

Or that in a tiny eastern Connecticut hamlet a restaurant, known locally for continental cuisine, specializes in mussels and in desserts that sound divine but sometimes flop.

But that's the way it is at Mansfield Depot, where a blend of formality and informality makes things interesting. Booted and blue-jeaned patrons have earnest

Interior of Mansfield Depot restaurant.

discussions (this *is* near the University of Connecticut) over $15 bottles of wine while strains of Vivaldi's "Four Seasons" fill the air.

The interior of this restored railway station glows at night as light from hanging green station lamps reflects off the shiny wood walls and bare, polished tables.

The handsome bar on the entrance level has a few tables for dining. Plans were in the works when we last visited for it to become another dining room when the lounge was moved to the far end of the building. Up a few stairs is the main dining room with high beamed ceilings, bare floors, mismatched chairs and a collection of old railway posters, including one of the 20th Century Limited.

At one side, a renovated railway car with fabric banquettes is used at lunch and on busy nights. In the daytime, there's a pastoral view through the back windows and once in awhile a freight train lumbers by.

We've eaten here for lunch and dinner and prefer dinner when the food seems to be taken more seriously. But it's fun at mid-day, too, when the day's specials are chalked on greenboards near the kitchen.

Mussels are usually on the docket; at noon, served in wine they are $5.50, with linguini $5.25. Big but tender, they come with a decent broth for soaking up the sourdough bread which is hot, dense and crusty.

Other entrees at noon include quiche (onion and tomato on the day we visited in winter with a group of friends), fettuccine Depot, which came with broccoli and a garlic cream sauce but was underseasoned, chicken marsala, grilled trout, broiled scrod and tortellini with tomato sauce. We liked best a large crepe, generously filled with a turkey-mushroom mixture and topped with a creamy cheese sauce.

There are numerous burgers and sandwiches (curried chicken salad is served in a plain or club sandwich, and as a salad plate). Other salads include tuna, Caesar, and one with cheese, mushrooms and artichoke hearts.

Hot entrees are $4.25 to $5.25; sandwiches go up to $4.75. The French onion soup, at $1.45 a cup, was worth it, with enough onions and stringy cheese to make it hearty. Beef vegetable and cream of mushroom were recent specials.

Of the desserts ($2 to $3), it was decided that the Russian cream, a goblet of heavy cream and raspberry puree, was the most scrumptious, with a very light, unadorned cheesecake second. Mississippi mud cake tasted like an ordinary chocolate cake, with whipped topping from a can. A German woman in our group, who had been looking forward throughout the meal to a poppyseed torte, was indignant when she tasted it. "This is a cream pie with a few poppyseeds in it," she decried, "and nothing like a real torte you would be served in Germany." Perhaps that is why it since has been taken off the menu and replaced with an apple torte.

At night, having dinner for two, we found our manhattan and gibson unusually good (the house brands must be better than the norm) and the atmosphere most pleasant, with a candle in a patio lamp shimmering on the bare table that was topped with fresh flowers in a small white vase.

The dinner menu lists 16 entrees ($6.95 to $14.95). The greenboard has interesting specials like charbroiled trout with lemon butter or grilled tarragon chicken served over fettuccine.

We were pleased to see an old favorite, Chateau Ste. Michelle chardonnay, on the wine list for $11.95; it was served without an ice bucket, but one was fetched after we asked. Owner Larry Ross prides himself on the wines, which include a number of French bordeaux from $15.95 to $75. There are a couple of local Hamlet Hill vintages, as well as a Marian white zinfandel for $6.95. The house wine is Domaine La Roux, $1.90 a glass and $7.50 a liter.

The appetizers run from $2.95 for mussels in white wine to $5.50 for lobster aioli, tossed in a homemade garlic mayonnaise. Also appealing are a duck liver pate and gravlax.

Again, the sourdough bread was perfect. The salad, served in a large glass bowl, was a mixture of lettuce and red cabbage, carrot strips and celery. We liked very much the house dressing, a creamy garlic with mustard seeds.

We also liked our entrees — mussels in wine ($7.95) and stuffed pork tenderloin ($11.95), rolled around apples, prunes and raisins with a savory sauce. Rice pilaf and just-done carrot and zucchini rounds with a pat of herbed butter were appropriate complements.

Among other entrees, red snapper en papillote, veal Dijonnaise, grilled shrimp with a marmalade-horseradish sauce and breast of chicken stuffed with brie sound like winners, as does the house filet mignon flamed in brandy and served atop a pate-covered crouton with mushroom gravy.

Mansfield Depot seems to attract a youthful crowd, but perhaps that's just because of its proximity to UConn. The staff is hip (and sometimes a bit flip — "it's my electric hands," quipped our waitress as she uncorked the wine and it fizzed a moment). But Mansfield Depot draws from all around the area and we middle-agers don't feel out of place.

One last word on the plethora of wood: the crowning touch is on one of the entrance doors — go up the far set of stairs and see for yourself!

Mansfield Depot, Route 44A, Mansfield Depot, Conn. (203) 429-3663. Lunch, Monday-Saturday 11:30 to 2, dinner 6 to 9:30, weekends 5:30 to 10:30; Sunday, brunch 11 to 2:30, dinner 5 to 9. Major credit cards. Reservations suggested on weekends.

Also in the Area

Altnaveigh Inn, 957 Storrs Road, Storrs. (203) 429-4490. The stone walls indigenous to the area surround this rambling 1734 Colonial farmhouse atop Spring Hall south of the university, marked out front by a striking sign centered with a pineapple logo. The pineapple is the symbol of the homey hospitality that new owners William and Victoria Gaudette try to convey, and they also are conveying a considerably spiffed-up image to a long-established restaurant. Since taking over

. in 1983, they have refurbished the two dining rooms — one, for non-smokers, with white linen and fanned blue napkins, all subdued with candlelight and stenciling on the walls; the other, larger and more colorful, with a large working fireplace and pink stenciled wallpaper, hand-stenciled curtains and pink and cranberry napery. Bill Gaudette, who does the cooking, has dinner entrees from $9.50 to $15.95; listed are salmon stuffed with sole and salmon mousse, roast duckling with a citron glaze, lobster newburg, beef Wellington and steak au poivre. They're served with a choice of green or spinach salad and potato or vegetable. Lunch is lighter and more casual: quiches, sandwiches, shirred eggs provencale and a few entrees like baked scrod or stuffed filet of sole, most in the $3.95 to $4.95 range. The domestic wine list has some exceptional bargains; the house Pere Patriarch is $7 a liter. The Gaudettes, who have refurbished four upstairs rooms for overnighters and planned to add a small cocktail lounge, serve breakfast and Sunday brunch as well. Lunch, Tuesday-Saturday 11:30 to 2:30; dinner 5 to 9 or 10. Sunday, brunch 9 to 2, dinner 2 to 9.

C.W. Walker's Cafe, 101 Union St., Willimantic. (203) 423-6628. Indefatigable Charles Wade Walker took more than five years restoring this old mill house and kosher meat market which had been converted into five apartments before opening his restaurant in 1983. Outside, it looks not unlike a Southern ante-bellum house; inside it's a roundabout maze of rooms and alcoves on three floors, including an airy new upstairs dining room with skylights and a popular outdoor deck. A framed collage of photos at the entrance shows the progress of the remarkable restoration; also notable is the salad bar ensconced in an old piano. Lunch is mainly salads and sandwiches, the latter all $4.25 and cutely named for presidents (the James Knox Polk has sliced turkey breast with avocado sauce) or Thread City landmarks ("Willimantic Falls," "Threadmill Square"). With a new kitchen in 1985, Wade Walker planned to add a more substantial dinner menu to complement nightly specials; entrees were to be in the $8.50 to $11.50 range. Open weekdays from 11, Sundays from noon.

The Clark's, 28 North St., Willimantic. (203) 423-1631. Very popular locally, the Clark's has been around and owned by the same family for more than 35 years — first in a ramshackle red wooden building, in the last few years in a large modern structure next door. The decor is vaguely Colonial with pine paneling and lots of red. Dinners are from $7.95 for chicken pie ("a perennial favorite here for more than 30 years," according to the menu), to $12.95 for tenderloin steak with mushrooms or baked jumbo shrimp. There are specials like scallop pie and roast stuffed pork every night. At lunch, you can get sandwiches, salad plates and entrees like baked fisherman's casserole with buttercrumbs and lamb fricassee with rice pilaf ($l.25 to $6.95). The sealegs saute, a recent luncheon special, was $3.90. Lunch, Monday-Friday 11:30 to 3, dinner from 5, Sunday noon to 8.

Sadler's Ordinary, Old New London Turnpike off Route 2, Marlborough. (203) 295-0006. Country food at country prices in a country atmosphere is the draw at this restaurant, part of the early American village in the Marlborough Country Barn complex. Popular with families, it stresses wholesome foods at both lunch and dinner. The hearty vegetable paysanne soup in a rich but light stock is $1.25 a cup, $2 a bowl. Continue with an omelet, a tuna or chicken salad plate or any of a dozen sandwiches ($1 for peanut butter and honey to $4.50 for open steak). Desserts ($1.25 to $1.75) run from tapioca and bread puddings to cream cheese pecan and French silk pies; all baking is done on the premises and available for take-out. Among dinner entrees ($5 to $9), the baked stuffed sole wrapped around an herb-vegetable-bread stuffing and the crab-stuffed chicken are favorites; there are also a variety of stir-fry items plus shrimp Creole and steak teriyaki. Beer and wine are available, and a half portion of any meal for children under 12 is half price. Lunch from 11, dinner from 4; closed Mondays.

Gillette Castle.

River View; Castle, Too

Gillette Castle/Hadlyme, Conn.

A nice way to approach Gillette Castle in Hadlyme, Conn., is as its owner first did, via the Connecticut River. It's possible, too — aboard the tiny ferry that plies its way between Hadlyme and Chester "on demand," carrying six cars and several foot passengers.

The ferry is fun and just a five-minute ride, but from the river you get a magnificent aspect of green hills with the castle nestled among them, a view that first enchanted the Connecticut actor, William Gillette. The Hartford-born Gillette wasn't on the ferry, but aboard his houseboat on a leisurely cruise up the river when he discovered the site. He was returning from Greenport, Long Island, where he had all but decided to build the home of his dreams, and had anchored for the night close to the spot where the Chester-Hadlyme ferry now docks.

Gillette woke up the next morning to a view that held him captive for a few extra days, long enough to abandon plans for the Long Island house and start planning on building one here. He purchased 122 acres of land with nearly a mile of shorefront. And in the next five years, between 1914 and 1919, he had a "castle" built to his exacting specifications. Gillette never called it one, but that is what it is, a massive stone building atop the southernmost hill in a series along the river known as the Seven Sisters. Gillette called his own home "The Seventh Sister."

For an actor it was a terrific stage set. No copy of a castle in Spain or England, Gillette's castle came from his own inventive mind. The aging actor, who was in his 60s at the time, drew all of the architectural plans himself. And not only the castle,

99

with its four-to-five-foot-thick granite walls, 24 oddly shaped rooms and marvelous stone terraces (wait until you view the river from them), but the furniture, too, was designed by Gillette.

Most of it is heavy, hand-hewn oak. The dining room table moves along on metal tracks on the floor; some of the bedroom furniture is built into the structure of the castle itself; even the lights were designed by the actor. Stout oak doors are fastened by intricate wooden locks reminiscent of Rube Goldberg; at every turn there is more evidence of Gillette's own personality.

But the actor-architect undoubtedly had the most fun creating a railroad on the castle grounds, a reflection of his favorite hobby — trains and locomotives. (Already at the age of 16 in his Hartford home he had built a stationary steam engine.)

The train in Hadlyme accommodated passengers and was, in fact, Gillette's favorite way to entertain his many visitors. They boarded at "Grand Central," a depot close to the castle itself, which survives as a picnicking site in today's park. With Gillette at the throttle (and we are told he was no overly cautious engineer), the group would travel through forest and glen to "125th Street Station," then to the east of the property, back to Castle Oak near the present entrance and finally around to Grand Central again. It was a three-mile ride.

The train has long since gone to Lake Compounce Amusement Park in Bristol, Conn., and most of the tracks have been dismantled.

But even without the train, the castle attracts more than 120,000 visitors a year under the auspices of Connecticut's state park system. It is probably as Gillette would have wished. The forthright actor, who wrote his will just months before his death at the age of 87, wanted his executors to see "that the property does not fall into the hands of some blithering saphead who has no conception of where he is or with what surrounded."

That didn't happen, for the state acquired the property in 1943, just six years after the actor's death. Inside the castle, in addition to the unusual inventions and furnishings, are the rich mementos of William Gillette's long and successful stage career. He was known best for his creation of the role of Sherlock Holmes in a play which he wrote himself as an adaptation of the Arthur Conan Doyle character, and was honored in his own day. He actually performed the role more than 13,000 times across the country.

Theater buffs will enjoy the stage memorabilia — in particular the room which is

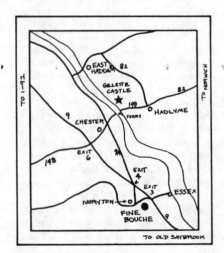

Location: Route 148. Exit 68-69 from Connecticut Thruway to Route 9. Exit 6 from Route 9 to take the Chester-Hadlyme ferry; Exit 7 to take Route 82 and the bridge to East Haddam; follow 82 south to 148.

Open: 11 to 5 daily, mid-May to Columbus Day, and weekends from Columbus Day to Christmas.

Admission: Park is free. To tour castle, $1 for those 12 and over; 50 cents apiece for children under 12.

Telephone: (203) 526-2336.

almost an exact replica of the stage set for the play in which Gillette starred. That room is on the third floor of the castle, approached by narrow staircases from the second floor balcony which overlooks the grand living room and massive fireplace.

There's an art gallery, too, with exhibits which change from time to time, a "bar" which transforms into a simple cupboard, and mini-greenhouses with bubbling fountains off the living room. You can see it on a guided tour if the day you visit isn't too crowded; otherwise, you will go on your own and interpreters throughout the building will be on hand to answer questions.

Prior to Christmas the castle is open weekends and decorated for the season as it would have been when Gillette was in residence.

The castle is not all there is to the state park. It serves as the focal point, but there are also views of river and woods, and trails leading through a dark and lush pine forest. A variety of spots are perfect for picnics and there is a snack bar.

On one visit we arrived just before noon via the Chester-Hadlyme ferry and went through the castle (it takes about half an hour) before spreading our lunch on a table in the Grand Central Station area. It sits nearest the river of any picnic spot and its thick stone walls make it welcomingly cool on a hot summer day. After lunch we spotted signs for the "Loop Trail" and hiked down the walkway to get closer to the water. It was not a strenuous walk — about a half mile — and rewarded us with natural loveliness.

Other trails wander through the park; there are also meadows and a lily pond. And recently the State of Connecticut has reconstructed a goldfish pond which will be stocked once it has filled with water from an underground spring.

Gillette is not buried on the property; his grave is in Farmington, Conn., next to his wife of six years, Helen Nickles Gillette, whose early death caused him great sadness.

A visit to Gillette Castle can be happily combined with a stops across the river at Chester and upriver at East Haddam. In both communities, the presence of the Goodspeed Opera House has encouraged the establishment of fine small shops and good restaurants.

Also in the Area

Chester-Hadlyme Ferry. Route 148 (either direction). Daily, April-November 7 a.m. to 8 p.m., 75 cents for car and driver.

Goodspeed Opera House, East Haddam. (203) 873-8668. Overlooking the Connecticut River, this Victorian opera house is enjoying a revival — of musicals, of interest, of enthusiasm. Three shows, mostly musical revivals, are presented each season, which extends from mid-April to early December. The Goodspeed's track record is fine in sending its productions on to Broadway, including "Man of La Mancha," "Shenandoah" and "Annie." You can attend the Goodspeed Tuesday through Friday evenings at 8, Wednesday matinee at 2:30, Saturdays at 5 and 9, and Sunday at 5. The house is dark Mondays. The smell of popcorn, from an old-fashioned popcorn wagon, fills the lobby and cocktails or champagne can be sipped during intermission on the porch which overlooks the river. Reservations are a must. **The Goodspeed at Chester,** located in a renovated factory building in the nearby river town of Chester, opened in 1984 and presents four new musicals a season. Open from mid-April through Christmas, the Norma Terris theater features a bar and candy shop in the lobby and is located in a charming town. Ticket prices are somewhat lower than those at the Goodspeed proper and performances are really fun. Curtain times: Tuesday-Saturday at 8, Wednesday, Saturday and Sunday at 2.

Dining 15 _____

Fine Bouche restaurant .

Fine Bouche/Centerbrook, Conn.

Rare is the restaurant whose menu is so well-chosen that you want to order every single item from soup to nuts. Rarer still is the restaurant whose menu changes so frequently and experiments so widely that you could happily go back and back and back, and never be bored nor sated.

Such is Fine Bouche, the petite paradise for gourmets in a Victorian house in Centerbrook, the creation and continuing triumph of young chef-owner Steven Wilkinson.

The inspired food is overseen personally by Steve Wilkinson, who apprenticed in London and San Francisco before opening his French restaurant and patisserie in 1979 to immediate acclaim. The variety on the menu reflects his wide-ranging tastes and a word-processing computer, which helps him change the menu daily to take advantage of what's fresh and available. "I can create and substitute on a moment's notice," he explained at our last visit.

And talk about creativity! For Easter Sunday, the menu was Russian; for Mother's Day, New Orleans and Cajun. In between was the third annual Baccanale di Primavera, a five-course dinner of Northern Italian regional dishes and wines. Following that was a week featuring the foods and wines of Spain and Portugal.

So it should not surprise one to find a dinner menu so appealing that the choice between selections is agonizing. Consider this recent offering for the five-course, $29 prix-fixe dinner:

For appetizers, papillotes of smoked salmon filled with a mousse of smoked trout and served with a sauce of creme fraiche and fresh herbs, stuffed shiitake mushrooms with a light garlic sauce, rabbit terrine, terrine of seafood with a fresh herb mayonnaise and puree of sweet red peppers, or a puff pastry with chicken quenelles and fresh asparagus in a tarragon and butter sauce.

For the soup or fish course, cream of asparagus, mussel soup provencale with garlic mayonnaise, filet of salmon with a red wine and butter sauce, or oysters, sole mousse and fennel with a cream and pernod sauce.

For entrees following the salad course, sauteed slices of veal with wild mushrooms, pepper steak with cognac sauce, sauteed breast of duck with petit sirah sauce and kiwi, or rack of lamb with herbes de Provence.

And for dessert, almond-hazelnut dacquoise, a strawberry-almond tart with apricot glaze, a heavenly marjolaine or fresh fruit sorbet.

Dining here is a fairly serious matter, as you might expect, with quiet classical music on tape and attentive but discreet service. Yet the experience is quite unpretentious and comfortable.

You enter through the patisserie, pausing for a look at the delectable things you might order for dessert, pass the handsome paneled service bar and wait for your table in a quiet reception parlor, where two lighted, glassed-in cases contain interesting memorabilia of the owner's career — special menus from London, empty bottles of rare wine, cookbooks, French plates and the like.

The two inner dining rooms, which seat 45, are small and inviting. One has cream colored walls with pictures of grapes and vines and reproduction Chippendale chairs with rust velvet seats. The other has pretty dark green and flowered wallpaper and old French prints. Linens are white and the flower arrangements are simple field flowers.

Especially nice for lunch is a cafe-style wraparound porch seating 15 to 20, a picture of pristine cheer with white, not quite sheer full-length curtains, arched lattice work over the windows, peach-colored walls and rattan chairs, the seats covered by a dark green chintz dotted with exotic lilies.

Lunch entrees, in the $7.95 range, might be sauteed scallops, chicken tarragon, ham and asparagus crepe, a salad of baked French goat cheeese served on a bed of radicchio and green leaf lettuce or a smoked fish platter with trout, salmon and sauce swedoise. You also can get a choice of soups and croissant sandwiches.

But it is dinner where the Fine Bouche repertoire is at its best. Although the prix-fixe dinner is a remarkable yet adventuresome bargain at $29, you can order the same appetizers and soups a la carte ($4.75 to $7) and a wider selection of dinner entrees from $14 to $19.

We remember with fondness a recent meal of warm duck pate in puff pastry, grilled oysters with fresh herb sauce, sweetbreads and filet of veal with mushrooms, Madeira and tarragon, and a rich genoise for dessert (and that was just for one of us), along with a bottle of Dry Creek fume blanc for a pleasant $12.50.

The wine list is exceptional, with an emphasis on French but an interesting selection of other European imports as well as Californias, fairly priced from $8.50 to $175.

Dinner is well worth the three-week wait for reservations on weekends. If you can't get in, do settle for lunch on the pristine porch, a sprightly tonic for a summer day.

Fine Bouche, Main Street, Centerbrook, Conn. (203) 767-1277. Open Tuesday-Saturday, lunch noon to 2 and dinner 6 to 9. Major credit cards. Reservations required at night, recommended at lunch.

Also in the Area

Restaurant du Village, 59 Main St., Chester. (203) 526-5058. Just a ferry ride across the Connecticut River from Hadlyme is the up-and-coming community of Chester and the prized Restaurant du Village, which also opened in 1979. It's about as provincial French as you can get, from its canopied blue facade to the white-curtained windows and French doors onto the side brick entryway which are kept open on warm nights for welcome breezes. The 40-seat dining room is charming in its simplicity: a few French oil paintings, white linens, carafes of wild flowers and a votive candle on each table, and blue flower-sprigged Laura Ashley-type service plates. The best French bread we've ever tasted comes with generous cocktails. Among appetizers ($5.75 to $7.50), the mussels with cream and curry are plump and delicious and the plate of terrines ranges from smooth to hearty. Entrees run from $16 to $20; we recommend the sweetbreads in a rich sauce of three mushrooms, the sauteed sole of the day, the marinated leg of lamb sauteed with garlic and the enormous rib eye of beef with peppercorn, tarragon and whiskey sauce. Desserts vary from a strawberry kirsch cream pudding-like affair served in a goblet and topped with walnuts to bitter chocolate granite with coffee sauce, served in a fluted pastry shell. The extensive wine list starts at $11.50. The lunch menu is fairly limited: soup and salad, $5, and five entrees from $5.75 for pate with salad to $8.75 for salad Nicoise. Lunch, Wednesday-Friday noon to 2; dinner, Wednesday-Sunday 6 to 9.

The Inn at Chester, 318 W. Main St., Chester. (203) 526-4961. Dining in this luxury inn which opened in 1983 takes place in the old John B. Parmelee House, the name of the first owner of the property, in a smashing high-ceilinged barn that was previously owner David Joslow's living room. The walls are of dark rough wood, but light pours through a greenhouse window addition, where geraniums and cacti in clay pots bake in the sun. Accent colors of deep blue, lovely flowered china and fresh flowers in blue vases give a rustic but elegant atmosphere here and on the outdoor patio with wrought-iron furniture. At dinner, the changing menu varies from $13.75 for a pork chop stuffed with herbs and garnished with spinach pancakes to $19.50 for rack of lamb coated with mustard and herbs. Among the offerings are cranberry roasted duckling, pecan trout, Cajun shrimp etouffee and rabbit in wine sauce — the last a superb dish served with onions on a bed of homemade spinach noodles. Appetizers start at $5.25, include a fine oyster and bacon brochette atop warm cucumber salad, baked garlic with goat cheese, salmon strudel laced with caviar and creme fraiche, and the chef's fancy, an assortment of appetizers that we've found worth the $6.50 tab. At lunch, soup and salad are $4.50 and entrees, $5.50 for cheese rarebit to $8.25 for salmon with leek sauce. Last time we lunched our party enjoyed a delicious scallop and corn soup and a black bean soup accompanied by chopped egg, onion and a small carafe of sherry to pour in, house salads dressed with raspberry vinaigrette, calves liver accompanied by fried apple slices and thread-thin fried onions, a Michigan pastie (meat and vegetable turnover) and a special chicken, almond and avocado salad. The Parmelee platter ($6.75) has rabbit pate, venison sausage, smoked cheese and Waldorf salad. Lunch, daily noon to 2, dinner 6 to 9, Sunday brunch 11 to 2; closed Tuesday.

Fiddler's Seafood Restaurant, 4 Water St., Chester. (203) 526-3210. A cheerful cafe atmosphere prevails in the two blue and white dining rooms of this new restaurant, which features three or four kinds of fresh fish poached, sauteed or grilled over mesquite. The prices are reasonable; at lunch you can get oyster stew with salad, lobster roll with fries or zuppa de clams or mussels for $4.50; pasta primavera with salad is $3.95. Dinner entrees ($9.95 to $13.95) include oysters imperial, scallops with black mushrooms, bouillabaiise, and lobster with peaches in a peach brandy and cream sauce. Lunch, Tuesday-Saturday 11:30 to 2, dinner 5:30 to 9 or 10, Sunday 4 to 9; closed Monday.

Gelston House, Goodspeed's Landing, East Haddam. (203) 873-1411. Just up the river from Gillette Castle next to the Victorian opera house and with a lovely view of the river is this recently refurbished restaurant-turned-inn under auspices of David Joslow of the Inn at Chester. The main dining room (newly carpeted in plush rust) has windows onto the river and couldn't be more romantic on a moonlit night after the pre-theater crowds have departed, and the new Winter Garden serves raw-bar type seafood, sandwiches, soups and salads from around noon to 9. Our favorite is the outdoor Beer Garden for casual dishes like bratwurst and potato salad, and for its smashing setting by the water. Inside, the menu is new American with a water theme and dishes like calves liver Lake Champlain and jambalaya for lunch ($5.50 to $7.25), Columbia River salmon or tournedos Casco Bay at night ($9.95 to $16.95). Lunch, Monday-Friday 11:30 to 2, Saturday noon to 4, Sunday brunch 11 to 2:30; dinner, 5:30 to 9, to 10 on weekends, Sunday 3:30 to 9.

Griswold Inn, Main Street, Essex. (203) 767-0991. Some things seldom change, and the immensely popular Gris is one of them. The always-crowded Tap Room is a happy hubbub of banjo players or singers of sea chanteys, and everyone loves the antique popcorn machine. The four atmosphere-laden dining rooms are nearly always full, offering a mixed-bag of seafood, meat and game for $8.95 to $16.95. You order the 17 wines by the bin number; better than half are available in half bottles. The inn's famous 1776 sausages, served with potato salad and sauerkraut, are available to take home and come four ways at lunch, when the fare is lighter and more varied. Did we say the Gris never changes? It's added three "Southern Secrets" at lunch, including fried catfish with hush puppies, barbecued ribs and chicken, and Cajun red beans and rice. Lunch, Monday-Saturday noon to 2, dinner 6 to 9 or 10, Sunday 5 to 9. The famed Hunt Breakfast is served Sundays from 10:30 to 2.

The Dock at Saybrook Point, Saybrook Point. (203) 388-4665. As if Griswold Inn owner William Winterer didn't have enough to do, he's acquired the old Dock 'n Dine and, after several false starts trying to upgrade its image, returned it to its basic seafood fare in 1985. "We've come back to the ocean," said the manager, which is not illogical considering the spacious establishment has perhaps the best water location around, where river meets Sound. The all-day menu has something for everyone; seafood platters are stressed, and you can create your own by combining two items for $10.95. Steamers are $4.95, three fish in a dish are $9.95 and the Nantucket bucket feast from smoked sausage to lobster is $19.95. Sea salt and tabasco sauce are at each papermat-covered table. A raw bar is near the entrance, there's a new ice cream bar for sundaes and an American wine bar offers wines by the glass. Open from 11:30 a.m. daily in summer, closed Monday in winter.

Seashell Cafe, Porter Plaza, Main Street, Old Saybrook. (203) 388-1510. Seashells are etched on the door of this small new cafe, open for breakfast and lunch, and on the handsome wallpaper. A grand sideboard holds a collection of whimsical artifacts; blue cloths are topped with flowered napkins in different colors, and the counter is dominated by a large copper espresso machine. A blackboard menu lists the day's wares — usually a couple of soups like clam chowder or split pea, a quiche, sandwiches on pita bread, brie baked with almonds and apple, even peanut butter and jelly on raisin toast. Rice pudding and cheesecake are a couple of the desserts. Prices are very reasonable. It's the coffees that owner Mildred Taylor prides herself on — a different flavor is offered each day, $1.75 for a small pot, $3 for a large. Amaretto, sambucca, cinnamon and Swiss chocolate almond are a few, and the beans are all for sale, for $6.25 a pound. Espresso and cappuccino, regular or pure water decaffeinated, are $1 and $1.50, respectively. Breakfast from 8 to 3, lunch from 11 to 6 or 7; closed Monday.

Daytrip 16 _____

Boat basin among the Thimble Islands.

Island Hopping

Thimble Islands / Off Stony Creek, Conn.

Vacation islands with pirate treasure? Yes, and you don't have to go to the West Indies to find them.

Right off the coast in Connecticut, so close in fact that one of them can be reached on foot at low tide, are the Thimble Islands, which legend says may be the hiding place for the treasure of that pirate extraordinaire, Captain William Kidd.

No one has found it yet. But the kids on Money Island spend hours and hours every summer searching in a cave on that island. And on High Island, which residents have renamed Kidd's Island, they paint their cottages black and fly the Jolly Roger in the pirate tradition. It's all in fun, of course.

There's a lot of that out on the Thimbles, which have been used as a summer resort since the Indians first paddled out in canoes and camped on Governor's Island.

The compact archipelago, which legend says number 365 islands in all (one for every day of the year), lies within a radius of five miles off the shore at Stony Creek, east of New Haven. There are probably nowhere near 365 islands, even if you count every rock that raises its head above water level at low tide, but the 32 inhabited Thimbles, ranging from three-quarter-acre Dogfish Rock to 17-acre Horse Island, represent nearly as many islands as can be found all along the rest of Connecticut's shore.

Like other islands off New England, the Thimbles are a gift of the glacial age, formed after the great ice cap melted and "drowned" huge portions of shoreline. From shore they look like great stone masses rising from the sea; for centuries, their very nearness has intrigued mainlanders, who could see them but for the most part couldn't quite reach them. It's that "couldn't quite" that makes the difference.

Thimble Islanders are enamored of their world apart and fiercely protective of their privacy.

For the 90 or so cottage owners — one cottage is actually a 27-room mansion, but most are much smaller — the Thimbles provide a way of life that is much simpler than the hustle and bustle of ordinary living. They have no electricity, no roads, few telephones, no stores. While a few people use generators to recharge batteries or run vacuum cleaners and irons, most are content with gas and kerosene lights and doing without television until the season is over.

Actually, the Thimbles (named for a wild thimbleberry which grew there) are much less commercial today than they once were. Their heyday was late in the 19th century when the islands boasted two hotels and there were at least five more in Stony Creek. Regular excursion boats made the run from New Haven, and from then until World War I the islands enjoyed real prosperity.

Now they are privately owned. The hotels have become private residences and other than invited guests, non-residents are clearly unwelcome.

But while tourists aren't free to walk (or more aptly, climb) around on the Thimbles, they can sail through them, and if they don't have their own boat, they can hitch a ride on a small ferry which winds its way among the islands, taking the islanders back and forth to Stony Creek and delivering groceries, messages, mail and other links with the mainland — sometimes even furniture.

Regular service is provided by Dwight H. Carter, who says he's a descendant of one of the oldest families on the islands (seven generations) and for a price he'll take tourists along for the ride. This is island-hopping in the truest sense of the word, as the "Volsunga III" with its 33-passenger capacity putts its way from island to island.

You can sit back in the boat, enjoy the breeze and listen to the "yarn" that Captain Carter spins about the islands as he goes. The story, since it's live each

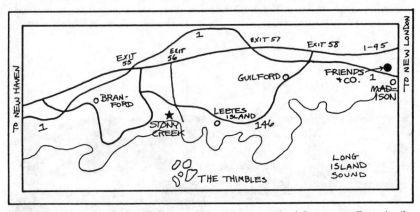

Location: Stony Creek, Conn., is east of New Haven, south of Connecticut Turnpike (I-95). Take Exit 56 from the turnpike and head south.

Boat trips around the Thimbles are provided by two sources. Dwight Carter and his "Volsunga III" give regular daily service from mid-May to early October. His boat leaves on the hour between 8 a.m. and 9 p.m. Sightseers pay $3 (adults) and $2 (children) and are not permitted to get off on any of the islands, which are strictly private. Commentary is live and usually given on trips from noon to 5 p.m. and in the evening. Call ahead to be sure: (203) 488-9978. Mike Infantino runs the "Sea Mist" daily on the hour from 10 to 5. A full narrated history is also given live. Prices are $3 (adults) and $2 (children).

Telephone: (203) 481-4841.

trip, is apt to change a bit from the script. But some of the facts and fancies are bound to be the same.

You're likely to hear about Captain Kidd, of course. Even though the infamous pirate's visit to the Thimbles has never been documented, it is known that he sailed around Long Island Sound in 1699 after his return from the Indies and before his capture and the Thimbles, some people think, would have been a great place to hide treasure. The Buccaneers (as they call themselves) on High Island even point to a hidden harbor between the island's two halves and ask if that might not have been the spot.

Governor's Island, to which the Indians went first, is said to have 16 cottages and 40 kinds of trees, thanks to a botanist who once summered there and planted them as a hobby.

Money Island is actually the most densely populated of the Thimbles, with all 30 cottages clinging precariously to the granite that makes up the island. Because of all that stone (the base of the Statue of Liberty is made of Thimble Islands granite), the islands have never been much good for farming or grazing, which is why they developed the only way they could — as resorts.

Horse Island was so named because some horses were found there long ago, presumably after they swam ashore from a nearby ship.

There's a good story about Mother-in-Law's Island. A young couple from one of the other islands was married and decided to begin their honeymoon on this island, which was, at the time, deserted. The girl's mother, concerned about her daughter, rowed over to the island to see how things were going. The irate son-in-law took his bride and rowed ashore, taking the mother-in-law's boat as well. Islanders who were sympathetic with young love didn't rescue the mother-in-law for three full days.

It's that kind of story, and more, that you'll hear out on the boat with Dwight Carter or with Mike Infantino, who runs another sightseeing boat, "Sea Mist."

Parking is tight in Stony Creek (all islanders must leave their cars on shore), so you may have to park some distance from the dock and walk the rest of the way. It

One of the more inhabited sections of Thimble Islands.

108

is a fun walk along the waterfront, and you might stop to watch the traffic in the harbor if you have the time and inclination.

The entire circuit of the islands takes between 30 and 45 minutes, but there is more to do in the area. The charming town of Guilford, with shops and art galleries, is right up the road. And if you have your own boat, you might drag it along and explore the Thimbles and the nearby shoreline on your own.

Also in the Area

Westwoods Trail System, Guilford (Call Town Recreation Department, Church Street, Guilford, at 453-2763). One and a half miles west of the Guilford Green off the Boston Post Road (Route 1) via Dunk Rock Road is this open space area of 2,000 acres in all. Part is owned by the State of Connecticut, part by the Guilford Land Conservation Trust, a small portion by the Town of Guilford; the rest is privately owned. Six marked hiking trails and a bridle path traverse the area that ranges from low and marshy to high and rugged. A map is available at the Guilford Recreation Department.

Whitfield House Museum, Whitfield Street, Guilford. (203) 453-2457. New England's oldest stone house (1639-40) was built as a stronghold, meeting hall and minister's house. Beautifully furnished with 17th and 18th century furnishings, the house also has a large herb garden. Open April-November, Wednesday-Sunday 10 to 5; November-April, 10 to 4. Closed Thanksgiving and Dec. 15 to Jan. 15. Adults, $1.25; youths 6 to 18, 50 cents; senior citizens, 75 cents.

 **Dining 16**

Friends & Company/Madison, Conn.

Yes, friends, this is a restaurant, as the words incorporated into the logo attest. And a good one, although you might not know it from its undistinguished dark wood exterior along busy Route 1 at the Guilford-Madison town line.

It is owned by Richard Evarts and Mack Walker, who were friends, and friends helped them open it in 1981. And a casual, friendly atmosphere prevails — hence the name.

The main dining room is good-looking with a fireplace, nine intimate booths, bentwood chairs at bare shiny pine tables except for four covered with linen along one wall, mixed fresh flowers (different at each table) and hurricane lamps, interesting crocheted and lace designs in glass dividers between booths, and dried flowers embedded in the front windows, which look out across Route 1 and the East River marshes toward Long Island Sound. Taped classical music plays in the background.

The limited menu is supplemented by blackboard specials, since Friends prides itself on seasonal produce and fresh fish, simply prepared. You'll probably want to order from the blackboard, but the problem is there's only one at the entrance and it doesn't move. So you must read fast and almost have to make your selection on the spot as the hostess waits to escort you to your seat. (Although the waitress will refresh your memory, the spiel is long enough that things get confusing if you haven't already made up your mind.)

The prepared lunch menu lists only five items (fresh flounder, chicken teriyaki, petite sirloin, hamburger and salad, ($3.25 to $5.95), plus "just for kids," a ham-

Dining corner at Friends & Company.

burger with salad and milk ($1.95), a half dozen side dishes and "finishing touches" — desserts and beverages. The blackboard was far more elaborate: entrees ($4.50 to $5.75) like broiled bay scallops, grilled mako shark with herbed butter, chicken Romesco, crab casserole with onion, green pepper, Swiss cheese, herbed bread crumbs and salad, and cheese tortellini with cream sauce, mushrooms and peas; sandwiches ($3.50 to $3.95) like curried vegetable and smoked turkey Florentine.

Service at lunch was lightning fast. A platter of the restaurant's special breads (for sale at $1.50 a loaf — the recipes are secret) with a ramekin of butter garnished with lettuce arrived at our table almost as we did. One was white and herbed with dill, fennel, basil and rosemary; the other was dark molasses-laden rye. Both were excellent.

A glass of the monthly featured house wine, Muscadet de Sevre et Maine ($2.25), arrived with our entrees. The flounder was stuffed with crabmeat and topped with a dill sauce, and was garnished with orange slices. Orange slices as well as green apple slices also came with the curried shrimp (mixed with chutney, cashews and coconut) in puff pastry, served cold, much to our surprise. A side order of vegetable fritters, a house specialty, was recommended as a tasty alternative to french fries.

At dinner, kids can still get a hamburger for $1.95 and chicken teriyaki for $3.50. The menu offers eight entrees ($7.75 to $11.50, things like veal saute, shrimp saute and New York sirloin), plus sliced sirloin with sauteed mushrooms for two (a bargain at $17.95).

Again the blackboard often is more interesting. There's an acclaimed Portuguese seafood stew with mussels, clams, sausages, leeks, saffron and chablis for $11.75, plus perhaps sauteed scallops, swordfish or lamb kabob. Breads and the house or spinach salad accompany. The dressings are homemade and, an unusual touch, a ceramic tray made by the sister of one of the owners and containing a variety of seeds comes with the salad.

The full dinner menu as well as sandwiches are served in the bar, which is helpful on weekends when the waits can be long (no reservations are accepted).

110

Although a few special wines are offered each month, the regular wine list is severely limited, although it has a couple of interesting offerings like Louis Latour pinot chardonnay and Chateau Ste. Michelle merlot in the $11 range. Firestone merlot was a special when we were there, $2.50 a glass and $9.75 a bottle.

The desserts are limited, too, but Friends makes its own hazelnut cheesecake, mud pie and ice cream crepe with hot fudge ($1.85 or $1.95). Otherwise it's all ice cream.

If you like fun and informality, Friends & Company is a fine spot for a good, quick meal.

Friends & Company, 11 Boston Post Road, Madison, Conn. 203 245-0461. Lunch, Monday-Friday 11:30 to 2; dinner 5 to 10, to 11 on weekends. Sunday, brunch 11:30 to 2:30 and dinner 4:30 to 9. Major credit cards. No reservations taken.

Also in the Area

The Bayberry Inne, 220 E. Main St., Branford. (203) 488-6544. A small 1850s house was converted at Christmas 1984 into a Colonial-style restaurant by Joyce Peterson, owner of a paint and wallpaper store, and her original business shows. The colorful exterior — beige with rust trim — continues inside with beige walls and deep blue trim, handsome wallpaper and stenciling and brass accents on the fireplace mantels. Even the waitresses are color-coordinated with dark skirts and beige blouses. The Colonial touches give way to a Victorian tea room atmosphere, what with dimpled glass plates and an intimate if rather cramped feeling in the two small dining rooms. The food is first-rate. At lunch, there are oversized sandwiches, a daily quiche and, among entrees ($4.95 to $7.95), tomato royale stuffed with crabmeat and a Mexican special of spicy beef with lettuce, sour cream, olives and tortilla chips. We enjoyed a huge salad plate called "fresh and fanciful" with cheese, chicken, bean sprouts, avocado and much more on shredded lettuce, and fettuccine with clams, heavy on the clams and resting in a delectable buttery sauce. Toasted breads and a croissant accompanied. Lunch was so filling we skipped such desserts as lemon meringue pie, linzer torte and lover's chocolate tart with raspberries. Dinners run from $9.95 for chicken cordon bleu to $14.95 for baked stuffed shrimp. Like the menu, the wine list is limited but well chosen and eminently reasonable. Lunch and dinner, Monday-Saturday 11:30 to 3 and 5 to 9 or 10.

The Sovereign, 225 Montowese St., Branford. (203) 481-4222. Serving "continental cuisine with royal flourishes" is this tiny but ambitious restaurant, opened in 1984 in a former Italian restaurant on Branford's green. The narrow room is made to feel wider by judiciously-placed mirrors; pink napkins, white cloths, a wine-colored carpet, posters of flowers and handsome and comfortable blond wood chairs add to the glamorous look. You can check out the delectable desserts on the cart as you enter. Mike Stevens, formerly of the Gelston House, and his British-born wife preside; the chef is 27-year-old Mark Baker, a Johnson and Wales culinary graduate. Luncheon entrees are mostly under $6 and include a sausage and herbed cheese puff pastry pie, crepes St. Jacques, chicken salad on a croissant, smoked roast beef sandwich and a spinach salad garnished with pignoli nuts and gorgonzola cheese with a hot bacon caraway dressing. For $7.95 at Sunday brunch, you can have a split of sparkling wine and a choice of things like schnitzel a la Holstein, finnan haddie cakes (all smoking of fish and meats is done on the premises), omelet boursin and tournedos with bearnaise sauce and eggs. At night, hors d'oeuvre include spatzle Liederkranz, smoked duck with raspberry sauce and mussels in a marinara sauce, $3.95 to $6.25. The extensive list of entrees includes four fish, four poultry and eight meat dishes, $12.95 to $18 (for venison scallops).

111

You could try pheasant stuffed with herbed rice, chicken tossed with morels, spiced shrimp in a saffron sauce or rack of lamb with a royal branston sauce. The house salad is usually Boston lettuce with a gorgonzola dressing. Finish, if you dare, with a lingonberry frangipan, chocolate walnut torte or fresh strawberry cheesecake. The limited wine list will soon give way to one of more sophistication, says Stevens, but the Rodet house wines ($1.75 a glass, $7 a liter) are fine. Lunch, Tuesday-Friday; dinner, Tuesday-Saturday. Sunday brunch, 10:30 to 3. Closed Monday.

L'Entree, Marina Village, 51 Boston Post Rd., Madison. (203) 245-1337. The pink neon duck stands out in the window of this small shopping-center restaurant, which used to be a cheese shop, Say Cheese. Owner Frank Paladino decided it would be more fun to run a restaurant, so in came his pal Bill Carroll (they grew up together in Madison), formerly manager of FitzWilly's in New Haven, to be chef and partner. They filled the cheese display counter with plants and a very pleasing restaurant has been created ("out of zero money," says Paladino) with lots of greenery, pink and gray linens, teacup roses on each table and some well-chosen baskets and posters for decor. At night there are generally four entrees, changing every night; usually a veal, beef, seafood and pasta dish, around $8 to $15. Sauces are light; herbs for them are grown by a gentleman in Killingworth. Carroll tries cuisines of many countries; he especially shines on his duck preparations, offered mostly on weekends. Of the appetizers ($3.25 to $4.95) the escargots en croute and the sauteed batter-covered mozzarella with a lovely fresh tomato sauce are outstanding. At noon there are salads, lobster croustade, seafood strudel, cheese board and interesting sandwiches, and nothing is over $5.95. Since you may bring your own wine (the owners hoped to get a beer and wine license one of these days), the resulting check is on the light side. Sunday brunch is planned for the fall of 1985. Lunch and dinner daily, 11:30 to 10; closed Sunday.

Chowder Pot, 560 Main St., Branford. (203) 481-2356. From a seafood shanty, the Chowder Pot has moved and expanded twice, and each time the crowds get larger. Seafood — fresh, fried and lots of it at reasonable prices — are the draw. Sandwiches start at $2.95 for breaded sole, a lobster roll is $6.25 and a dozen seafood platters are from $7.95 to $9.95. The decor at the newly expanded (again) Chowder Pot is dark and nautical in an upscale sort of way; there's dancing in the lounge. An artistic display of crab legs, huge shrimp and the like is a feature of the raw bar near the entrance; in a glass tank in the wall, lobsters, up to six pounds, swim around. Open daily from 11:30.

The Dock House, Lower Whitfield Street, Guilford. (203) 453-6884. Seafood with a rare (for this area) water view is the specialty of this long, low fieldstone building with an outdoor patio, captain's tables in the windowed dining room and a sprightly bar with turquoise deck chairs and rose-colored cushions on benches. The menu is fairly standard; dinner entrees start at $8.95 for beef kabob and rise to $19.95 for the seafood special (lobster, broiled fish, two stuffed shrimp and steamers) or combination prime rib and lobster. There's a good, nicely priced selection of wines, plus a children's menu. Lunch daily, April-Thanksgiving, 11:30 to 2:30; dinner nightly year-round, 5 to 9; Sunday brunch.

La Cuisine, 25 Whitfield St., Guilford (on the Green). (203) 453-0483. A food shop, bakery and cafe are in this small and appealing establishment on Guilford's green, where you can have a very reasonably priced breakfast or lunch. Take it out, or sit on bentwood chairs at one of the six tables covered with blue and white checked cloths. Danish, muffins, croissants (one filled with scrambled eggs and ham is $3.95) are breakfast choices. At lunch there are always a couple of soups (maybe spicy tomato or mushroom shrimp bisque), two or three kinds of quiche, sandwiches and six or seven salads set out on ice. The display of desserts might include a lime mousse cake, mint chocolate chip cheesecake or Patty's Revenge, a brandied chocolate mousse in a thick brownie crust with chocolate ganache covering. Breakfast is 9 to 11:30 Monday to Friday; 8:30 to noon on weekends. Weekday lunches are until 3:30; desserts until 4:30, and on weekends from noon to 4.

Serino's at Short Beach, 126 Shore Drive (Route 142), Branford. (203) 481-6707. The counter at this former luncheonette and grocery store is now the service bar at a simple continental restaurant with all the character you might find at a neighborhood place in southern Italy. The outstanding bread comes from Judie's Bakery next door and the creative dinner specialties are the work of the young owner and his chef who trained in Manhattan and at the Homestead in Greenwich. Entrees ($10.50 to $12.95) include three kinds of veal and chicken, medallions of pork with green peppercorn sauce or vinegar peppers, sea scallops and pepper steak. Country-style curtains shield the view of passing cars, but sometimes are opened for a glimpse of Long Island Sound down the street. Pink carnations grace the tables, chairs are delightfully mismatched, and the trolleys stenciled on the walls reflect the time when this was "the end of the line." Dinner nightly except Monday, 5:30 to 9 or 10; reservations imperative well ahead on weekends.

Chez Bach, 1070 Main St., Branford. (203) 488-8779. Madame Bach Ngo, whose cookbook "The Classic Cuisine of Vietnam" won the prestigious Tastemaker award as the best of the year, runs this well-regarded establishment and opened a smaller place in Westport in spring 1985. Twenty-five items from soups to entrees are offered on the menu billed as gourmet Vietnamese cuisine. Singing chicken, "Good Mother" pork chops, lemon grass beef, sea ghost fingers and puff shrimp are some of the entrees, priced at $7.50 to $12.95, slightly less at lunch; daily specials and some dishes that must be ordered a day ahead are listed on the back of the menu. The dessert cart is exceptional, as is the sophisticated wine list. The predominantly black color scheme is brightened by white and yellow napkins and maps of Vietnam under glass in the booths. Lunch, Tuesday-Friday noon to 2:30; dinner, Tuesday-Sunday from 5.

Century House, 2455 Boston Post Road, Guilford. (203) 453-2216. The exterior is deceiving at this barnwood place that looks by day like a roadhouse almost on top of Route 1. Inside all is luxury with a capital "L" at this five-year-old restaurant on the site of an old foundry. The main dining room is large but intimate, with soft lighting from lanterns on walls and candles in hurricane lamps; covered by heavy linen cream-colored cloths, the tables are spacious and seats are leather armchairs. The adjacent Library, even nicer, is all pink and rose with velvet chairs, burgundy-rimmed china, and weathered shelves filled with books and artifacts. The French menu, bound in leather and printed on parchment, starts with appetizers from $4.95 for a subtly flavored, large slice of duck pate to $28 for beluga caviar with Russian vodka. Entrees, served with a house salad and vegetable, are $14.95 for coq au vin or stuffed sole on a bed of lobster sauce to $18.95 for lamb chops chasseur, beef Wellington and steak Diane. The steak was cooked tableside in a great flurry of brandy, brown sauces, garlic and what-not, and the end result was superb. We passed up delectable items on the dessert cart for a parfait framboise with raspberries and a special coffee done with liqueurs bursting into whooshes of flame by the table. The large well-explained wine list climbs from the low teens to $300. Dinner nightly except Monday, 6 to 9 or 10.

Daytrip 17 _____

Sign denotes Whitlock Farm book barn.

Books in a Barn

Whitlock Farm/Bethany, Conn.

If you're one of those people who can't pass a bookstore without going in and can't seem to leave once you're there, heaven is waiting for you in Bethany, Conn. Here, off a winding road in the pleasurable ambience of old red New England barns, you can browse, and buy, books to your heart's delight.

Sometimes there's a bowl of red cinnamon candies sitting on the counter at Whitlock Farm. But the wares are infinitely sweeter to those who love to read: old and rare books in categories from antiques to zoology at half or much less than half the original purchase price.

The farm doesn't look much like a bookseller's place at all — at least from the outside. That's because it was and still is a working farm where two brothers, Gilbert and Everett Whitlock, also run a book business.

Gilbert was a farmer when he started his book buying — and selling — back in the late 1940s, nobody is quite sure when. It was just that following the Depression the farm wasn't doing as well as it might, and Gilbert began to do the only other thing he knew how: buy books. First he filled his bedroom and the adjoining rooms on the third floor of the family homestead; gradually he filled the rooms downstairs, one after the other. And all the time he was developing a thriving business, selling books to other booksellers, mostly by mail.

When the house was nearly filled, Gilbert moved some of his inventory across the road to the hayloft of a large barn. The decision was made to "go public."

114

In those days the barn was left unmanned, open 24 hours a day, and people were on the honor system to pay for their books by leaving money in an open cigar box on the counter at the top of the stairs. Most of the books cost five to 50 cents then and it was paradise for insomniacs who would, indeed, arrive in the middle of the night and read away their sleepless hours.

Now Whitlock Farm Booksellers is a full-scale operation — the largest used and rare bookseller in the state, one of the largest in the country, one of the best-known in the world. But it hasn't lost much of its flavor, and Gilbert and Everett Whitlock, the soft-spoken brothers who run the business, are seeing that it doesn't.

To the average customer, not knowing or being able to buy rare books doesn't make a lot of difference. Everyone is welcome in the barns, where the good smell of hay lingers, where there's the candy to munch, and where nobody, but nobody, will tell you to hurry up.

This is the turkey barn, the lower barn, which is the main office and sales desk for Whitlock Farm. The older, rarer and more expensive books are shelved here. In the sheep barn, just a few steps up the hill, are the less expensive books (often $5 and under) and upstairs is a print loft with old maps, children's book illustrations, calendars and prints of hundreds of subjects. It's a place to sit on the floor and pore over the treasures.

The feeling at the barns is almost spartan: Just books and more books, filling the shelves from floor to ceiling and lighted only by bare lightbulbs which dangle from cords. Everything is arranged systematically, according to subject matter, and then alphabetically by author within each section, so it's easy to find something special if you're looking for that. More often people are just apt to walk up and down the rows until something happens to catch their eye.

The Whitlocks will buy almost anything — Gilbert has said that's his weakness — but they usually don't sell an edition of Goethe (as they once did) in which some marginal notes turned out to have been made by Goethe himself. The purchaser realized a profit of thousands.

The brothers know books very well because they more or less grew up in the business. Their father, Clifford, operated Whitlock's, Inc., a bookstore in downtown New Haven, for years, and it was from experience with their father's store that the brothers were able to get into the business.

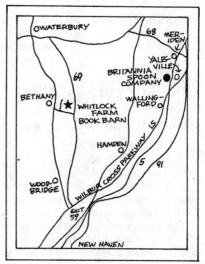

Location: 20 Sperry Road, Bethany, Conn. Exit 59 from the Wilbur Cross Parkway (Route 15); take Route 69 north four miles. Left onto Morris Road to Sperry Road. Right on Sperry Road. Farm is a short distance on right.

Open: Year-round, Tuesday-Sunday 9 to 5. Closed Monday.

Telephone: (203) 393-1240.

In good weather some of the paperbacks and less expensive books are displayed in outdoor stalls and on tables, lending an almost carnival air to the spot. Picnic tables are placed nearby. In rainy weather it all moves indoors and then, in the warmth of the barns, with the patter of raindrops on the roof, there is a different, no less wonderful, experience.

Best-sellers are not the Whitlocks' stock-in-trade, although some can be found, after about a year, at 50 percent or more off the original price. Better to look for old, less-known books; better to browse and see what you come up with.

Actually the major part of their business is not to Sunday book lovers, but to other booksellers and a few collectors. Much of it is mail-order. When he comes up with a really rare book, Gilbert might offer it first to nearby Yale University, with which the family has strong ties. Professors and students also have long been customers.

But people who visit Whitlock Farm are just as likely to be from rather far away. A recent entry in the guest book — yes, there's a guest book to sign if you want — was by visitors from Australia with the notation "we finally found you again after many years."

If you haven't found Whitlock Farm yet, you'll discover that the ride itself through the roads of rural Connecticut adds to the experience and like most people before you, your first trip will probably not be your last.

Also in the Area

Beinecke Library, 121 Wall St., on the Yale University campus, New Haven. Believed to be the largest building in the world devoted entirely to rare books and manuscripts, the Beinecke is a place of hushed reverence, dark and tranquil, where the light coming through translucent marble "panes" exposes the striated patterns in the stone. It is rather like a cathedral and for a lover of books, the atmosphere could not be more appropriate. When you stand at ground level you can view with special appreciation the central tower of glass-enclosed bookcases which rises to the top of the building, making the old and rare volumes the focus of attention. On display are a Gutenberg Bible, original Audubon bird prints and medieval manuscripts. Open year-round (except for the Christmas recess), Monday-Friday 8:30 to 5.

Walking Tours of Yale. Meet at the South Gate at 344 College St., across from the New Haven Green. Tours are offered weekdays at 10:30 and 2, Saturdays and Sundays at 1:30. They last about one hour and are free.

 Dining 17_____

Britannia Spoon Company/Yalesville, Conn.

With the best choices for dining in this area spread across some distance from New Haven to Waterbury, you must expect to drive a bit for a worthy meal.

It's worth the trek to the out-of-the-way Yalesville section of Wallingford, where an appealing restaurant with a spectacular setting beside the Quinnipiac River has been fashioned out of an old red brick mill.

The roaring falls at this point of the river powered a grist mill, where early Colonists ground their corn and wheat from 1687 on. In 1805, the Yale brothers, after whom the hamlet is named, built a factory which manufactured, among many

View onto Quinnipiac River from Britannia Spoon Company.

other houshold wares, Britannia spoons. You can see a few of these antique utensils in a glass case beside the front desk at the entrance.

You can't see the river from the front of the building, with its elaborate Victorian-type sign and masses of flowers in brick planters. So it is an unexpected treat to walk through the attractive bar and onto a two-level outdoor deck with a lovely view of the river and falls, an oasis of water amid a forest of green. Blue deck chairs, green and white umbrellas on each white table and lantern-like lights on wood standards add to the color. When the weather is warm, this is a great place for an al fresco lunch or snack.

The inside makes the most of its riverside location as well, and the decor is a treat to the eye, although it is hard to take in everything at once: tile, parquet and patterned carpeted floors, Tiffany lamps, stained glass in unexpected places (like around the top of the large square bar), barn-type bric-a-brac atop the ceiling crossbeams, little nooks and crannies in which to have a drink, an upstairs lounge with antique sofas and, for a few lucky couples, tables for two on the mezzanine where you can dine ensconced in wing-back upholstered chairs.

The airy main dining room, with surely one of the highest beamed ceilings in any restaurant, is uniquely situated to take advantage of views of the water through large windows on three sides. It is large enough to provide a rather serene and uncrowded atmosphere, despite the hustle and bustle out front.

Small clay pots with fresh flowers are on each bare wooden table. Chairs are charmingly mismatched. All kinds of old manufacturing artifacts as well as the mandatory dozens of plants decorate the room. In another, smaller dining room, the walls are lined with displays of old dinnerware under glass. The lighting is low enough for diners, most of whom have a view of the outdoors, to appreciate the effects of spotlit falls and trees as the dusk deepens.

117

Like the restaurant, the limited menu is casual/elegant, sticking mainly to steak, chicken and seafood offerings, with a few snacks and sandwiches available on the deck or at the bar at night.

Dinner entrees, priced from $9.95 to $17.95, are served with bread, salad and baked potato or fries.

The soup of the day on our dinner visit with a teen-aged son was cioppino, served in a large bean pot and left on the table for seconds. It was thick, spicy and hearty, although you couldn't distinguish what seafood had been used. Beef and barley, French onion and chicken vegetable soups are other possibilities, as are a few appetizers like mushrooms stuffed with crab or cheese, steamed artichoke, clams or oysters on the half shell and shrimp cocktail. The french-fried zucchini ($2.50), an ample portion in a tempura-like batter with sweet and sour dipping sauce, was absolutely delicious.

The salad, topped by a lone cherry tomato, was a mix of fresh greens and the house poppyseed dressing was a standout.

The bread, which looked more like one Portuguese roll for the three of us, came on a bread board with butter in a crock. It was replenished cheerfully several times.

We all chose steak for entrees, and found the filet mignon ($15.95), the New York strip ($14.75) and London broil ($10.50, served on sourdough bread) perfect examples of what good steaks should be — rare, tender and enhanced by a pat of herb butter. The accompanying french fries were no disappointment either, and each plate was heaped with watercress and — a novel touch — grated horseradish root.

The wine list is limited but interesting and most reasonable, with reds ranging from $6.75 for Sebastiani burgundy to $18.95 for Napa Clos de Val. Whites include a Parducci chardonnay for $9.95. The house wine is Settlers Creek delicato, red or white, $2.25 a glass.

For dessert ($1.95 to $2.95), the zucchini yogurt cake, strawberries with sour cream and brown sugar, and taffy apple pie in a graham cracker crust and topped with caramel custard sounded interesting. But the only one of us who could manage was the teenager, who chose Haagen-Dazs ice cream.

At lunchtime, appetizers and dessert remain the same, while the rest of the menu includes sandwiches, salads, burgers and omelets. Specialties include totalito ("the ultimate enchilada"), mandarin spinach salad, ratatouille and a healthworks salad, all $3.95 to $4.95.

Britannia Spoon's combination of exceptional location, interesting decor, good food and, in general, nice laid-back feeling make it a popular spot any time of day or night.

Britannia Spoon Company, 296 Church St. (corner of Routes 68 and 150), Yalesville, Conn. (203) 265-6199. Lunch, Monday-Saturday 11:30 to 2:30, dinner 5 to 9, weekends to 11, Sunday noon to 8. Credit cards. Reservations accepted.

Also in the Area

Elm City Diner, 1228 Chapel St., New Haven. (203) 776-5050. The old Mountainview Diner, at this site since 1955, was transformed in 1981 into the trendy, theatrical Elm City Diner. Still very much a diner on the outside, it's anything but on the inside — all mirrors and shiny green tables, black and chrome chairs, candles in votive glasses, a mass of flowers atop the grand piano and 700 small ceiling lights ("we call them golf balls," says co-owner Steve Klass, "and at night the reflections are magical"). The food is trendy as well. Dinner entrees like spinach fettuccine, cheese tortelliini primavera, chicken sardou, pasta with shrimp and broccoli plus the obligatory baked stuffed shrimp, filet mignon and surf and turf are $6.50 to $13.95; you can get all kinds of appetizers, salads and burgers at dinner as well as on the late-night menu, which is served until 1:45 a.m. or later. The lunch menu is basically sandwiches, while the weekend brunch ranges from crab mornay to Greek salad to the "gingersnap," pecan waffles with whipped cream and maple syrup. Supplemented by daily specials, the eclectic fare is staggering in its variety — as it has to be to appeal to the diverse tastes that fill its 65 seats plus the bar from as early as 9:30 a.m. to as late as 2:45 a.m. on weekends. Closed Mondays most of year.

The Rusty Scupper, Long Wharf, New Haven. (203) 777-5711. The harbor view is everything at this large new eating and drinking establishment which packed in the crowds since it opened in mid-winter of 1985. The circular bar area has two levels of intimate seats by the windows, as well as sofas in the lounge. At night, the lights of New Haven are reflected in the shimmering waters just outside the two contemporary-style dining rooms, and a deck beside the water appeals during warm weather. The lengthy menu (its cover containing a nautical map of New Haven Harbor) is typical of the chain, with everything from prime rib and mesquite-grilled salmon and tuna to shrimp tempura and pastas (dinner, $8.95 to $16.95). Prices are less than half that range at lunch, when soups, sandwiches, salads and such are featured. Open, Monday-Thursday 11:30 to 10, Friday and Saturday to 11, Sunday noon to 9.

Scribner's Downtown Oyster Bar, 9 Elm St., New Haven. (203) 776-1828. The late, lamented L'Avventura, which took over from the late, lamented Curious Jane's and spent a fortune in decor, gave way in late 1984 to Scribner's of Milford seafood fame. Chef-owners Scribner Bliss and Wayne Kregling kept the stunning decor, naturally, adding some fishy prints and maritime scenes to the basic blue and white color scheme. The emphasis is on seafood in many styles, from broiled, baked, garlicked and stuffed to stir-fried and steamed. Six Louisiana specialties comprise the Cajun part of the menu. Dinner appetizers are $4.50 to $5.95 and entrees $9.95 to $21.95 (for combination dinners, broiled or steamed). Depot and French silk pies are popular desserts, and the adjacent lounge has a raw bar. Lunch is salads, sandwiches, deep-fried seafood and six hot entrees, $4.95 to $6.95. The extensive wine list is well-chosen and reasonably priced. This is seafood dining at its most elegant. Lunch, Monday-Saturday 11 to 2:30; dinner, 5 to 10 or 11; closed Sunday.

The Boston Brahmin, 399 Whalley Ave., New Haven. (203) 777-8014. Opened in January 1985, this Indian restaurant looks like a veterinarian's office (which it was) outside, but inside, what a treat! Owner Nalini Srinivaean, born in England, raised in New Delhi and educated at Johns Hopkins University, has fashioned a quiet oasis for enjoying many of the cuisines of India. Comfortable chairs are upholstered in a tweedy fabric, each glass covered table holds a single rose and a a basket of the crispest and most peppery pappadum; exotic Indian music plays softly in the background. The owner's collection of Indian art enhances the walls. Entrees are in the $9 to $11 range; one of the best dishes we tried was chicken korma, done in a paste of nine spices, fresh coriander leaves, poppyseeds and cashews. The assorted platter of appetizers containing pakora, samosa, marinated chicken wings and the like is a meal in itself, and the house hot and sour chutney is a tearjerker. There's a full bar and some good wines on the list, but beer (many are imported) is the drink of choice with this kind of food. Lunch, Monday-Sunday 11 to 2, dinner 5-10, Sunday 5 to 9.

119

500 Blake St., 500 Blake St., New Haven. (203) 387-0500. Nestled in the interesting Westville section of the city is this tavern-style place with an immense menu featuring huge portions and highly spiced Italian food. It's also a favorite watering hole with not one but two long bars, plus a piano bar where we hear the singing gets pretty rambunctious at night. The decor is plain, with scarred oak tables and carpeting that has seen better days. Appetizers include lots of clam, mussel, calamari and scungilli dishes; cherry peppers stuffed with tuna, olives, capers and anchovies are often ordered. Entrees are quite expensive (most over $9 at lunch, $12 at night), but you get king-sized portions. Garlic and oil are evident in many dishes and the house salad and the Italian bread are great. Open daily from 11:30 to midnight, Sunday from noon.

Audubon's Cafe & Restaurant, Audubon and Orange streets, New Haven. (203) 785-0277. Floor-to-ceiling windows by day and neon signs and gas lights on poles by night brighten this simple but chic restaurant with American cafe-style snacks and side orders plus a dozen heartier dishes at night. But the barbecued ribs, chicken breast Florentine and almond sole a l'orange ($6.75 to $13.75) generally take a back seat to nachos, potato skins, frittata, eight kinds of burgers (one called "no-name") and pasta salad. Open from 11:30, Saturday from 4.

Cap'n Nick's, Hemingway Avenue, East Haven. (203) 469-2937. From its original waterfront shanty location at Branford Point, Nick Colavolpe's family-owned operation has moved into a large, modern building across from Trolley Square Shopping Center. The seafood remains as popular as ever: sole, scrod, swordfish, shrimp, scallops in the $5.95 to $9.95 range. The blackboard menu listed boiled lobster at $8.95 the last time we were there. The captain's platter, quite a bargain at $8.95, was piled high with all kinds of deep-fried seafood including clam strips, scallops, shrimp and flounder and was too much to finish. The side order of onion rings ($1.75) was the best we've had. The chocolate fiesta combining moist chocolate cake, ice cream, hot fudge sauce and whipped cream is an irresistible dessert for $1.95. Sections of the menu are devoted to children and senior citizens, two groups which comprise a fair part of the devoted clientele. The limited wine selection is printed on wine-bottle vases filled with flowers. Nautical decor prevails in the high-ceilinged dining room; the large lounge has a striking copper ceiling. Lunch, Tuesday-Friday 11:30 to 2:30; dinner nightly from 5, Sunday 1 to 8:30.

No Fish Today Cafe, 457 W. Main St., Waterbury. (203) 574-4483. When Frederick J. Hall once visited a friend's restaurant in Baltimore, "No fish today" was chalked across the blackboard menu. The words struck Hall as a neat name for a restaurant, which 10 years later he opened just west of the Waterbury green. Don't let the name mislead you, for fish is very much the thing here, listed daily on an enormous blackboard menu which slides along the floor on a wooden stand ("meals on wheels," quipped our waitress). Dinner entrees range from $7 to $15; the San Francisco cioppino, mako shark Dijonnaise and New Orleans scampi are standouts. At lunch, prices are about half those at night; we remember an incredibly fresh and tasty sole meuniere, served with peas and a rice pilaf ($5), and scampi al Parma, four huge shrimp in a zesty red sauce on mountains of linguini. A few Italian and meat dishes round out the menu. The cafe is narrow and tiny, seating 36 diners in nine high-backed wooden booths with dark blue leatherette covering the tables, or at a few comfy seats at the old mahogany bar. A huge mirror on one wall helps prevent claustrophobia. Lunch, Monday-Saturday 11:30 to 2:30; dinner 5 to 9, to 10 Thursday-Saturday; closed Sunday.

Victorian home built in 1874 for Samuel Clemens family.

The House That Twain Built

Mark Twain Memorial / Hartford, Conn.

They say that Edward Tuckerman Potter was the architect and Louis Comfort Tiffany the decorator. But there is so much of Samuel Clemens, a.k.a. Mark Twain, in this tri-colored brick mansion high above Hartford's Farmington Avenue that the beloved author must be given most of the credit for the way it looks.

And today the Mark Twain house looks very much the way it did when Twain and his adored family — a loving wife and three lively daughters — lived there from 1874 to 1891.

The Clemenses came to Hartford from Buffalo in search of a literary community and because Twain's publisher — Elisha Bliss of the American Publishing Company — was located in Connecticut's capital city. They found a literary community in Nook Farm, a section not far west from the downtown area, where writers Harriet Beecher Stowe and Charles Dudley Warner and the actor William Gillette lived.

The Clemenses arrived in Hartford in 1871 with their first child, a baby boy, Langdon, who died in infancy. Their daughter, Susy, was born in a house rented by the Clemenses before their own wonderful and fanciful place was built; in the Farmington Avenue house were born two more daughters, Clara and Jean.

It was a joyous place. The visitor is immediately struck by the lavish hand that chose the decorations, by the touches of whimsy. Your guide will tell you, for example, that the circular velvet sofa in the center of the foyer was the place for putting birthday presents for the children when guests arrived for a party; that the figures across the mantelpiece in the library were used as "characters" in romances Twain concocted frequently for his daughters before bedtime, or that the butler, George, would stand behind the serving screen in the Clemenses' dining room, but

121

couldn't refrain from laughing when Mark Twain told one of his frequently funny after-dinner stories.

Entertaining was a way of life in this Victorian literary community in Hartford and the Clemenses were among the great hosts and hostesses of their day. Of the 19 rooms in the house, several were reserved for guests; among them were the writers Bret Harte and Joel Chandler Harris, inventor of the Uncle Remus stories. Actually, Twain is said to have complained of Harte that if he stayed much longer, they would be forced to take out a listing in the Hartford phone book for him.

The Clemenses had a telephone, but it was not something Twain was fond of. Because he preferred not to hear its insistent ring, it was placed in a closet off the foyer; the visitor can see today the tiny little cubicle to which was relegated Mr. Bell's invention. Twain even gave up an opportunity to invest in the telephone, insisting it had no future. Instead, he put thousands of dollars — and lost them all — in the Paige Compositor, an automatic typesetting machine, which lost the race against the linotype machine.

But Twain made money while in Hartford as well. These were the years when his great books were written and published — among them *The Adventures of Tom Sawyer* and *The Adventures of Huckleberry Finn, Life on the Mississippi, The Prince and the Pauper* and *A Connecticut Yankee in King Arthur's Court.* The centennial of the publication of Huck Finn was celebrated in 1985.

Twain did some of his writing in his third-floor billiard room, where he also liked to smoke cigars, drink whiskey and entertain his men friends. That room was the author's retreat and it was off-limits during the day to all but his beloved wife, "Livy." If it is nice weather when you visit, you may get to step out onto the "Texas deck" off the billiard room for a look around the environs.

Our favorite room is the library on the first floor. Entered from the more formal parlor, it is a room with floor-to-ceiling bookcases, an elaborate carved wooden mantel which the Clemenses found in a Scottish castle, and an Emerson quotation carved in brass above the fireplace: "The ornament of a house is the friends who frequent it." Here is the grand piano where Twain would sometimes play a tune (his daughters hated to sing along, because whenever their father made a mistake he would insist on starting again at the beginning) and the place where he told his famous stories. It was here that the Christmas tree stood, in the bay-windowed alcove. And off this room is a marvelous conservatory, with its softly trickling fountain, its lush green plants, and the whimsical Japanese lanterns which hang above just as they did in Mark Twain's time.

The dining room is dark and formal in the manner of the day. But in this room, on the northern wall, is a fireplace with a double flue and a window directly above the fire. Twain liked to watch this fireplace — especially in winter when, he said, he loved to see the snowflakes fall to meet the rising flames.

The master bedroom is a marvelous spot, and the black walnut bed which crowns it, a delightful piece of furniture. Purchased by the Clemenses in Venice, it features removable carved angels on the bedposts with which the children were allowed to play when they were sick. The Clemenses slept in the bed with their heads against the footboard, we're told, so that they could view the elaborately carved headboard for which they'd paid so dearly.

By now you've gathered there are lots of original pieces of furniture in the house. In addition, the wallpapers and hand-stenciled patterns on walls and ceilings are faithful re-creations of the originals — thanks to the diligence of the trustees, who voted in 1955 to restore the house and who have been faithful to that promise ever since.

Other rooms of particular interest include the schoolroom where the girls were taught by a German tutor. They were only permitted to speak in German while in the room, and although Mark Twain was facile in the language, it is said he called his daughters out into the hall whenever he had a message for them, so that he could deliver it in English. The room is furnished as it would have been, cluttered with books and games for children including Chinese checkers and "Pin the Tail on the Donkey."

One of the second-floor guest rooms was used most often by Olivia Clemens's mother, who was a frequent guest during the winter months, and a very welcome one at that. The delicate furnishings in the room are Mrs. Langdon's, and something of a departure from the heavier taste of the Clemenses.

Susy had her own room; Clara and Jean shared a larger space that contains the crib in which all of the Clemens babies slept, as well as a plethora of dolls and toys and a large and lovely dollhouse similar to that which the girls would have had. This is a happy room in a happy house; one can't help but imagine the loving family life that was shared during these 17 joyful years.

The mahogany guest room on the first floor is the saddest room in the house. Oh, yes, it was here that the many gifts were wrapped for Christmas, and here that some guests — including Bret Harte — were assigned, but it was in this room, in the large mahogany bed, that the Clemenses' oldest daughter, Susy, died of spinal meningitis. Her death came several months after her parents and sisters had gone to Europe for a speaking tour. Susy had stayed behind to attend school, and was planning to sail to Europe to join the family when she was stricken.

Their daughter's death devastated Samuel Clemens and his wife and surviving daughters; it is said the family never fully recovered. What is certain is that they did not move back to the Hartford house for they couldn't bear to be reminded of the sadness of Susy's death.

Location: 351 Farmington Ave., corner Forest Street, Hartford, Conn. Exit 46 (Sisson Avenue) from I-84.

Open: June-August, daily 10 to 4:30; September-May, Tuesday-Saturday 9:30 to 4, Sunday 1 to 4 p.m. Closed Jan. 1, Easter, Labor Day, Thanksgiving, Christmas.

Admission: Adults, $3.25; 16 and under, $1.25. A combination ticket to visit both the Twain house and the Harriet Beecher Stowe House on the same large property is $5.50, adults; $2.25 for 16 and under.

Special Events: Nook Farm Day, a Victorian children's festival, is held on a Saturday in early June. Check the Visitors Center for the exact date. Mark Twain and Harriet Beecher Stowe works, plus Victorian decorations, children's toys, and other appropriate memorabilia are sold in an unusually creative gift shop at the Visitors Center.

Telephone: (203) 525-9317.

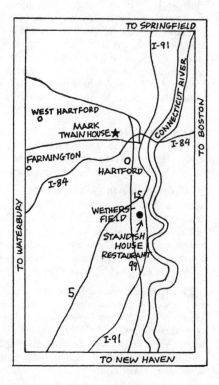

Still Twain was grateful that she had died in the house which had always meant so much to all of them, the house about which he had written, "To us our house was not unsentient matter — it had a heart, and a soul, and eyes to see us with; and approvals and solicitudes, and deep sympathies; it was of us, and we were in its confidence, and lived in its grace and in the peace of its benediction."

Also in the Area

Harriet Beecher Stowe House. The author of *Uncle Tom's Cabin* lived for several years in this lovely home on the Nook Farm property, some of them while Mark Twain was also in residence. Harriet Beecher Stowe reveled in the design of her house; her lighter decorating touch is very much evident. Tickets to the Harriet Beecher Stowe House alone cost $2.75 for adults and $1 for those 16 and under. Hours are the same as those at the Mark Twain Memorial.

Noah Webster House, 227 S. Main Street, West Hartford.(203) 521-5362. Located just a few miles west of the Mark Twain Memorial, this is the Colonial saltbox house in which the famed lexicographer was born. The house has period rooms as well as a museum addition in which are mounted changing exhibits. The annual Noah Webster birthday party in late September is a festive event with visiting authors, authentic Colonial foods, crafts and games, and usually the music of a fife and drum band. Open Monday-Thursday 10 to 4, Sunday 1 to 4. Adults, $2; children, $1.

Hill-Stead Museum, Farmington Avenue, Farmington. (203) 677-9064. This 29-room white clapboard home sits atop a hill in the posh Hartford suburb which is also home to the private Miss Porter's School, alma mater of Jacqueline Kennedy. Built in 1901 from designs by Stanford White for the Alfred Atmore Popes of Cleveland, the house was really the idea of the Popes' daughter, Theodate, also a graduate of Miss Porter's, who had fallen in love with the town. As stated in the daughter's will, the house and its contents are exhibited as she left them upon her death in 1946. The art collection — primarily works by French Impressionists — is extraordinary, as are the furniture and furnishings. The museum is said to be the only one in America where the French Impressionist paintings can be seen as they would have been by their contemporaries. Open Wednesday-Sunday 2 to 5. Closed mid-January to mid-February. Adults, $2.50; children, $1.

Old State House, 800 Main St., Hartford. (203) 522-6766. This Bulfinch-designed Federal structure is a gem; its restored Senate and House chambers are lovely; there are changing exhibits in main floor galleries and a really good museum shop. Open daily 10 to 5, Sunday, from noon. Free.

Wadsworth Atheneum, 600 Main St., Hartford. (203) 278-2670. This museum, said to be the nation's oldest public art museum, has many fine collections, among them the outstanding Nutting collection of early American furniture. There are also a Lions Gallery of the Senses, where exhibits can be very creative; a Matrix gallery for new and emerging artists, and many other galleries showing the museum's own fine collections and visiting exhibitions. Open Tuesday-Sunday 11 to 5. Adults, $2; children over 13, $1.

Picnicking is not allowed on the grounds of the Mark Twain Memorial, but can be enjoyed in two nearby parks. Elizabeth Park, 915 Prospect Avenue, on the Hartford-West Hartford line has more than 100 acres including the first municipally owned rose garden in the country with more than 14,000 plants and 1,100 varieties. Greenhouses are open free. Bushnell Park, in the shadow of the State Capitol in downtown Hartford, is a popular lunchtime spot with office workers in nice weather and is often the scene of special events on weekends.

Upstairs dining room at Standish House.

Standish House/Wethersfield, Conn.

"People have a hard time finding us because they think this is a museum," said our waiter during dinner at the Standish House. Although Old Wethersfield dwellers know what the big white house across from the First Congregational Church is, others might drive right by its discreet sign.

And that's the point. The grand old (1790) house, given by the Myles Standish family to the town in 1929, is an historic treasure and the town wanted to keep it that way. The Wethersfield Historical Society proposed its use as a restaurant, leased it to a developer who could envision what they had in mind, and together they put together a restaurant of quiet elegance and taste.

With an entirely appropriate atmosphere for those visiting the historic house museums in Old Wethersfield, the restaurant has two small dining rooms on the first floor with Queen Anne reproduction chairs, a comfortable waiting area with sofa and upholstered chairs in front of a fireplace, and upstairs, two more small dining areas and a larger room on the street side, altogether seating about 100.

White damask covers the spacious tables, topped with a single candle in a silver candlestick and a perfect freesia bloom in a clear glass vase. The china, heavy silver and delicate wine glasses add more elegance, and the service couldn't be more correct, with cutlery being whisked away, fish service delivered, more cutlery whisked back for the main course and so on.

The rooms are done in muted but pretty Williamsburg colors, with the wavy-paned windows swagged by printed drapery trim. Brass chandeliers with tiny lights and wall sconces add atmospheric lighting. Upstairs, plush area carpets and oriental rugs cover the original wide board floors. And the upholstered chairs are comfortable — this is a place in which to be pampered.

For its opening in 1984, at the request of the historical society, the restaurant devised a two-sided menu — one-half containing entrees that could have been served in the 18th and 19th centuries; the other half more nouvelle. The latter side proved more popular, and now the seasonal menu is strictly contemporary.

We started with most generous drinks and crusty, hot rolls served with curls of sweet butter. The assorted smoked fish with a horseradish and apple mayonnaise ($5) was a super appetizer, with large portions of smoked Scottish salmon, bluefish and trout (the latter two smoked in the restaurant's kitchen).

Other appetizers are bluepoints on ice, chicken liver mousse in port aspic, scallops with basil mayonnaise and rust (red pepper and garlic puree) sauce and crabmeat tortellini with tomato sauce ($4.25 to $5.50). We passed up halibut chowder and sweet potato and sausage soup as a bit hearty for a warm spring night.

For entrees, we had sweetbreads with cepes and the loin of veal stuffed with goat cheese with mousse of leeks, $16 and $17 respectively. Both were lavish portions, served with light spinach gnocchi and carrot souffle, and could not have been better. The sauce on the sweetbreads and the leek mousse were highlights of a memorable meal. From the interesting, reasonably priced wine list we chose a Dry Creek fume blanc for $14.

Other entrees range from $9.50 for feuilletee of wild mushrooms and braised fennel to $17.50 for rack of lamb with herb sauce. They include braised sole with cream and sorrel sauce, shrimp with champagne vinegar and caviar, sauteed duck breast with port sauce and baby vegetables and grilled salmon with basil and olive butters.

According to new chef Blake Brousseau, who learned the subleties of the new American cuisine as sous chef under Richard Scully, now departed for New Jersey, the menu will change every six to eight weeks to take advantage of seasonal products.

Desserts change daily, and might be chocolate velvet cake with grand marnier mousse in the center, frozen strawberry souffle, raspberry puff pastry tartlets, bread and butter pudding, a selection of fruit and cheese, and, almost always on the menu because it is so popular, a flourless French chocolate cake with vanilla rum creme anglaise. In the summer, seasonal fruit desserts are always offered; perhaps strawberries in a champagne saboyan. We sampled a wonderful trifle, a huge serving that was more than ample for two, filled with raisins, blueberries, pears, oranges and strawberries, and topped with almonds. With coffee steaming from a silver pot, what a way to end a meal!

Lunch entrees are in the $4.25 (for welsh rarebit) to $7.95 range. They include calves liver with bacon and onions, crab cakes with shallot butter sauce, veal Nicoise, smoked turkey and endive salad and an interesting duck, orange and avocado salad.

Sunday brunch, $8.50 to $12.95 depending on the entree, includes a complimentary cocktail, juice and breakfast pastries. There are a seafood ragout in puff pastry, French pancakes with fruit filling, mixed grill with fried eggs and an English cold platter with perhaps a half roast game hen, various smoked fish, a salad of almonds, wild rice and oranges, or whatever the chef feels like putting together.

With all the sense of history, luxurious furnishings, discreet and tuxedoed waiters, and classical music, we have seldom had a more comfortable evening in a restaurant. And it's truly amazing what the chef can turn out from his small kitchen.

Standish House, 222 Main St., Wethersfield. Conn. (203) 721-1113. Lunch, Tuesday-Saturday noon to 2; dinner Tuesday-Saturday 6 to 9, Sunday 5 to 8; Sunday brunch, noon to 2:30. Major credit cards. Reservations recommended.

Also in the Area

L'Americain, 2 Hartford Square West (just south of downtown), Hartford. (203) 522-6500. Since it opened in 1982, this has been widely acclaimed as the city's top (and most expensive) restaurant. A luxurious foyer leads to two dining rooms — we prefer the smaller, Gray Room, with spotlit oil paintings, brass chandeliers, tall windows with rose draperies and Queen Anne reproduction chairs, and two striking stained-glass windows with intricate and colorful depictions of vegetables and herbs. Chef Chris Pardue changes the menu seasonally. At lunch, entrees are $6.75 for minced lamb to $10 for tenderloin tips in puff pastry with a port wine glaze; other choices might be watercress sea scallops or veal in paprika cream, and the duck and mushroom soup is an indication of L'Americain's flair. The six dinner entrees ($19 to $23) include sauteed breast of duck with shiitake mushrooms and honey-ginger game sauce, hunter-style tournedos, saffron orange scallops and Atlantic salmon in a red zinfandel sauce with cucumber and caviar. You might start with pears poached in beaujolais and topped with goat cheese, and finish with a tart filled with kiwi, strawberries and pineapple. Lunch, Monday-Friday 11 to 2; dinner, Monday-Saturday 5 to 10.

Panache of Hartford, 357 Main St., Hartford. (203) 724-0810. Created in 1984 and doubled in size in 1985, Panache is a jewel box of a restaurant seating 75 in a smashing black, gray, rose and pink color scheme. Suave posters adorn the deep-rose walls, and unusually attractive bouquets are in black bowls on each table. Lunch is Hartford's priciest — four appetizers from $5.95 to $7.50 and four entrees from $8.95 to $14.95, plus a fish of the day. But what wonderful seasonal offerings they are: a gratinee of shrimp and scallops with fresh herb butter sauce, medallions of veal sauteed with shrimp and scallions, and noisettes of lamb with veal sweetbreads. At dinner (five entrees are $17.95 to $21.95), you could begin with an assortment of pates or escargots in puff pastry, enjoy veal tenderloin sauteed with shrimp and mushrooms or sliced loin of lamb with morels, fresh basil and curry sauce, and finish with a white chocolate mousse or a hazelnut and praline genoise. The expanded restaurant has a small, six-seat bar. Lunch, Tuesday-Friday noon to 2; dinner Monday-Thursday 6 to 9, Friday and Saturday to 10.

Shenanigans, 1 Gold St., Hartford. (203) 522-4117. Mark Twain would have loved this lively, informal spot in the Bushnell Tower complex, complete with a relocated diner in its center. It's usually jammed from breakfast right through to closing. The food is what gregarious owner John Chapin calls "cleaned-up American," light and not expensive and perfect for "grazing." Lunch might be a "blue plate special, an American diner tradition" or steamed mussels, spinach and sausage pie, curried chicken platter or hot fish and vegetable salad (a super dish for dieters), $4.25 to $6.95. Dinner offers many of the luncheon items plus salamagundi stew, stir-fried shrimp, chicken and vegetables, and lobster Shenanigans — sauteed with mushrooms and brandy, served in a puff pastry cap and the most expensive item at $12.95. The Hartford cream pie is notorious, as are some of the special drinks. Open daily, lunch 11:30 to 2:30; dinner 5:30 to midnight. Late-night menu and Sunday brunch.

The Parson's Daughter, Route 17, South Glastonbury. (203) 633-8698. A dear little cream-colored structure with small-paned windows and dating back to 1753 houses this charming, country-style restaurant which reminds us of an English tearoom, a pub and a French country inn all wrapped up into one. The dinner menu runs from $11.95 for chicken Freda to $15.95 for beef Wellington; rack of lamb Dijonnaise, steak au poivre, veal piquante and seafood medley are among the possibilities. We particularly liked the mushrooms stuffed with crabmeat, the lively sour cream and dill salad dressing and, among desserts, a moist carrot cake and a white cake studded with strawberries. Lunch items ($4.25 to $8.75) include salads, omelets, quiche and the like, and the Sunday country brunch is a Glastonbury tradition. Open Tuesday-Saturday, lunch 11:30 to 2, dinner 5:30 to 9 or 10; Sunday brunch, 11:30 to 3.

The Blacksmith Tavern, 230 Main St., Glastonbury. (203) 659-0366. A blacksmith shop was once attached to this sprawling house, part of which is thought to date from around 1700, in the center of Glastonbury. Nicely restored, it was turned into a restaurant in 1978, with additions since then. One can dine in a well-proportioned main dining room, in one of the five small dining rooms named after local historical figures or, at lunchtime, in the spacious upstairs bar and lounge and in season on a small outdoor roof garden. For lunch, try the clam chowder ($2.50), a local favorite, very thick and laced with thyme. The shrimp salad platter ($5.95) is also a winner — generous with the shrimp and garnished with hard-boiled eggs, olives, cole slaw and tomatoes. Several beef, veal, chicken and seafood hot entrees are $5.95 (for seafood crepe) to $9.95 (New York strip steak). At night, several appetizers are $4.50 to $5.95; entrees ($10.95 to $16.50) include veal moutarde, breast of chicken Rossini (stuffed with veal pate and wrapped in bacon, topped with a bordelaise sauce) and shrimp Genevieve. A small loaf of warm bread served on a wooden paddle and a salad topped with sprouts with a good sweet and sour house dressing accompany. For dessert, everyone loves the buttercrunch pie, the recipe for which has been published in the Ford Times. Open daily for lunch and dinner; lunch served until 4 in lounge. Sunday brunch, 11 to 2:30, dinner 4 to 9.

Apricots, 1593 Farmington Ave., Farmington. (203) 673-5405. Ann Howard, of local catering and cooking lessons fame, opened her long-awaited restaurant in an old trolley barn at a scenic turn of the Farmington River in late 1982. With a pub on the ground floor, two dining rooms (one a porch-like affair overlooking the river) upstairs, and a patio with raw bar in season right by the river, Apricots is going great guns. Patrons are attracted for casual dining with moderate prices in the pub for lunch and dinner; upstairs things are a little more formal, with dinner entrees from $13 for pasta of the day to $21 for rack of lamb with mustard hollandaise and garlic provencal sauces. We like the Portuguese sailors' stew, $15.95. An exceptional prix-fixe dinner for $32.50 is also available. Check the pretty apricots and leaves painted on walls, posts and exposed pipes by Farmington artist Tom Rose. Lunch, 11:30 to 2:30; dinner, 6 to 10. Sunday, brunch 11:30 to 3, dinner 5:30 to 9. Light meals in pub until closing.

The Reading Room, Helen Winter's Grist Mill, Mill Lane, Farmington. (203) 677-7997. In a complex of antique and art shops (and one of our favorite book stores, the Millrace), with large picture windows overlooking an especially scenic part of the Farmington River rapids and waterfalls, is this small and well-regarded restaurant. Among appetizers ($4.50 to $6.25), baked brie pommery (for two) and oysters wrapped in bacon are standouts. For entrees ($12.50 to $19.95), try the veal princess or rack of lamb. The lunch menu includes sole calvados and mussels mariniere; several blackboard specials are listed each day — maybe swordfish with garlic butter, scrod with capers or chicken tarragon. Prices are in the $6 to $8 range. The tollhouse cookie pie is always a favorite here. At the Sunday champagne brunch try the crabmeat rarebit or a lobster and asparagus omelet. Tables on the lawn beside the river provide the setting for lunch or cocktails in summer. Lunch, Monday-Saturday 11:30 to 2:30, dinner 5:30 to 9:30. Sunday brunch, 11 to 3.

🚗 Daytrip 19_____

Wall of early implements at Sloane-Stanley Museum.

Tools of the Trades
Sloane-Stanley Museum/Kent, Conn.

When artist Eric Sloane died early in 1985, he left an enormous legacy — not the least of which is the Kent museum that bears his name and displays a collection of his beloved early American tools.

Sloane lived for years in nearby Warren. The idea for the museum grew out of a meeting between the artist and industrialist Donald W. Davis, chairman of the board of the Stanley Works of New Britain, Conn., which donated the land on which the museum stands.

Sloane met Davis at the New Britain Museum of American Art, where the artist's then-traveling collection of early American tools was being exhibited. Sloane said Davis told him he should think of preserving the collection permanently for the public and added that the company would donate the land if the artist would turn over the tools. They shook on it.

The barn-like structure which is the museum was designed by the artist and writer specifically to house the collection. And one of these days it will have an addition. Shortly after the artist's death, Donald Davis announced that he would build a new wing on the museum to house a reproduction of the painter's studio.

Sloane's interest in early American artifacts was deep and long-lived. In his book, *A Museum of Early American Tools*, he wrote, "Finding an ancient tool in a stone fence or a dark corner of some decaying barn is receiving a symbol from another world, for it gives you a particular and interesting contact with the past."

The Sloane-Stanley Museum displays these symbols from the past in a most ambient setting. All of the tools in the collection were personally arranged and

129

lighted by Sloane. The baskets and the pitchforks, the wooden shovels and bowls, the sawhorses, axes, yokes and scythes are grouped in an exceptionally attractive arrangement. An assortment of early planes would be of interest to anyone who likes to work with his hands.

In the background is classical music — a surprising but apt choice since the tools are classics, too. For the approximately 10,000 visitors who stop in annually, the most popular item is a pale aqua, dog-powered butter churn, according to a guide. Sloane liked it, too. The winnowing machine prompts the most questions (it was used to separate the chaff from the grain). For us the best part were the baskets, some of them Shaker, and the wooden forks, ranging from two to six-tined, which are grouped to good effect on one wall.

A new gallery was opened not long before the artist died: in it are horse-drawn sleighs and other early artifacts.

Those who know Eric Sloane's paintings are not surprised that he chose to build his museum in the shape of a barn. To some, Sloane was preeminently a painter of barns, although he disagreed with the description.

"I'm known as a barn painter," he said once in an interview. "But I'm not really painting barns. I'd rather be known as a thinker than as an artist."

Nonetheless, several of Sloane's paintings — some of them barn paintings — are also on display in the museum.

Visitors to the site can also visit a tiny cabin that Sloane built when a television

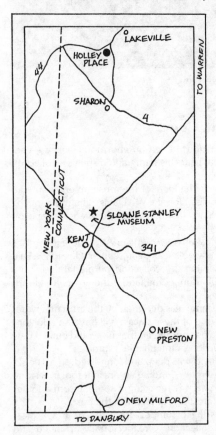

Location: Route 7, Kent, Conn., just north of the village in the northwestern corner of Connecticut.

Open: May-October, Wednesday-Sunday 10 to 4:30.

Picnicking: At tables on the site.

Admission: Adults, $1.25; senior citizens, 75 cents; children, 50 cents.

Telephone: Connecticut Historical Commission, Hartford (203) 566-3005.

station was preparing to make a TV film of his book, *The Diary of an American Boy.* The book is based on the 1801 diary of Noah Blake which Sloane found. The actual diary is exhibited in a glass case in the museum.

Sloane built the cabin in two weeks. It has a dirt floor, a single room split into kitchen and sleeping space with a loft reached by a ladder notched from a single log. On a crude wooden table in the fireplaced kitchen is a little vase often filled with fresh flowers.

The Sloane-Stanley Museum, which is run by the Connecticut Historical Commission, is on land which also contains the remains of an old blast furnace used to produce pig iron for more than 70 years during the 19th century. The site is located at the bottom of a hill behind the museum and can be visited by those who wish.

Eric Sloane took his first name from the middle letters of the word American and his surname from an artist with whom he studied when he was young. He dedicated a lifetime to writing, thinking, collecting and giving away in an attempt, as he once put it, "to recapture the spirit of America that is lost."

The Sloane-Stanley Museum is a splendid monument to that life.

Also in the Area

Kent Falls State Park, Route 7, north of the Sloane-Stanley Museum. Scenic roadside parkland dominated by 200-foot cascade. Wide path follows falls to the top. Picnicking and recreation area. Free.

Covered Bridges. Two of three covered bridges in the state can be found in this area. The closest to Kent is Bulls Bridge, just south of the village, west of Route 7. The bridge crosses a deep gorge of the Housatonic River. One car at a time, please. Another, larger bridge spanning the Housatonic leads into picturesque West Cornwall.

 Dining 19

Holley Place/Lakeville, Conn.

If megabucks can turn an old factory into a first-class restaurant, then Holley Place would succeed in spades. Fortunately, the food and presentation are equal to the stunning structural restoration, and Holley Place has become one of northwestern Connecticut's best restaurants in tiny Lakeville, a community with more than its share.

Two historic markers out front signify the site of Holley Place, which occupies the lower floor of the imposing red brick mill-type structure that formerly was the Holley Manufacturing Co. knife factory at Pocketknife Square.

Outside is a secluded terrace for outdoor dining in season. Inside is a tavern with light fare and one of the longest bars in New England, and beyond on two levels, a skylighted dining room, whose most noticeable feature is its granite walls of huge honey-colored stones, effectively illuminated by track lighting so that the contours show. A large oriental carpet adds to the luxury.

Windsor bow chairs flank the tables, which are covered with peach-colored cloths and napkins, a color scheme repeated in the poppies gracing the elegant Villeroy & Boch china. A few tables have blue dotted overcloths under glass. A gas fireplace shines its light into both tavern and dining room on cool nights. Fresh flowers, mirrors and photographs of old Lakeville scenes complete the decor.

At dinnertime, appetizers are $3.50 to $5.75 (for mushrooms stuffed with crab-

Interior dining room at Holley Place.

meat and glazed in hollandaise). The country pate is excellent, urbanely dotted with pignoli and served with rough mustard and cornichons. Also appealing are escargots in puff pastry with a garlic cream sauce.

The house salad of mixed greens is garnished with fresh mushrooms, red onions and tomatoes and dressed with a nippy vinaigrette.

For a restaurant of such elegance, entrees are pleasantly priced from $9.95 to $14.95, the higher for filet mignon with honey bordelaise sauce. We enjoyed a wonderful dish of calves liver and bacon, the bacon crisp, the liver grilled pink as ordered and served with a crumb-topped broiled tomato and a mound of dark brown fried onions, as thin as thread, that melted in the mouth. Another fine offering was tender veal in lemon butter ($14.50), accompanied by mashed squash and a delicious braised fennel.

There are usually several specials (one at our visit was veal breast stuffed with pork). Quennelle of scallops with shrimp sauce, venison stew with gorgonzola polenta and Creole-style shrimp sauteed with pernod are among other choices. The menu changes seasonally, and in summer you might order cool poached fillet of beef with basil sauce, chilled cream of watercress soup or a hot spinach pasta with cold tomato sauce.

The wine list, which is part of the menu, is a pleasant surprise with a number of bottles at $12 and under. Our Caymus Liberty School Napa cabernet sauvignon ($12) was smooth and spicy; Fetzer zinfandel and Cotes du Rhones were both under $10.

Desserts are $2.25 to $4.50 and might include Paris Brest, Yankee apple crisp, chocolate souffle, grand marnier layer cake, creme brulee and poached pears with Poire William custard. We shared the assortment of sherbets and fresh fruits ($4.50), which was far more than one could have tackled. A dinner-size plate contained an appealing array of sherbets — pear, cantaloupe and kiwi fruit — plus slices of apples, cantaloupes, tangerines and grapes, all on a bed of raspberry sauce. Coffee is served from a large pot of the same V&B china, left on the table for seconds.

The lunch menu offers some of the dinner specialties, plus omelet, soup and sandwich ($4.95) and hamburger on kaiser roll with cole slaw ($4). Entrees range

132

from $6.25 for cassoulet, linguini in mushroom cream sauce with smoked ham or Greek spinach pie to $9.75 for baked sole with a white wine cream sauce. The limited tavern menu, served all day in the sleekly rustic tavern, includes hamburger, smoked turkey club sandwich on rye or roast beef on seeded roll and the cassoulet, a hearty stew of lamb, sausage and duck ($6.25).

Local entrepreneur Ralph Schwaikert spared no expense in making Holley Place a model of how to restore an old building, from the etched glass in the doors to the 40-foot long mahogany-tipped serpentine bar to the lighting fixtures. Even the restrooms couldn't be more tasteful, with brass fixtures, color coordinated wallpaper and framed photographs of old Lakeville.

Holley Place is a picture-perfect setting for a casual tavern lunch or a fairly fancy dinner.

Holley Place, Pocketknife Square, just southwest of intersection of Routes 44 and 41, Lakeville, Conn. (203) 435-2727. Lunch, Wednesday-Saturday and Monday, noon to 2:30; dinner 6 to 9 (tavern only on Wednesday); Sunday 11:30 to 2 and 4 to 8; closed Tuesday. Reservations accepted. Major credit cards.

Also in the Area

The Woodland, Route 41, Lakeville. (203) 435-0578. A stylish lounge with slate floor and curved greenhouse windows has been added to this classy looking establishment in a wooded area south of Lakeville. Beehive lights hang over the smart red booths in a dining room striking for the art work on the walls, interesting woven placemats and profusion of fresh flowers. Eight luncheon salads are $3.25 (spinach) to $7.95 (shrimp platter), and salad Nicoise is $4.50. There's a large variety of sandwiches, and you can create your own omelet for $3.95. Vegetable frittata and vegetables Woodland (sauteed with ginger and garlic and topped with melted cheese) are specialties. At night, there are a few salads and sandwiches, plus eight entrees from $7.50 (chicken Kiev or sole meuniere or amandine), to $12.95. Only two, scampi and sirloin steak, are over $10. Finish with such delectable homemade desserts as cranberry linzer torte, chocolate fudge cake with kahlua sauce, pear custard cake or kiwi sorbet, all in the $2.50 range. Lunch, Tuesday-Saturday 11:30 to 2:30, dinner 5:30 to 9, weekends to 10; Sunday brunch, noon to 3; closed Monday.

The Milk Pail, Route 7, Kent. (203) 927-3136. Old milk pails and an ancient sled flank the facade of the small brown house that houses the Milk Pail in the center of Kent. The late Eric Sloane painted the logo for the restaurant. At night you order from a blackboard; entrees ($9.75 to $15.95) include veal forestiere, mustard chicken and crab-stuffed shrimp, but light eaters could get chili and salad for $5.95. Seasonal soups like cream of asparagus or parsley and herring in white wine sauce are among appetizers. Salads, sandwiches and a few blackboard specials are the fare at noon; a soup and sandwich combination is $4.75. The chocolate lovers' pie is a cross between chiffon and mousse, says owner Ernie Schmutzler (whose wife Penny makes the desserts); it has a graham cracker crust and is topped with whipped cream and shaved chocolate. A large outdoor deck in back affords stunning vistas of the Housatonic River valley. Lunch, Tuesday-Saturday 11:30 to 2:30; dinner 5 to 9:30. Sunday, lunch-brunch noon to 3, dinner 4 to 9. Closed Monday.

Fife 'n Drum, Route 7, Kent. (203) 927-3509. A red wood and fieldstone building, accented by large lanterns and the ubiquitous American eagle, might make you think this is a place for New England food, but the menu features French and Italian dishes. Inside are a tavern, a tap room and a dining room, with white linen against a backdrop of dark barn wood and small-paned windows. Dinner entrees are from $9.95 for fettuccine Alfredo to $17.95 for steak au poivre, finished tableside with brandy. Duckling is also flambeed tableside, and sweetbreads are broiled with thyme, herb butter and hollandaise sauce. The blackboard lunch menu offers items like eggs benedict, quiche, beef goulash, seafood crepe, baked sea trout, chicken Portuguese, cold marinated seafood salad or cold pasta salad with scallops, $4.25 to $5.95; there are also four sandwiches and three soups, one of them raspberry when we visited. The tap room menu has sandwiches, munchies and mini-meals, most $2.95 to $5. Owner Dolph Traymon sometimes entertains with piano show tunes; he and his family have been so successful in their 14 years here that they recently added a gift shop and inn with seven guest rooms across the way. Open daily, lunch and Sunday brunch 11:30 to 3, dinner 5:30 to 9:30 or 10:30, Sunday 3 to 8:30.

Iron Kettle, Route 7, New Milford. (203) 354-1809. After some years in Atlanta, chef-owner Ronnie Shelnutt and his wife Meredith took over the Iron Kettle late in 1984, refurbished the Colonial house considerably and added some New Orleans touches to the menu. The blackboard dinner menu features appetizers like Canadian smoked goose and entrees ($9.95 to $15.95) of bluefish Parker House, shrimp bayou, chicken pecan or linguini fra diavolo. The interesting lunch menu goes from $4 for Creole omelet to $6.95 for sole with crabmeat, calves liver English style, or fried oysters remoulade. There are several pastas and "a red and white symphony" (bagel, cream cheese and smoked salmon). Among desserts (about $3) are gooseberry tart, raspberry creme cake and amaretto Napolean. Lunch, Monday-Friday noon to 2; dinner, 6 to 9, weekends to 10:30; Sunday brunch, noon to 3; closed Tuesdays.

Woodstoves, Route 37, Sherman. (203) 355-1179. Personable chef Robert Ausbury no longer opens his creative restaurant for lunch, but dinners and Sunday brunch are still as special as ever. The blackboard menu usually lists a curry (Ausbury's sister once owned an Indian restaurant in New York and he inherited some of her recipes), served with a tray of interesting condiments. Appetizers could be a heavenly shrimp in beer batter ($5) or artichokes beurre noisette ($3.25) or clams casino ($5.75). The four or five entrees, in the $14 to $19 range, generally include swordfish Allison (named for Ausbury's wife, who does much of the baking here), with a crumb, shallot and clam topping, or en brochette, with a scampi sauce, on a bed of rice, and "reeking of garlic butter," says the chef. The $10.75 brunch includes a glass of house wine or bloody mary; eggs benedict, eggplant crepes and artichoke stuffed with mussels are some main dish dishes and everyone loves the homemade fruit muffins. Meringues sprinkled with kirsch and topped with fresh fruit are a favorite dessert here, and you can buy many of the desserts like strawberry mousse pie, chocolate mousse tartlets and a very special bread, rhubarb nut. Wines are also listed on the blackboard and specials change often — a Dry Creek cabernet sauvignon is $14; Rutherford Hill sauvignon blanc $12. The two small dining rooms have yellow linens and in the smaller is a fireplace and the bar, in an old church pew. Check out the stained glass and collages. Woodstoves, which has one in the corner, was once a barn and was moved from a nearby lake. Dinner, Wednesday-Sunday 6 to 9; Sunday brunch, noon to 3.

Andre's, Low Road, Sharon. (203) 364-5405. The various herbs in small containers in the front garden at Andre's, a natural foods store which in 1984 added a restaurant, are used with a free hand in many of the dishes served there. Owner Andre LaFontan, a man of many interests, hosts a farmers market on the lawn on Saturdays from Memorial Day to October, and runs several animal shelters. The new dining room has polished wood floors, tables covered with calico cloths of different colors, pots of flowers all over the place, stained-glass hanging lamps and candles of various colors in antique glass holders. A marble-topped sideboard holds the luscious desserts, including the chocolate almond rum cake that, says La-Fontan, is "too strong for children." Walter Fairservis, a professor at Vassar College, makes many of the soups devised from historical recipes; Seven Nations is an Indian concoction of corn, fish and white beans and Henry VII includes leeks and potatoes. Besides the blackboard specials, lunch is mainly soups, sandwiches, salads and quiche; a veggie pita pizza is $3.50. At night, appetizers include baked brie with almonds, smoked trout and spinach feta triangles, in the $2.25 to $4.50 range; entrees ($6.95 to $11.95) could be stir-fried chicken and vegetables with rice, broiled fish of the day (the fish truck from Rockland, Maine, is parked in front of the restaurant on Fridays) or, for vegetarians, baked acorn squash stuffed with vegetables, nuts and cheese. For Sunday brunch ($5.95, including salad, dessert and coffee), you could have banana french toast and bacon or eggs Europe, poached eggs and ham on homemade muffins with a mushroom onion cheese sauce. A liter of Cuvee blanc de blanc is $7; $2 for a glass. Lunch, Monday-Saturday 11:30 to 2:30; dinner, Friday and Saturday 5 to 9:30, Sunday and Monday 5 to 8. Closed Tuesday.

Rudy's, Route 202, 2 1/2 miles north of New Milford. (203) 354-7727. Swiss-born Peter Lang, who once worked for Rudy Hilfiker when he owned the Hopkins Inn, took over his restaurant last year, after 13 years at the Mileaway in New Hampshire. A handsome solarium dining room overlooking a small pond was added, but otherwise the nice rustic alpine atmosphere has stayed the same. Rudy's is the kind of a place where the waitresses ring the three immense cowbells for customers' anniversaries and birthdays. Shutters inside the dining room are painted as they are in the Alps; an alpenhorn and a collection of plates of the Swiss cantons are part of the decor. The continental specialties are listed on a blackboard; gravlax, marinated mushrooms, raclette and bundnerteller, a kind of Swiss antipasto, are a few of the appetizers. Entrees, most in the $10 to $15 range, include sauerbraten, wiener schnitzel, veal zaza (in a garlic sauce), duck a l'orange and sweetbreads cafe de Paris. Some seldom-found Swiss wines are on the list, and a coupe toblerone, served with hot Swiss chocolate sauce in a pitcher on the side, is a popular dessert. Dinner, Tuesday-Saturday 6 to 9, Sunday 3 to 8; Sunday brunch, noon to 3.

Hopkins Inn, Hopkins Road, New Preston. (203) 868-7295. Beautiful Lake Waramaug sparkles below the popular outdoor terrace, with the Litchfield Hills rising all around. You could easily imagine yourself beside one of the lakes in the Alps, and Austrian chef-owner Franz Schober must feel quite at home. Lunch or dinner on the terrace, shaded by a giant horse chestnut tree and distinguished by striking copper and wrought-iron chandeliers and lanterns, is great from spring into fall. One dining room is Victorian, while the other is rustic with barnsiding and ship's figureheads. The blackboard menu changes daily, but always includes Austrian and Swiss dishes. Dinner entrees are $10.25 to $14.50 for dishes like wiener-schnitzel or sweetbreads that we remember fondly from years past; the roast pheasant with red cabbage and spaetzle is especially popular. For vegetables, you may get something unusual like braised romaine lettuce, and appealing desserts are strawberries romanoff and grand marnier souflee glace, each about $2.50. The varied wine list has half a dozen from Switzerland as well as three from Hopkins Vineyard next door. Lunch prices start at $5.25 for spinach salad or lamb curry and top off at $8 for smoked salmon or shrimp Dewey. Lunch, noon to 2; dinner, 6 to 9, Sunday 12:30 to 8:30; closed Monday and January-March; dinner only in early spring and late fall. No credit cards.

Colonial structure is home of Aldrich Museum.

Contemporary Art; Colonial Setting

Aldrich Museum/Ridgefield, Conn.

Contemporary art is served up in a Colonial setting at the Aldrich Museum of Contemporary Art in Ridgefield, Conn. — and it's the setting that gets you at first. Driving along the conservative old town's gracious Main Street, with its Colonial homes, fine churches and ancient trees, you don't quite expect to be confronted with Robert Morris's L-shaped beams or Robert Perless's kinetic sculptures. The Aldrich Museum is, in fact, the only contemporary art museum in the state of Connecticut.

Actually the sculpture isn't all that obvious at first. You must pull up to the side of the 1783 landmark building, with its demure white clapboards and black shutters and walk out back to see the enormous pieces of contemporary sculpture that sit on the great expanse of lawn as it slopes away from the building. There are 30 sculptures in all, mostly massive, and they provide a startling and stunning contrast to the building itself, which is not allowed to alter its exterior and so blends in with the rest of Ridgefield's Main Street.

By this time, though, everyone has gotten over the inhibiting idea that antiques have to be exhibited in old houses, or contemporary art in glass and steel buildings, and so the mix at the Aldrich is quite splendid the way it is. Local kids who cavort

136

in front of the Eduardo Paolozzi stainless steel sculpture, which acts like a mirror in an amusement park fun house, have a good time even if it's taken a while for the rest of the local populace to accept it. And it has.

When the Aldrich Museum opened in 1964 under the private ownership of Mr. and Mrs. Larry Aldrich, its patrons tended to be the cognoscenti from New York, who would tool out to the country on nice weekends from spring until fall to view the art. In those days the museum closed during the winter. But gradually the reputation of the Aldrich grew; it went public in 1969, began to open year-round in the mid-1970s, and now gets support from the entire area. The focus has changed, too, from strictly paintings and sculpture to include photography, drawings and special events: films on art, concerts, art tours, panel discussions and regularly scheduled evenings when leading artists discuss their work.

Recently the museum has mounted a number of exciting exhibitions which have drawn wide critical acclaim. Arakawa and Warhol are two artists who have had successful one-man shows. "American Neo-Expressionists," which featured the work of 24 leading contemporary painters, was the first museum survey of this group of artists.

Another show, "Intermedia — Between Painting and Sculpture," presented the work of 36 internationally known artists who were represented by works which were neither painting nor sculpture but fell somewhere in between. "The Classic Tradition in Recent Painting and Sculpture" surveyed a group of well-respected artists whose work has references to the classical period in art.

All of this means that the Aldrich keeps a commitment to the new, the emerging, the avant-garde, very much the way its founder would have it. Larry Aldrich, although now in his 80s, continues to exert influence and to pay great attention to what is happening at "his" museum. He may not tramp through lofts in SoHo to select paintings personally, as he once did, but his original intentions live on, and he stays in close touch.

The Aldrich is an exciting place to visit, mostly because of the art that's on display, but also because of the way it is done. The interior of the old building has been pretty much gutted to allow for broad expanses of white walls where the canvases (many of them huge) by contemporary artists can be shown to best advantage. The polished wood floors and good track lighting add to the ambience.

Outside, the sculpture garden is a place to walk, to chat, and finally to sit at wrought-iron chairs and tables thoughtfully provided by the museum. Picnicking is welcomed and it's a glorious spot to do so on a terrace just behind the building,

Location: 258 Main St., (Route 35), Ridgefield, Conn. Reached via Merritt Parkway or I-84, then Route 7 to Route 35.

Open: Year-round, Wednesday to Friday 2 to 4, Saturdays and Sundays 1 to 5. Concerts and films on Friday evenings.

Admission: Adults, $1; children, students and senior citizens, 50 cents.

Telephone: (203) 438-4519.

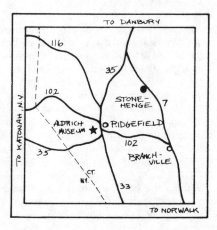

where you can feast your eyes as well as the rest of you. The sculpture garden is always open, so if you're in the area at a time when the rest of the museum is not, you can stop to view the sculpture alone. It is worth the time.

As you might expect, children enjoy this museum. They have a grand time playing on the grass around all those "funny shapes" and are inclined to respond to the contemporary work inside, as well. Your trip to the Aldrich makes a good focal point for a day which might also include shopping in Ridgefield's splendid stores, and a meal at any of the many outstanding restaurants in the area.

Also in the Area

Keeler Tavern, 132 Main St. (junction Routes 33 and 35), Ridgefield. (203) 438-5485. And now for a change of pace. This meticulously restored tavern, a short and pleasant walk from the Aldrich Museum, was operated as an inn from 1772 to 1907. A British cannonball from the Revolutionary War remains imbedded in the wall of the building. Furnishings are largely original. Guides dressed in colonial costume are on hand. Open Wednesday, Saturday and Sunday 1 to 4. Adults, $1.50; children, 50 cents.

Putnam Memorial State Park, Junction Routes 58 and 107, Redding, This was the winter encampment (1778-79) of the right wing of the Continental Army under General Israel Putnam. The historical area recreates the area of the encampment with some buildings recreated. There's a Revolutionary War museum and facilities for fishing, hiking and picnicking. The park is open all year with the museum open Memorial Day-Labor Day 9 to 5. Free.

 **Dining 20**_____

Stonehenge/Ridgefield, Conn.

Connecticut's most famed inn, perhaps, is Stonehenge in Ridgefield — famed for its food and, since the rooms were greatly upgraded and expanded in 1984, famed for its accommodations as well. In an early 19th century Colonial-style white building, the restaurant is enhanced by its surroundings of towering trees, spacious lawns and a lake where swans, ducks and a gaggle of Canada geese carry on their affairs.

Judging from the bits of conversation overhead inside the dining rooms, one wouldn't be surprised if a few affairs were being carried on there as well! Stonehenge has that kind of romantic, escapist atmosphere.

At night, dining in the dark-paneled, cozy and intimate bar is especially romantic, when red shaded candles inside glass lamps cast a seductive glow on the tables elegant with cream cloths and red napkins.

By day in the large and airy main dining room and especially on the new dining porch adjacent, the lovely grounds and the lake can be viewed through the sparkling windows. Handsome draperies add a luxurious note to the unusually beautiful main room, as do the wood paneling and corner cases filled with rare china and silver. Fresh flowers are on every table, and the same red lamps enhance the red and cream color scheme as at night.

Stonehenge has been known for distinguished cuisine since the famed Swiss chef, Albert Stockli of Restaurant Associates in New York, became co-owner in 1965. Although he died in 1972, present owners David Davis and Douglas Seville

Main dining room at Stonehenge.

are doing a grand job in keeping up the traditionally elegant food and service and enhancing the inn's overall appeal.

We've had both lunch and dinner here several times and each meal has been memorable indeed. Although lunch is less expensive than dinner, entrees cost $8.50 for omelet of shrimp and scallops or curried chicken madras to $16.75 for medallion of venison or tournedos with bordelaise sauce.

The menu changes seasonally, and at lunch we've started with the famous and hearty Stonehenge barley soup and an intense, bisque-like mushroom soup. Among entrees we've sampled the marvelous shrimp in beer batter with pungent fruit sauce, brook trout meuniere, a fabulous chef's salad and a beautifully arranged seafood salad in an avocado shell. Country pate is rough-textured and delicious, and chicken livers in an excellent sauce are served on crisp toast.

At dinner the cost is a prix-fixe $34, with several items carrying a surcharge. Or you can order some items a la carte — appetizers $4.75 to $8.75, entrees $19.50 to $21, desserts at least $4 and coffee $1.50.

Drinks are large and served in pretty, long-stemmed goblets. The wine list is extensive and expensive, starting at $14 for a good selection of Californias and rising into the $20-$60 range (a page of rare vintages goes from $100 to $450 for a 1947 Chateau Mouton Rothschild, and co-owner Seville says they're selling well since they cannot be purchased in stores for less).

At dinner, our appetizers were simply superb. Mushroom crepes with a mornay sauce and gruyere cheese were out of this world, rich yet delicate. Sausage, smoked in the Stonehenge kitchen, is well worth a try; with a mustard wine sauce and garnished with grapes, it's served sizzling, the edges slightly curled from the broiler. The sauce is extraordinary.

Stonehenge also has its own trout tanks — we watched in fascination the fish flopping in their pails as they were unloaded outside the window during a late-Saturday lunch. You can sample the trout as an appetizer, smoked and served with grated horseradish ($4.50 at lunch, $6.25 at night), or as brook trout meuniere, boned at tableside ($9.50 at lunch, on the prix-fixe menu at night).

A whole roasted squab chicken Grandmere was a tasty if formidable dish, garnished with mushrooms and and carrots, and swathed in a rich brown sauce. Vegetables of the day were carrots, glazed to a candy-like perfection, and a discreet small boiled potato with the trout, dusted with parsley. In season, you can get pate-stuffed roast quail with truffles or saddle of venison; filet of beef Wellington is offered Saturday evenings.

The house salad, served following entrees, was a nice mixture of greens, gleaming with its coat of mustardy vinaigrette.

There is a luscious selection of desserts, although we thought the Black Forest cake rather ordinary. A strawberry tart was really special, with an abundance of fresh fruit on a shortcake crust, topped with a deep and shiny glaze. Chocolate mousse, coupe aux marrons and selections from the cheese tray are other choices.

Service is distinguished, quiet and efficient, with many dishes heated and served tableside.

And if you think you are spending a bundle on your meal, consider the tale of the group of eight who flew in two helicopters from New York, landed in Danbury since Stonehenge wouldn't grant landing privileges, hired a limousine to the inn, entered holding their glasses full of Dom Perignon, and ordered three bottles of the more expensive wine. It was a birthday party for the manager of a noted rock group, and the bill in today's dollars came to more than $1,500!

Stonehenge, Route 7, Ridgefield, Conn. (203) 438-6511. Reservations recommended. Major credit cards. Lunch, daily noon to 2, dinner 6 to 9:30, weekends to 10:30. Sunday brunch at noon and 2:30. Closed Tuesday.

Also in the Area

Le Coq Hardi, Big Shop Lane, Ridgefield. (203) 431-3060. Serenely pretty and "nouvelle" in the lower level of a 19th century blacksmith shop at the end of a row of stores, this restaurant has a sophisticated French country look in its front greenhouse and two dining areas. Lunch entrees range from $8 for omelets to $13 for quail with red currant sauce; we had a fine breast of chicken with lingonberries and an interesting salad concoction of scallops and vegetables. For dinner, appetizers like sweetbreads forestiere and poached oysters are $6 to $7, entrees (perhaps grilled monkfish with pink peppercorns or veal chop with plum tomatoes) are $17 to $21, and desserts start at $5.50. Lunch Tuesday-Friday noon to 2, dinner Tuesday-Sunday 6 to 9 or 10, Sunday brunch 11 to 2.

Le Chateau, Route 35 at Route 123, South Salem, N.Y. (914) 533-6631. A few miles west of Ridgefield on a hilltop with a commanding view of the rural countryside, the huge baronial stone mansion built by J. Pierpont Morgan is a favorite with locals. Dining is in several formal, high-ceilinged rooms, a couple facing onto the garden patio. The eleven lunch entrees go from $6.25 for a cheese omelet to $15 for veal Normande. Dinners are $13 for calves brains to $20.50 for veal chops with morels. Frog legs, Dover sole meuniere, bouillabaisse, sweetbreads and steak au poivre are among the choices, and escargots Paul Bocuse are popular appetizers at lunch as well as dinner. Desserts include grand marnier souffle and cherries jubilee. Displays of appetizers and desserts tempt diners near the entrance. Lunch, daily noon to 2; dinner 6 to 9, Saturday to 11, Sunday 2 to 9; closed Monday.

Old School House Cafe, Cannon Crossing, Wilton. (203) 762-8656. The quaint one-room school in June Havoc's complex of antiques shops has had a succession of owners, but the latest — Westport caterers Henni Payne and Linda Keeler — offer the most interesting fare, with a variety of regional American food and specializing in Cajun and Tex-Mex. A "country platter" for $5.50 might contain watercress soup, pate, French bread, mushroom salad, grapes and brie. Seating is at tables covered with gray-green country prints, at a counter facing the creek or outside on a patio. Lunch and Sunday brunch except Monday, 11:30 to 4; BYOB.

Cafe Natural, 3 Big Shop Lane, Ridgefield. (203) 431-3637. The menu changes weekly at this intimate spot with its old posts and beams and stenciled watermelon slices on the walls. Young chef-owners Mark and Beth Ostad put in long days, serving breakfast and lunch starting at 8 a.m. and dinners three nights a week until 9. The soups, omelets, salads and sandwiches are interesting and reasonable ($1.75 to $5.95). Complete dinners, all under $10, might be chicken cacciatore, roast leg of lamb, veal Dijonnaise or shrimp-stuffed sole. They are served with a complimentary glass of wine, or you can bring your own. Breakfast and lunch, Monday-Saturday 8 to 4, Sunday 9 to 3; dinner, Wednesday-Friday 6 to 9.

A Taste of Paris, 20 Prospect St., Ridgefield. (203) 438-576l. Another casual place, part of a charcuterie and with a few tables outside under umbrellas, this French deli-bistro offers great croissants, heavier breakfast items and salads, quiches and crepes for lunch. A country pate plate is $5.50; a pastry shell filled with scallops $3.50. The Ridgefield special — homemade sausage with Swiss cheese, alfalfa sprouts and mustard with homemade cole slaw — is $3.50. You can pick out a wine from the interesting wine shop next door. Open daily except Sunday, 9 to 6.

The Kitchen Shop Cafe, Ridgefield General Store, Copps Hill Common, Ridgefield. (203) 438-1984. Ten tiny tables on the bright lower-level of a new shopping complex offer patrons an interesting variety of lunch choices: shrimp salad, chicken pie and salad, beef vegetable soup with cornbread, zucchini and three-cheese pie with salad, from $2.50 to $5.95. Among desserts are three cheesecakes, one a "serious chocolate cheesecake." Lunch, Monday-Saturday noon to 3.

Gates, 10 Forest St., New Canaan. (203) 966-8666. Authentic Austrian gates at the entrance lead to more gates inside at what is generally acclaimed New Canaan's most interesting restaurant. Towering ficus trees in the two-story green-house portion, interior arches, red tile and parquet floors, a veritable art gallery on the walls and newspapers on racks in the bar enliven an exceptionally bright, eclectic place. Cuban black bean soup, salads like Mexican and vegetarian and burgers are served at lunch and dinner, as are changing entrees. Lunch ($4.95 to $8.95) might be chicken oriental or calves liver madeira. Dinner ($9.50 to $14.95) includes lemon or curried chicken, filet of sole with soy and ginger served with snow peas, sauteed scallops or veal lacoste. Wednesdays and Thursdays are Fulton Fish Market nights, with an appealing array of seafood specials from sea trout in a three-onion butter with asparagus or scrod el Rosario to swordfish dijon ($10.95 to $14.95). The beer list numbers 42 varieties from the Philippines to Czechoslovakia. The elaborate Sunday brunch includes eggs, waffles, entrees, salads and sand-wiches ($4.95 to $9.95). Open daily, 11:30 to 3:30, dinner from 6.

Main Roosevelt house at Hyde Park.

Eleanor and Franklin

Roosevelt Sites/Hyde Park, N.Y.

For those of us who were babies or young children during World War II — and certainly for those born shortly after — it was Eleanor Roosevelt that we knew. F.D.R. died in 1945; Eleanor was with us until 1962, living to bless the Presidential candidacy of John F. Kennedy.

It was Eleanor at the United Nations, Eleanor in Washington, D.C., Eleanor in India or on an around-the-world tour. Now, and since 1984, it is Eleanor in Hyde Park. And for those of us who long to walk behind the scenes of a famous person's life, it is a treat indeed.

The site is called Val-Kill, after the rushing stream which flows through the property. It is land which was part of the holdings of her famous husband, land loved by the First Lady and originally used as a place to picnic or to walk in the woods. In the late 1920s, the property was given to Eleanor and two friends to build a cottage upon — a charming Dutch-style stone building designed by F.D.R. and intended as a retreat.

Just a five-minute ride from the main Hyde Park mansion where the President had grown up, and where he lived (at least part-time) until his death, the Val-Kill property was used for picnics and parties throughout the President's lifetime. More important to Eleanor Roosevelt was its quiet seclusion, a chance to get away from the turmoil of public life, and a home, truly, of her own. The President's mother, Sara, had proved to be a dominating mother-in-law and made all household decisions at the main Hyde Park mansion.

One reaches Val-Kill by shuttle bus from the main Roosevelt house and library-museum on property overlooking the Hudson River. The Val-Kill property is open from April until November; when we visited in late April, daffodils nodding by the stream gave a special loveliness to the scene.

In addition to the Dutch Colonial cottage which was the original building, there is a larger building which was erected by the First Lady and her friends in 1926 for use by local craftsmen, who made reproductions of early American furniture and tableware. That industry was the women's response to an exodus from rural America to the cities in search of work. Val-Kill Industries endured for 10 years, but in 1936 even that experiment became a victim of the Depression.

It was soon after the departure of the craftsmen that Mrs. Roosevelt had the larger building remodeled to include two apartments, one for herself and one for her secretary, Malvina "Tommy" Thompson. As a way of warming up the stone building, she had the interior walls redone in knotty pine, which gives them a cozy, if somewhat dark, feeling.

Visitors are introduced to the site and to Mrs. Roosevelt through a 20-minute audio-visual presentation in yet a third building, known as the playhouse. The building, we were told, was used by the Roosevelt clan and visitors when a picnic was planned and rained out.

The First Lady's home, used both as a retreat and more or less full time when she was a widow, is memorable, most of all, for the photographs on the walls and tables, everywhere it seems. They provide a glimpse into a life filled with and devoted to people: her great humanitarianism extended to rich and poor alike, and she entertained many famous people at Val-Kill. Among them were Nikita Khrushchev, Marshal Tito, Haile Selassie and Jawaharial Nehru. John F. Kennedy had tea with the First Lady, we were told, at a round mahogany tea table in the parlor of her apartment prior to his seeking the Presidency. Although she had supported Adlai Stevenson in the past and was still a great admirer of his, she gave Kennedy her blessing during the visit.

Location: Route 9, Hyde Park, N.Y.

Open: Roosevelt house and library, daily 9 to 5 except Thanksgiving, Christmas and New Year's Day. Val-Kill is open only from April until November and is reached by shuttle bus from the Roosevelt site.

Admission: A $1.50 combined ticket admits visitors to the Roosevelt Home and library and to the Vanderbilt Mansion (see below). A visit to Val-Kill requires a separate $1.95 ticket. Senior citizens and visitors under 16 are admitted free.

Telephone: (914) 229-8114. For information on Val-Kill, (914) 229-9115.

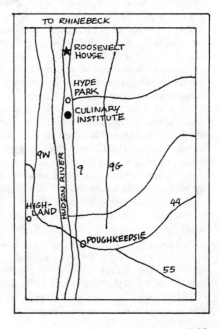

Val-Kill, the house where Eleanor Roosevelt lived.

Val-Kill is simple and unpretentious, very much what we would expect of Eleanor Roosevelt. She was an egalitarian at heart, and it is very apparent at this home. Outdoors, an enormous fieldstone fireplace for picnics, a pool, a tennis court, and a playhouse for children complete the compound. There are trails through the woods and a rustic bridge across the stream. All is quiet and lovely, and much removed in spirit from the public life which the once-shy First Lady inherited with her marriage.

The main mansion at Hyde Park is really Franklin's home, and perhaps even more than Franklin's, his mother, Sara's. It was here that the future President grew up, the adored son of a wealthy father and a cultured mother. The house has great spirit and personality. The enormous living room, which fills the entire first floor of the south wing, has massive fireplaces at either end. It was here that the family played, rested, read and entertained.

Other first-floor rooms include the dining room, the so-called Dresden Room, which is like a formal parlor and has an exquisite chandelier; a small room called the Snuggery, where the President's mother organized her household, and a large entrance foyer. The Office, which was used as a Summer White House, is viewed from outdoors; the visitor may press a button which brings a recording of F.D.R.'s voice. It was in this room that Roosevelt and Winston Churchill signed an historic agreement which resulted in the world's first atomic bomb.

Since a devastating fire in 1982, this is all of the main house that has been open to the public. The second floor was expected to be reopened by the summer of 1985.

The second-floor bedrooms express an even more personal side of the Roosevelt family: the boyhood bedroom was used by Franklin as a child, and by his four sons after him. The President's bedroom contains favorite memorabilia: family photographs and naval prints, plus the leash and blanket of the President's dog, Fala.

The Franklin D. Roosevelt library and museum, a sizable stone edifice to the northeast of the house, is most absorbing. Established in 1939, it contains an exhibit of the "First Fifty Years" of the President's life, beginning with the wicker bassinet used for him as a baby, and including touching letters in his childish hand to his mother, as well as from the Groton School in Groton, Mass., where he matriculated as a high school student. His Harvard years, and his courtship of his fifth cousin, Anna Eleanor Roosevelt, are all recounted.

Roosevelt's tragic encounter with polio, which left him severely crippled, and his courageous public life that followed, are all represented in the gallery.

Equally absorbing is the wing devoted to Eleanor, which tells of her sensitive nature, the death of her mother when she was but eight and of her father when she was 10, and her British schooling.

Downstairs is a gallery known as "America on the Seas," containing just a small part of F.D.R.'s large and valuable collection of sea memorabilia; there is a portion of the stamp collection he began as a child, as well. His office in this building — for he worked here at times over a period of six years before his death — has a simple wheelchair (we are told he eschewed the more institutional variety), a massive desk and several other pieces of furniture.

In the gallery devoted to his years as President, the visitor can read copies of drafts of his famous speeches; see the Dutch Bible on which he took the oath of office, even his famous fedora, and be reminded of the extraordinary times — from 1933 to 1945 — during which he led the nation.

His favorite — and famous — car, a Ford Phaeton convertible, is on display in a separate gallery.

No matter what your politics, the Roosevelt homes and the library-museum provide a rare and precious view of life at the time of the Great Depression and the Second World War, of the family that stood at the helm of the ship of state, and for better or worse influenced a world and a century far more than most.

Also in the Area

Vanderbilt Mansion, Route 9, Hyde Park. Just a short distance north of the Roosevelt sites on Route 9, with an enchanting view of the Hudson River, this 54-room mansion was the home of Frederick W. Vanderbilt, grandson of Commodore Vanderbilt. It was Frederick's brothers who built the Marble House and the Breakers in Newport, R.I., and our guide reminded us that this was, indeed, the most modest of the Vanderbilt mansions built during the gilded age. An Italian Renaissance palace created by the famed architectural firm of McKim, Mead and White, the "house" was used during the spring and fall by Frederick and his wife, Louisa, a social woman who entertained — didn't they all? — lavishly. The circular plan of the first floor, with a dining room which could be turned into a ballroom and where the Roosevelts' only daughter, Anna, was once feted, is in marked contrast to the home of F.D.R. Perhaps it's all that marble which makes it seem so formal, but this is a pretentious place — in spite of its modest size for the social set the Vanderbilts were a part of. Especially nice, however, is the property. A road leads down to the banks of the Hudson River, where there are ample parking and picnic tables along the river's edge. The so-called "guest house" — only 16 rooms here — is now a visitors' center. A short slide presentation precedes a visit to the house. Daily, 9 to 5, except Jan. 1, Thanksgiving and Christmas.

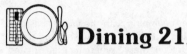

Dining 21_____

Culinary Institute of America/Hyde Park, N.Y.

"I am the Emperor of Germany, but you are the Emperor of chefs," said Emperor William II to Auguste Escoffier, the great French chef whose career spanned the years from 1859 to 1921.

In the fast-food days of pizza spots, Big Macs gulped on the run, and soups and sauces straight out of cans, Escoffier would be pleased to know that his traditions are being carried on in the famed dining room named after him at the Culinary Institute of America, where many of the nation's restaurant greats receive their training. The spirit of Escoffier also reigns in the institute's American Bounty restaurant, a more casual and experimental room opened in 1982 to espouse the joys of America's regional cuisine, and in the new, still more casual St. Andrew's Cafe, specializing in nutritious foods.

This is not a traditional school campus, you think to yourself as you head from the parking lot toward the main building and watch budding chefs in white hats and coats scurry across the green, some clutching their long red knife kits that look like giant toolboxes. It couldn't be, when you find out the rallying chant for the hockey team is "mirepoix, mirepoix, roux, roux, roux; slice 'em up, dice 'em up, drop 'em in the stew!"

As a former Jesuit seminary, St. Andrews-on-Hudson, high above the river, the old red brick building has an institutional tinge. But the tantalizing aromas that waft from the Escoffier Room or American Bounty at opposite ends of the long, somewhat gloomy main hallway are anything but institutional.

Cooking and serving in the restaurants are the final courses in the 21 months of study for the institute's 1,900 students, who arrive and graduate in cycles every three weeks. The final fruits of their labors are sufficient to draw diners from far and wide, with reservations booked several months in advance at peak season.

Our first of several memorable dining experiences at the CIA was in the **Escoffier Room,** which reminds one of a small, solid and comfortable hotel dining room and seats about 50 people. It is cheery and well lit, with gold and white lattice-work walls and handsome brass chandeliers, comfortable black leather-like chairs and banquettes, and spacious tables on which gigantic wine glasses take an inordinate amount of room.

Lunch is $16 prix-fixe and worth every penny. In fact, it's a bargain when you compare it with dinner ($34), which offers only one more course, fruit and cheese. Expect to spend more than two hours and to not have any appetite for dinner that night.

Menus, consisting mostly of classic French items with some international dishes, change every week for three weeks and then the cycle starts over. In classic French style, most dishes are served from rolling carts.

At lunch or dinner, you choose from among five appetizers and four soups. They include such delights as oysters Rockefeller, galantine of pheasant, clams casino or rumaki. Our hors d'oeuvre varies added up to a colorful and filling plateful of salads, ham, tuna and pepper, eggs a la Russe, dried beef, prosciutto, sardines and marinated mushrooms. This, with the excellent croissants and rolls served with curls of sweet butter, would have been enough for a soul-satisfying lunch.

Following the soup course (the onion was the best we've ever had), you tackle the main course, a choice of eight or nine entrees plus a daily special. We remember a tasty chicken in a spicy and well-blended curry sauce, accompanied by a large tray of chutneys and condiments. The tender sweetbreads were topped with two large slices of truffle and a subtle sauce. Other luncheon entrees might be coquilles

American Bounty restaurant at Culinary Institute.

St. Jacques au gratin, grilled salmon bearnaise, English mixed grill, chicken with Hungarian paprika cream sauce, entrecote bordelaise or broiled lamb chops served with an artichoke bottom filled with julienne of tongue, mushrooms and truffles. A seasonal salad follows the main course.

We groaned as the dessert cart filled with noble tortes, rich cakes and more rolled up, but had to taste an incredible many-layered pastry square, filled with sweet whipped cream and raspberries.

You wouldn't expect such a repast to be surpassed, but it was, to our minds, some years later in the new **American Bounty** restaurant. Fashioned from offices and corridors, two cloister-style dining rooms seat 118 people at tables spaced well apart. A gorgeous array of America's bounty spills over in an arrangement in front of the glassed-in kitchen window, where you can watch students at work and ducklings turning on the rotisserie. The effect is stunning, from the pirate's trunk filled with fresh fruit to the voluptuous (that's the only word for it) display of breads of all shapes and sizes on a nearby sideboard.

The menu, edged in the dark green, rust and beige color scheme of the restaurant and sealed with a gold sticker, changes every meal. It's one of those rare creations in which every item appeals and only the New England clam chowder seems old hat. Here, the prices are a la carte and, as opposed to the Escoffier Room, a full-course lunch can be nearly as expensive as dinner.

For appetizers ($3.75 to $4.75), how about diced veal sweetbreads and shiitake mushrooms, Savannah Bay hot scallop salad with cheddar rusks, Southwest beef tortilla with guacamole and sour cream or California wild mushrooms with cream

147

and herbs on toasted croutons? We settled for tomato and celery mousse on cold fresh tomato hash, and a sampling of the three soups ($2.50) served in tiny cups, a chilled fresh strawberry, clam chowder and New Orleans chicken and sausage gumbo.

With these came a basket with at least nine kinds of bread and rolls, from corn sticks to biscuits, served with a crock of sweet butter.

Entrees are $9.75 to $11.50 at lunch, $11.75 to $16 at dinner. You might try shrimp and Cajun sausage with pecan rice, Mr. Prudhomme's blackened red snapper with tomato and green chili salad, beef tenderloin with Arizona chili butter and barbecued mushroom stew, pork medallions with corn cakes and creamed crab meat or Atlantic swordfish with caviar butter sauce and fried enoki mushrooms. From the rotisserie, you could have Cornish game hen with cream gravy and barley with pinenuts or roast Wisconsin duckling with raspberry sauce.

For a spring lunch, we sampled two seasonal dishes: fresh asparagus on sour-dough toast with creamed salmon and sweetbreads, and a popular item called "baked fresh seafood variety, new garden style" — crabmeat, clams casino, mussels, clams, salmon and more topped with butter and crumbs and baked, pretty as a picture in an iron skillet rimmed with tomato wedges. Vegetables, served family style, were stuffed cherry tomatoes, yellow squash and tiny new red potatoes, boiled in their jackets.

Desserts ($2 to $2.50) are to swoon over, from poached pear half with port wine syrup and fresh blueberries or bread pudding with fresh strawberries to coconut and banana fritters with white chocolate sauce and fresh fruit cobbler with Wild Turkey sauce. We loved the Mississippi river boat, a pastry shell filled with intense chocolate mousse topped by kiwi fruit, and fried strawberries with a sour cream and orange dipping sauce.

The wine list is all American and contains some real bargains, due to a small markup. Service is less formal than in the Escoffier Room (the garb is green aprons), but correct and cordial — after all, these kids get *graded* for this.

If you don't feel up to the price or the calories, you might try some of the students' fare in the new **St. Andrew's Cafe** in the old Wexler Coffee Shop, open evenings part of the year for pastas, salads, sandwiches, light entrees and "energizing beverages," all with an eye to health and nutrition values at bargain prices.

But we'd suggest planning ahead for a lunch or dinner in either the Escoffier Room or American Bounty, depending on your taste. Either way, it will likely linger in your memory as one of the meals of a lifetime.

Culinary Institute Restaurants, Hyde Park, N.Y. (914) 471-6608 for reservations. Escoffier Room, Tuesday-Saturday, lunch noon to 1:30, dinner 6:30 to 8:30. American Bounty, Tuesday-Saturday, lunch 11:30 to 1, dinner 6:30 to 8:30. Reservations with deposits required; booked long in advance in summer, but there may be cancellations. Major credit cards accepted.

Also in the Area

Beekman Arms, Route 9, Rhinebeck. (914) 876-7077. The Culinary Institute has a monopoly on fine dining in the Hyde Park area, and otherwise for better restaurants you have to head north to Rhinebeck or south to Poughkeepsie. Billing itself as America's oldest hotel (1766), the venerable Beekman Arms is thoroughly up to date with an appealing garden room out front, covered with a brown canopy, hanging plants and ferns, and brightened by redwood window boxes filled with geraniums. White linened tables surrounded by deck chairs are perfect for lunch on pleasant days; inside, the dark, low-beamed Tap Room, the Pewter Room and Wine Celler Room ooze a sense of history. The menu is fairly straightforward. At lunch, sandwiches, salads, build-your-own omelets, crepes, quiche and blackboard specials are $4.75 to $7.95. Dinners include a crock of herbed cheese with a cracker basket, salad, homemade bread, vegetable, and rice pilaf or potato. Entrees range from $11.95 for buttermilk pecan chicken to $16.50 for prime rib; roast duckling with raspberry sauce, veal with artichokes, Cajun blackened redfish and shrimp tempura are among the more adventuresome choices. The extravagant Sunday brunch buffet spread out on tables in the Wayfarer Room, $11.95 for adults and $6.95 for children, is a local institution. Open daily for breakfast, lunch 11:30 to 3, dinner 5 to 10; Sunday brunch 10 to 2.

Jacaruso's Trottoria, 37 Montgomery St. (facing Route 9), Rhinebeck. (914) 876-7272. The brown-shingled, 1825 First Baptist Church now houses a good-looking dining room and bar; outside is a colorful sidewalk cafe. Low black booths, tan and brown linen, two striking floral paintings between the three stained-glass windows and a mass of plants make a colorful setting. The small lunch menu offers two salads, four pastas and four sandwiches, $3.50 to $5.95. At night, pastas are $6.50 to $11.95 (with shrimp and scallops), entrees run from $8.95 for eggplant rollatini to $12.95 for scampi garnished with mussels or filet mignon with a mush-room and sherry sauce. The fish of the day ($9.50) is baked in paper. The house antipasto is $5.95 for two. Cannoli, carrot cake and ice cream are among the homemade desserts, Italian coffee is served with amaretto and the house soave and valpolicella are $2 a glass, $7 a carafe. Hours and days vary by season; lunch and dinner daily in summer; off-season, dinner 5:30 to 10, lunch weekends, closed Tuesday and-or Wednesday.

Victoria Peak, Route 9, Rhinebeck. (914) 876-7933. The roadhouse exterior of this unlikely looking establishment just north of the village belies its ornate interior, with mahogany bar, crystal chandeliers, pink linen and deep red velvet-backed and cushioned chairs. The Szechuan-Hunan-style Chinese food is memo-rable, according to our CIA guides; unfortunately when we visited in May 1985, lunch no longer was being served. The 59-item dinner menu lists eight appetizers, $2.50 to $5.75, plus an assorted plate for $11.95, as well as poultry, pork, seafood, beef and vegetable entrees from $8.50 for King Pao chicken or pork with tiger sauce to $15.75 for Peking duck. Szechuan orange beef is $11.25 and Hunan-style shrimp, $12.50. Dinner, Tuesday-Saturday from 5, Sunday from 3.

Denmarc, 221 Dutchess Turnpike (Route 44), Poughkeepsie. (914) 473-0399. A discreet sign, "Denmarc, A Restaurant," barely identifies the large white house transformed into a suave new restaurant with one of the more imaginative menus we've seen lately, one that changes five times a year. A spare but good-looking decor marks the five small dining rooms, three with fireplaces, plus a porch with brightly cushioned wicker chairs for cocktails. Classical music plays in the back-ground and you might well imagine you were a guest in the home of Danish chef-owner Better Nielsen. For dinner, start with snow pea salad, flower oysters, fresh asparagus with shrimp, gravad laks or roasted quail with maple syrup and walnuts ($2.50 to $7.50). Spring soups were mushroom, quail's nest and chilled straw-berry-buttermilk. Main courses vary from $8 for a dinner of assorted seasonal vegetables ($8) to $20 for tenderloin of lamb or chilled lobster. Others might be Louisiana redfish with black pepper, poached salmon with dijon sauce, Cornish hen with rhubarb sauce, warm chicken salad, sweetbreads "meuniere-ish," lamb stew or medallions of pork tenderloin with oranges, scallions and ginger. After an optional salad or cheese course, finish with melon and port, kiwi with creme cointreau, rhubarb cheese cake, mandelkage or honey walnut crepes, $2.50 to $3.50. The lunch menu, though smaller, is equally creative — anything from flapjack sandwich or Welsh rarebit to lobster or squid salad, marinated chevre, cod roe blintzes with sour cream and caviar or "a meal of melon and such;" prices are $4 to $8. The extensive American and French wine list is priced from $9 to $100. Open daily, lunch and weekend lunch-brunch 11:30 to 3. dinner 6 to 10:30, late-night supper 10 to midnight.

Vassar College Alumnae House, Raymond Avenue at College Avenue, Poughkeepsie. (914) 485-3700. The imposing Tudor mansion that has served for more than 60 years as headquarters for Vassar alumnae now is an inn, restaurant and pub open to the public with reasonably priced, straightforward food in a club-like atmosphere. Generally overlooked locally because of traditional town-gown coolness, afficionados sing the praises of the bountiful weekend brunch and, new in 1985, a lavish Wednesday night buffet. Lunch in the paneled, high-ceilinged dining room with cushioned, heavy wood chairs covers a range of soups, salads, platters and sandwiches plus house specialties (served with soup or salad and breads, $4.25 to $6.95) like lemon chicken, lobster salad sandwich, stir-fried oriental vegetables and quiche or omelet du jour. At night, there are light salads and pastas ($4 to $5), plus cheese and beef fondues ($8.25 and $11.95) and entrees from $5.25 (omelet or quiche) to $10.95 for steak au poivre, filet mignon or shrimp scampi. For dessert, try the Vassar devil (devil's food cake heaped with vanilla ice cream and chocolate sauce) or a frozen brandy Alexander. A light menu is served in the rear pub or on the outdoor terrace with everything from pizzas to shrimp in a basket, soup to kahlua milkshake, $1.10 to $5.75. Open daily, lunch 11 to 4, dinner 4 to 10 or 11; light menu, 2 to midnight.

Springwood Inn, Route 9, Hyde Park. (914) 229-2681. Add a greenhouse with slate floor and bentwood chairs to the old Howard Johnson's and, voila! You have a casual place with a bit of the Ho-Jo's air. There's something for everyone on both lunch and dinner menus as well as the Wednesday night seafood bonanza buffet ($11.95) and the Sunday buffet brunch ($8.95). Lunch is sandwiches, salads, things like chicken in a basket with cole slaw and a few blackboard specials like seafood newburg crepes or bluefish provencal ($2.50 to $6.50). Steaks are the only items above $10 on the dinner menu. Lunch daily, 11:30 to 4, dinner 4 to 10, Sunday brunch.

Coppola Brothers Italian Kitchen, Route 9, Hyde Park. (914) 229-9113. One of three Coppola restaurants in the Poughkeepsie area, this is in a pleasant, awninged building, has two nondescript dining rooms and serves "food like your mom used to make," a secretary at the CIA told us. The elaborate luncheon menu, supplemented with two inserts and daily specials, starts at $3.95 for a complete meal, with 15 more from $4 to $5 (standards like mussels marinara, chicken cacciatore, eggplant parmigiana and stuffed clams). Dinner entrees start at $6.95 (chicken or eggplant parmigiana and chicken livers saute); most are under $10, with zuppe di pesci (including lobster or crab) tops at $28.75. Lunch and dinner daily.

Easy Street, Route 9, Hyde Park. (917) 229-7969. The outside looks like a Wild West saloon, and the sign over the long, Western-style bar says "Relax, enjoy and take it easy." That's what the locals do here, over burgers, sandwiches, salads and a handful of specials like fettuccine with scallops and turkey or sole baked with shrimp (about $5). Dinner entrees are hearty, from Yankee pot roast ($7.95) through seafood, chicken and pork chops to steak au poivre ($13.50). Easy is the theme, in decor (rustic wood tables and booths) as well as in food. Open daily, lunch 11:30 to 4:30, dinner from 4:30.

Van Cortlandt Manor at Croton-on-Hudson.

Hudson River: History and Lore

Sleepy Hollow Restorations/Tarrytown, N.Y.

Three centuries of Early American history and culture are recreated for visitors at the properties of Sleepy Hollow Restorations in the Tarrytown area and north along the Hudson River.

There the Revolutionary War estate known as Van Cortlandt Manor; the northern headquarters of a mighty 18th century trading empire, Philipsburg Manor, and the cozy home of one of America's most beloved authors, Washington Irving's Sunnyside, are handsomely restored and brought to life by interpreters in period costume.

Together they make a full day trip, and there is something to be said for visiting them all in one shot. This is especially true if the sun is shining, as it was for us, the spring flowers are in bloom, and if one of the houses (in our case, Philipsburg Manor) has a special festival under way. What happens is an immersion into life along the river which enhances the visit and transports the visitor from the suburban bustle of Westchester County to the lives of early Dutch traders and politicians and the cottage retreat of the writer who immortalized Dutch lore.

We started at **Sunnyside,** the home at the river's edge, which was bought by Washington Irving in 1835 when he was 52 years old and already something of a success. Of the three houses, this is the only one directly on the Hudson (the others are on tributaries) and the majesty of the river so enchanted Irving that he would sit for hours in a green chair in the dining room, marking its moods.

The chair is still there, as are most of the furnishings used by the beloved writer when he was in residence. In fact, Sunnyside is especially nice a place to visit since it is filled with so much personal memorabilia; the re-creation is to the mid-19th century period when Irving lived here.

The parking lot is above; the shop (where tickets are purchased) and the house itself both below the roadside, set into the hilly river banks. Still farther below, at the river's edge, are the tracks for the railroad which were cut through during Irving's residency.

Born in New York City, the author of *The Legend of Sleepy Hollow, Knicker-bocker's History of New York, The Story of Rip Van WInkle,* and a five-volume biography of George Washington (for whom he was named), vacationed in the Hudson River Valley as a boy and loved it. But it was not for many years that he finally managed to buy the riverfront property and settle down with a melange of relatives, including one brother and his family.

Early in life Irving attained a law degree and practiced for awhile in New York City. He fell in love with the daughter of one of his law partners, a girl who died of consumption at the tender age of 17. Irving never married, and spent much of his life traveling. He and a brother went into an import-export business in England (it was while there that he wrote *The Legend of Sleepy Hollow*), but the business was unsuccessful and for more than 15 years Irving traveled around the Continent, picking up various assignments in American embassies.

By the time he returned to this country and could purchase 10 acres and a small cottage on the Hudson, he was a reasonably successful writer, actually making a living from his books. He put a great deal of himself into Sunnyside, one of the factors that makes a visit such fun. Even the huge, gnarled wisteria vines that climb over the entryway were planted by Irving.

The house is a treat both outside and in. The beige stucco structure with green shutters and red gabled roof has a whimsical quality; inside there are surprises such as a second-floor skylight, arched ceilings and keystone arches between the rooms. Irving's hand was in it all, although we're told he had an architect friend with whom he consulted.

Students of American literature will be especially interested in the library, the first room to be entered on the tour. The books here were Irving's own and he did much of his writing in this room. A sofa bed to the rear of the room was actually used by the author for awhile, we were told, when the house was too crowded with family for him to have his own room; later he moved upstairs to the bedroom where he eventually died.

The dining room opposite the library (these two rooms are on the site of the original cottage) is a gracious spot, where Irving enjoyed entertaining friends and where he sat and watched the river. A rear parlor is another convivial area; the piano in the corner was bought by Irving for two of his nieces. A conversation room adjoins this parlor, and nearby is the room with a bathtub, which for 1847 was considered a very modern convenience. Our hostess told us it was gravity-fed from a pool above the house, but only cold water was available.

A narrow staircase leads to the second floor. The bedroom has a bed in an alcove, striped wallpaper ordered by Irving because it reminded him of a circus tent, and the author's walking stick in his clothes cupboard. The skylight which brightens the hallway was the author's idea.

All of the kitchens at the Sleepy Hollow homes are active, a real highlight of the tours. The cook at Sunnyside was making rhubarb wine when we visited in May because, she said, rhubarb was about the only fruit in season at the moment. Don't forget to check out the laundry room, part of the 1840s addition to the house, with three washtubs and a collection of irons, some of them displayed on a special "laundry stove" where they were heated. The Spanish tower which was an addition to the house and is off this room (Irving spent many years in Spain) is closed to the public because of its one narrow staircase, but can be seen from outside.

Also outdoors are the separate ice house and root cellar. Gorgeous gardens and paths along the river also should be explored.

From Sunnyside we headed north about 10 miles to **Van Cortlandt Manor,** located in Croton-on-Hudson. This impressive house was home to several members of a family that came to New York in the 1600s and produced (in Stephanus Van Cortlandt) the first native-born mayor of New York City. It was Stephanus who began to purchase land in Westchester County, including the property here.

Stephanus's oldest son, Philip, inherited this chunk of land which, in addition to the manor house, came to include a gristmill, retail store, church, school and the Ferry House, an inn providing food and lodging for travelers along the old Albany Post Road at the spot where they had to cross the Croton River.

Visitors today tour the Manor House with its many sets of Dutch doors, and the Ferry House, between which stretches a long brick walk flanked by spectacular beds of perennials. We'd never before seen green and yellow striped tulips!

The stone Manor House with its pillared porch wrapping around on three sides is approached by a double staircase in front, reminiscent in look to some of the Acadian homes in Louisiana. A formal front parlor is interesting for its painted floor (meant to resemble marble tiles), casement windows and beautiful furniture. The wooden Venetian blinds, which seem so modern to us, were also used back in the 18th century, our guide told us.

The wealth of the family is particularly apparent when one views the large set of Chinese export porcelain in one of two cupboards flanking the fireplace in the dining room. Chippendale chairs there are elegant as well.

Location: Off Route 9 just south and north of the Tappan Zee Bridge in Tarrytown, North Tarrytown and Croton-on-Hudson, N.Y. Write for information to Sleepy Hollow Restorations, 150 White Plains Road, Tarrytown 10591.

Open: Daily, 10 to 5. Closed Thanksgiving, Christmas and New Year's Day.

Admission: For one house, adults $4, senior citizens and children $2.50; for two houses, adults $7 and others $4.50; three houses, adults $10, others $6.50.

Special Events: There are many. Pinkster Day is actually a weekend, usually the weekend in May prior to Memorial Day weekend, at Philipsburg Manor; there is often a Sheep to Shawl festival in early June at Van Cortlandt Manor; summer concerts in July on Sunday evenings at Sunnyside; a fall marketplace in October at Van Cortlandt Manor; Appletime at Sunnyside in October featuring tastes of historic apple varieties from the restorations; storytelling at Sunnyside the weekend before Halloween, featuring Irving's famous tales; King George II's birthday at Philipsburg Manor in November and candlelight tours for Twelfth Night at Van Cortlandt Manor. There are many more; call for a schedule.

Telephone: (914) 631-8200.

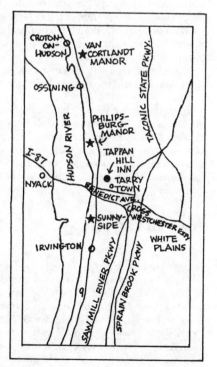

The two main-floor bedrooms, narrow but long, were the master and guest bedrooms. Upstairs, the children and their tutors slept dormitory-style. Downstairs at ground level is the immense kitchen where slaves cooked the Van Cortlandt meals.

When we visited, tarts were being made in the Dutch ovens, heavy pots with lids upon which coals were heaped, which were then hung by a crane over the hot fire. The Van Cortlandt family collection of receipts and two cookbooks from the 1700s serve as resources. Next door is a parlor used much as a family room would be used today.

The Ferry House gives insight into the way people traveled in the early years of the country. Women and children were not allowed into the tavern room proper and had to remain in a ladies' sitting room (this one is especially pretty with red and white checked coverings and curtains). A Dutch baroque clock, early Dutch painted chest, beautiful collections of English and American pewter and Country Queen Anne furniture are of particular interest.

Philipsburg Manor, back in Tarrytown, is extraordinarily picturesque. It was particularly so the day we visited — the annual Pinkster Festival, which recreates an early Dutch community's celebration of spring.

Philipsburg Manor was the northernmost site of the Philips family's trading empire; here on the Pocantico River (which empties into the Hudson nearby), tenants ran a gristmill and also farmed. The visitor approaches the site via a long wooden bridge above the dammed-up river; spread out ahead are the reconstructed gristmill, the tenants' house, a barn, sheep pen, and pretty grounds along the river.

Because of the festival we were treated to more activity than usual: one costumed interpreter was dying eggs with natural dyes (in this case beets, onion skins and Brazil wood) in the kitchen of the tenant house; another was operating the gristmill, which was converting corn into cornmeal. We watched a fiddler and a group doing English country dances on the lawn, listened to a black storyteller, saw the cows being fed in the barn and the sheep and their lambs in the sheep pen. We could have eaten sausage sandwiches and washed them down with lemonade cider; we did buy a loaf of bread made from the gristmill's own wholewheat flour to take home.

Since the setting is so picturesque, possibly what we enjoyed most was simply strolling along the river's edge while happy voices rang out in the background.

John D. Rockefeller Jr. was the benefactor who saved most of these areas for restoration and we are grateful. The interpreters in period costume (every woman in a dust cap, men in leather breeches and boots) are welcoming and helpful. And the houses are kept in exquisite condition — they're truly a pleasure to visit.

Also in the Area

Lyndhurst, 635 South Broadway, Tarrytown. (914) 631-0046. Lyndhurst is a museum property of the National Trust for Historic Preservation. Considered one of America's finest Gothic Revival mansions, the residence was designed by Alexander Jackson Davis and features a comprehensive collection of Victorian decorative arts. It was occupied at various times by former New York City Mayor William Paulding, merchant George Merritt and railroad magnate Jay Gould. Open April 14 to Nov. 4, Wednesday-Sunday, 10 to 4:15. Several special events include Rose Day in June and a dog show in September. Adults, $4.

View from upstairs dining room at Tappan Hill Inn.

Tappan Hill Inn/Tarrytown, N.Y.

It's about the priciest place in the area in which to eat, and you may find, as we did, the mixture of valet parking, salad bar and canned elevator music at lunch rather curious, but the Tappan Hill Inn has a lot going for it as well.

For starters, it has the best view around — atop the 490-foot hill with a magnificent panorama of the Tappan Zee, widest part of the Hudson River, the Tappan Zee Bridge (sparkling like a fairyland at night), and the Palisades and Ramapos beyond. The area between the inn and the river is heavily treed, and you would not know that busy Tarrytown is somewhere below.

The lavish mansion, built by the Halle banking family in 1925, is on land once owned by Mark Twain (between 1902 and 1905) and originally intended for his daughter Jean. Beautifully landscaped, with formal gardens and terraces, it has a spacious outdoor dining area under a striped awning, which is naturally popular in summer.

Entrance is into a large and formal rotunda, where a portrait of Mark Twain hangs over a fireplace. A welcome sense of humor is introduced in the darkly-paneled Polo Bar, through glass doors to the right, where a life-size sculpture of Twain, white suit and all, sits at the end of the bar, a glass of Jack Daniels before him. It was done by Barbara Gordon, the owner's wife, and a sign reads "Please do not handle. Mark Twain is an original soft sculpture and is due the respect of an older generation." Another original touch is the Dow Jones News Service machine on a table, installed for all the businessmen, according to the bartender, who come to what obviously is an expense-account place.

The big and comfortable, if not distinguished, main dining room is at the back, with expansive windows on three sides to catch the view. Linens are white, and chairs have leather-like seats of a butterscotch color. (When it is being used for weddings and other special functions, which is often, two dining rooms up the

155

beautiful curving staircase from the rotunda are put into service.) Four ficus trees in white containers, adorned with tiny lights, flank the sizable dance floor in the middle of the room.

Just inside the entrance, the salad bar is set up in front of a fountain. The bowl of greens includes a fair amount of watercress; the vinaigrette and blue cheese dressings are good, and there are red onions, peppers, radishes, fresh mushrooms and sprouts to lavish on top. But there is no getting around it: a salad bar is out of place in this restaurant.

Appetizers, soups, salads and desserts are the same (and priced the same) at lunch as at dinner. Lunch entrees run from $8.50 for eggs benedict New Orleans style or zucchini, sausage, cheese and tomato frittata, to $17.50 for steak or double lamp chops. A blackboard lists the day's specials, which we found more interesting than the menu; cold salmon with cucumber salad, shrimp salad in a beefsteak tomato and chicken salad with papaya were a few at our visit.

Appetizers run the gamut from mushrooms in herbed wine sauce ($2.50) to smoked northwestern salmon ($6.50). Smoked goose breast with celeriac is $4.75; baked goat cheese with walnuts, $4.50. Spinach salad with warm bacon dressing is $4.50, and the five soups, $2.50 (chicken consomme or chilled vegetable) to $3.95 (baked onion).

We tried a blackboard special, sauteed soft-shell crabs for $12.50, and a dish of Cornish hen and smoked pork sausage, $10.95. The latter was served on a bed of apple slices and golden raisins, and, curiously, included one gigantic kilbasa-type sausage and three breakfast sausages. The four or five tiny crabs were sauteed to a turn. Both dishes were served with crisp long green beans with little flecks of onion, and crusted mashed potatoes.

A basket of Italian and pumpernickel-raisin breads with several pieces of lavasch, the Middle-Eastern flat bread, accompanied nicely, as did our wine, Chateau Ste. Michelle riesling, $10.75 and good and fruity. House wine is soave or valpolicella, $3 a glass, and several other wines are available by the glass, $3.50 to $5.50.

Other lunch choices (the menu changes seasonally) included sauteed chicken breast stuffed with goat cheese and prosciutto, broiled filet of sole stuffed with crabmeat, and a steamed vegetarian plate with red pepper sauce.

Among the desserts ($2.75 to $4.50), you could choose raspberry cake with ice cream, cinnamon rice pudding, apple fritters with vanilla sauce or chocolate satin decadence. Then you might end with espresso or Viennese coffee with whipped cream ($2) or cappuccino that has chocolate in it ($3).

Dinner entrees are $13.50 (for the vegetarian dish mentioned above) to $19.50 for rack of lamb. A dish of shrimps, scallops, fish filet and mussels, Louisiana style; the sauteed veal chop with wild porcini mushrooms, and sauteed calves liver with onions and Iowa bacon sound appealing.

Upstairs, in the larger of the two dining rooms, there are three tables for two by huge arched windows that look out over the Tappan Zee bridge, an even better view than from the first floor. Here there are hunting prints on the wall and a rust and brown carpet.

Service is quite continental, with many dishes finished on a cart with a burner. It can also be a bit haughty and aloof, and we had long, inexplicable delays as five waiters stood nearby and chatted.

But not to quibble, when you can stroll around the lovely grounds, or sit on the terrace and watch the barges ply their trade on the mighty Hudson. No wonder Mark Twain liked the property so much that he built a cabin here.

Tappan Hill Restaurant, Tappan Hill off Benedict Avenue, Tarrytown, N.Y. (914) 631-3030. Lunch, Monday-Saturday noon to 2:30; dinner, 5:30 to 9:30, to 10:30 Friday and Saturday. Sunday brunch, noon to 3; dinner, noon to 9:30. Major credit cards accepted. Reservations advised.

Also in the Area

The Gallery Restaurant, 24 Main St., Tarrytown. (914) 631-4409. This is the kind of place we love — small and charming, and reflecting the personality of its owner. In this case he is Radovan Trnavac, known to one and all as "Micha," in this country only a few years from his native Yugoslavia. A well-known artist, he opened the restaurant in 1984 with money he had won in a painting competition. All black and white, the setting is a perfect foil for his gigantic and colorful mural on one wall; his large paintings on another. A tall, thin young man with a salt and pepper beard, Micha sits outside his restaurant at a tiny cafe table, drinking coffee and welcoming patrons — at night, that is, for he paints all day. At lunchtime, the black-clothed tables are covered with white shelf paper and crayons are provided in a wine glass, so that one may experiment with art. In the evening, the paper is replaced with white overcloths, hurricane lamps glow and there is gentle classical music. The several Yugoslavian wines on the list, under the Dutchess label, are good bets at $9.50 to $10.50; our pinot noir was excellent. The basket of rolls was also first-rate; the poppyseed and sesame seed rolls are baked by a local bakery. Entrees ($8.95 to $15.95) include, for the former price, a wonderful linguini orientale with pork, clams and vegetables stir-fried in sesame oil on homemade pasta, the dish ringed by mussels on the half shell. We also liked the rack of lamb, five bite-sized chops with a mint hollandaise sauce. House salads of mixed lettuce are garnished with fresh mushrooms and a good herb vinaigrette. The most unusual dish is poached salmon and sole tricolore, a filet of sole filled with salmon mousse and hollandaise sauce, plus poached salmon filled with sole mousse and topped with lobster sauce. Scampi, veal, chicken and beef dishes, plus a couple of interesting pastas, make up the rest of the menu, with two or three special entrees each night. Desserts change nightly and at our visit, we couldn't resist a peach crepe in hot brandy sauce, topped with shaved chocolate, although the hot apple strudel just out of the oven sounded mighty good. Espresso was the perfect ending. At noon, salads, sandwiches, omelets, hamburgers, the same pastas as at night and five or six entrees make up the choice, from $3.50 for a club sandwich or burger with fries to $8.95 for a sirloin. Appetizers are similar to those available at night and include smoked trout, clams casino and mussels mariniere ($2.95 to $4.25). Lunch, noon to 3; dinner, 5 to 10; closed Monday.

Santa Fe, 5 Main St., Tarrytown. (914) 332-4452. Featuring the foods of Mexico and the Southwest, Santa Fe is a small and attractive restaurant, opened early in 1985 by Rick and Janice Dumas, he a former New York restaurateur. "We painted the walls four times to get the right shade of pueblo rose," Dumas told us, and, indeed, the rosy beige bricks look stunning with the tables topped with quarry tiles (which he made himself) and blond wood chairs and banquettes. A beamed ceiling, track lighting and unusually nice posters, plus many Indian artifacts, complete the decor, and on each table is a small cactus in a basket. You could start with a margarita ($2.75, or $15 for a big pitcher) or sangria, or select one of a number of Mexican beers. These are served with homemade tortilla chips and a nice spicy salsa (with fresh coriander, much to our liking). The special blue corn tortillas are flown in almost weekly from Santa Fe. The lunch/dinner menu is huge; a card listing daily specials is brought around as well. A concept we like is the taco basket, $5.95 a person for two or more, where you get a stack of warm tortillas and all the makings. Soups (the gazpacho and black bean are good), quesadillas, tostadas, enchiladas, burritos and combination plates make up most of the menu, but there are entrees you don't often see in a Mexican restaurant in the North, such as red chile ribs, stuffed sole Monterey, chicken mole poblano and fajitas (marinated skirt steak wrapped in corn tortillas). Prices start at $1.50 for a cup of soup, rising to $12.95 for a 12-ounce Texas rib eye steak, but not many items are over $8. At lunch, we thought the shrimp and crabmeat tostada was a little light on the seafood; the Santa Fe salad of lettuce, tomato, pinto beans, guacamole and cheddar ($2.95 for small size) was very good. At Sunday brunch there are some interesting "huevos" dishes like a southwestern fritada with chorizo and green chiles ($4.50) and a guacamole omelet, $4.25. Chimichangas dulces are the Southwest's version of stuffed French toast and you can get them with apple and raisin, guava and cream cheese or peaches and cream. For dessert, how about a margarita mousse ($2.75) or a chocolate chalupa, a sweet flour tortilla deep fried, dipped in chocolate and stuffed with fresh strawberries, topped with strawberry puree and whipped cream? How could you even think of the Santa Fe especial coffee, $3.50 and a lovely creation of kahlua, tequila, chocolate and cinnamon? Open, Sunday-Thursday 11:30 to 10, Friday and Saturday to midnight; Sunday brunch.

Cory's, 27 Main St., Tarrytown. (914) 631-7227. Three partners bought the old greasy spoon at this location, and with a lot of hard work and elbow grease turned it in 1984 into a rather suave space with taupe-colored or mirrored walls with fine paintings and posters, dark green accents, much blonde oak and brass, and a handsome bar which you pass to get to the dining room at the back. On each table is a yellow carnation; the Jackson china service plates feature yellow roses. At noon the menu is a melange of soups, sandwiches (a Monte Cristo with warm raspberry sauce for $4.95 sounds special), omelets and quiches, salads, and extras like chicken fingers with peach brandy dip and fried zucchini sticks with horseradish sauce. Cory's specialties include fettuccine Alfredo, sauteed filet of sole on spinach with champagne sauce and ham, turkey and broccoli baked in cheese sauce. You could finish with a double chocolate fudge cake or Swiss apple pie. Most dishes are in the $3.95 to $5.50 range. At night, entrees, most named for friends, are $11.95 (for filet of sole Jean) to $16.95 for twin lobster tails. Red snapper is sauteed with capers, tomato and avocado, and medallions of lamb with red wine, shallots, mushrooms, red pepper and parsley. You could begin with escargots baked in a crock or sausage and cheese in pastry, and end with a grand marnier chocolate mousse or a raspberry torte. Lunch, Monday-Friday 11:30 to 3, dinner Tuesday to Saturday 5:30 to 11; Sunday brunch, 11 to 3; dinner, 3 to 9.

Horsefeathers, 94 North Broadway, Tarrytown. (914) 631-6606. Funky and offbeat, this place has four tables outside in front by the Broadway and Horsefeathers street sign, colorful cafe curtains painted on the windows, booths surrounded by bookshelves and a wall of portraits of famous authors, ending with not Karl, but Groucho, Marx. The gigantic (and cutesy) menu lists, under numbered chapters, all kinds of burgers, omelets, salads, chili, crepes and the like, at moderate prices. The Englebert Pumperdinck is a sandwich, on pumpernickel, of course, combining turkey, ham, bacon, onion, tomato, Russian dressing and melted Swiss cheese, $4.95. A separate menu lists specials of the day, with dinner entrees like pasta with seafood, $10.95. The beer list is long, the wine list is short, and all kinds of fancy frozen drinks are offered. For dessert, you could try a piece of chocolate satin pie or strawberry shortcake, with homemade biscuits. Open Monday-Saturday, 11:30 to 11 or midnight.

The Irvington Cookshop, 12 North Astor St., Irvington. (914) 591-8096. Seating 35 lucky diners in two tiny rooms, this storefront restaurant in a turn-of-the-century building is tucked away across from the Irvington railway station. It is crammed with antiques, all for sale, from dainty china in a cabinet to old samplers and tea cosys. Even the red enamel pot that holds a bouquet of flowers on the bar has its price. The old wooden floors are painted green; quarry tile-topped tables sport flower-printed napkins and pewter side plates, and track lighting adds a modern touch. The most expensive dish at lunch is stir-fried vegetables, rice and shrimp ($8.95), but most are under $6. Chunky chicken salad with walnuts and fruit, "our famous fluffy scrambled eggs" with caviar and sour cream, burgers on a kaiser roll with tomatoes and onion, and, especially, the chunky beef chili over rice topped with onions, cheddar cheese and sour cream ($5.95) are renowned. Dinner entrees ($10.95 to $16.95) are accompanied by complimentary hors d'oeuvre — perhaps celery root remoulade — then a salad brimming with vegetables, even jicama, and wonderful whole grain bread. Spaghetti primavera with scallops, sirloin of beef with four kinds of peppercorns, and breast of veal with spinach and pistachio nuts are some entrees on a menu that changes seasonally. At our visit, soft-shell crabs with a Madeira butter sauce, coho salmon, brook trout and red snapper were listed on the blackboard. For dessert, a giant goblet of old-fashioned strawberry shortcake is $2.95; Patti's brownie pie chantilly the same. Although there's a full bar, because of limited storage space the only wine available is Boucheron, $2 a glass and $7.95 a carafe. Patrons may bring their own for a $3.50 corkage charge. Lunch, Monday-Friday 11:30 to 2:30; dinner, Wednesday-Saturday 6 to 9 or 10.

Dudley's of Sparta, 6 Rockledge Ave., Ossining. (914) 941-8674. In the historic section of Ossining known as Sparta, you sure can't miss Dudley's. It's the only house painted purple — an intensity of purpleness not to be believed. The place has quite a history, dating back to Prohibition when booze was smuggled in from the Hudson via an underground tunnel through a trapdoor that you can still see behind the bar. Two years ago Ralph Rink, a former IBM executive and his son, Mark, took it over and with a CIA chef have turned it into a well-regarded spot. The decor is elegant, with a rose on each pink-linened table along with a votive candle in frosted glass; plants hang around a skylight in the middle of the pressed-tin ceiling and stained-glass panels abound. Up a few stairs is a small rear dining room with dark paneling and old etched-glass light fixtures. The extensive dinner menu is listed on several blackboards placed around the room; among standard entrees like chicken divan, steak au poivre and scallops Dijonnaise are some interesting Creole dishes — shrimp and crayfish etouffee, seafood jambalaya and blackened redfish, to name a few. Prices are in the $11.95 to $17.95 range. Veal Amadeus has a sauce of veal stock, port wine, fresh diced tomatoes, minced prosciutto and chanterelles; among seasonal entrees at our visit was poached shad roe with caviar. For lunch, sandwiches, egg dishes, salads and a few entrees are $4.95 to $8.95 (for paillard of beef). Mediterranean seafood salad contains scallops, calamari and shrimp. You could begin with truffle mousse pate and end with white chocolate mousse atop a puddle of raspberry melba sauce, or fresh sliced kiwi fruit and strawberries topped with saboyan. Several wines are available by the glass; the wine list is extensive and fairly priced. Lunch, weekdays; dinner nightly.

For those who would like to get close to the Hudson River, be aware that two private boat clubs right by the Tappan Zee bridge have opened their doors to the public in the past few years. The **Tarrytown Boat Club** serves lunch and dinner in its main-floor dining room seven days a week; the decor and menu are standard but the view superb and prices reasonable. A house special is shrimp bianco, broiled with garlic, onion, peppers and mushrooms, over linguini, $11.95 including salad, vegetable and potatoes. A deluxe cheeseburger at noon is $3.55. Just beyond is the **Washington Irving Boat Club,** with even less in the way of decor, but with a pleasant deck overlooking water and bridge. Go in and push your way through the regulars at the bar and you can get a darned good martini for $1.50 or beer for $1.25 — take it out to the deck and, as we did after a hectic day of sightseeing, relax and enjoy. Lunch daily; dinner Friday-Sunday.

Daytrip 23_____

Elephants at the Bronx Zoo.

Where the Wild Things Are

Bronx Zoo, The Bronx, N.Y.

Take the Bengali Express and see Siberian tigers.

Or, perhaps you'd like to have a ride on an elephant.

With the Safari Tour Train you can get the whole picture.

And, if you want to be above it all, try Skyfari.

No, it isn't Disney World or Busch Gardens in Florida. It's the good old (86 years in 1985) Bronx Zoo and it's better than ever.

The largest urban zoo in the United States, that in the Bronx is 265 acres exhibiting 699 species and 3,600 animals in all. Plus: cotton candy, popcorn wagons, snack and souvenir stands, shady walks and benches for resting. All in all, it's one of the best places we can think of for families (all generations, please), lovers, friends and anyone who gets a kick out of zoos.

We're zoo freaks; we admit it. We stand by the sea lion pool and watch the seals and sea lions for nearly an hour — until we're forcibly removed by family members who've seen enough. We cannot believe giraffes: mythical beasts to be sure. At the Bronx Zoo they parade around in the company of enormous ostriches — more mythology at work.

Then there are the pink pigeons. This nearly extinct species is on display at the World of Birds, one of the permanent buildings at the zoo. Here birds fly around happily in pleasant habitats which recreate their natural surroundings.

The Bronx Zoo is a venerable, memorable place, which most of us visited as kids. We remember the Children's Zoo (it's still there — a zoo within a zoo) and the wonder of it all. But returning is still special because the zoo is constantly being upgraded, new areas built, buildings remodeled.

The Children's Zoo was reopened in 1981, for example, after extensive reconstruction. Located on the site of the original Children's Zoo, the new one features participatory educational themes which are intended to teach children how animals function and feel. The kids who enter the Children's Zoo get to sit on a child-size bird's nest, crawl in an enormous spider web, or climb through a child-size prairie dog tunnel . They can compare their own jumping ability to that of a bullfrog, or try to move like a snail in a giant snail shell.

The Children's Zoo also allows them to check out porcupine quills, try on a turtle shell and escape down a hollow tree the way a lizard does (via a spiral slide). There are still farm animals which they can pet and feed. And, when it's all over, there's a place to have your photo taken with a bunny on your lap. What kid wouldn't love it?

For big kids there are bigger thrills (and bigger animals). Among the biggest is the gaur, the largest of all wild cattle, located on the open plains of Wild Asia, which has outdoor habitats for rare Asian wildlife, such as tigers and elephants. You board the Bengali Express, a monorail train, at Wild Asia Plaza and take a two-mile, 20-minute ride around it all.

It's apparent that the Bronx Zoo is into conservation and propagation of wildlife, and Wild Asia is one of the places it's taken most seriously. The zoo is a producer of wildlife and a place for endangered species. In Wild Asia we saw red jungle fowl, Formosan deer, peafowl galore, an Indian one-horned rhinoceros (wallowing in the mud), the Nilgais (largest antelope found in Asia), black-hooded vultures and a couple of Siberian tigers.

After the ride, or before, you might get an all-American snack (hamburgers, hot dogs, ice cream and popcorn dominate the snack bar menus) and stop at the Wildlife Theater in Wild Asia Plaza where, during one of five daily programs, you might be introduced to a python, a boa constrictor or a small alligator.

Next on our agenda was the African section of the zoo, where we saw our favorites, the giraffes, as well as cheetahs, lions and the silly-looking ostriches.

Located nearby is World of Darkness, where day is turned into dark and visitors can get a view of nocturnal animals like bats, foxes and sugargliders. Unfortunately, the buildings are not air-conditioned and if the day is hot — as it was when we visited — the buildings can be almost suffocating. Still, this building has a special fascination.

Location: Bronx River Parkway at Fordham Road, The Bronx, N.Y.

Open: Daily, year-round. March-October, 10 to 5, until 5:30 Sundays and holidays; November-March, 10 to 4:30.

Admission: November-March, Friday-Monday, adults $1, children 50 cents; April-October, adults $3, children $1.25. Tuesdays, Wednesdays and Thursdays, free. Safari Tour Train, adults $1.25; children $l; Skyfari, adults $1, children 75 cents; Bengali Express, adults $1.25, children 75 cents; elephant and camel rides, $1 each.

Telephone: Information, (212) 367-1010; all departments, (212) 220-5100.

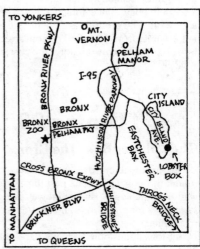

Darwin's theory of evolution gets reinforcement in the Great Ape House, where gorillas and gibbons reside — and put on entertaining shows for their descendants. An otter, swimming happily in his pool outside this area, was fun to watch. Not far away is the 1908 Elephant House, now under reconstruction. But outdoors you'll still find elephants, even some to ride. Camels for riding are also available.

The Aquatic Birdhouse is an indoor house for exotic waterfowl such as tufted puffins (who seem to be having a wonderful time), the scarlet ibis and snowy egrets. This building is also home to the nearly extinct Bronx boatbill; all of those on display were bred in the zoo in a colony begun in 1964. Outside, flamingos are exceptionally photogenic, as are penguins in a seabird colony with several other birds.

We skipped the Reptile House (crocodiles, snakes, turtles, frogs and a reptile nursery) because we were hung up for so long at the Sea Lion Pool, a fairly new pool in the Zoo Court area. Here the seals and sea lions swim, sun, push each other into the water and fight the seagulls for fish. We could have stayed longer.

As it was, we were at the zoo for five hours and couldn't see it all. We never did take the Skyfari ride, an aerial tramway which runs from the Wild Asia area to a spot near the Children's Zoo, nor did we hop aboard the Safari Tour Train to get a narrated tour through the zoo. If you have grandparents along, and they need a rest, this is a good way to see that they get it.

The animals are only part of the fun at the Bronx Zoo. For suburbanites or rural dwellers, the melange of people is an experience to be valued on its own. We saw Hispanic families and Indian families, black families and white families, old people and young, and everyone having a good time together. The trees at the zoo are large and spreading, shading the walks and the benches and providing a pleasant retreat on a hot day. Some people sleep on the benches. Some people rest on them. Some use them to change babies' diapers.

While security police are in evidence, their presence is subtle and there is a generally relaxed atmosphere. A day at the zoo is simply one of the best investments any family can make.

Also in the Area

New York Botanical Garden, Southern Boulevard, The Bronx. (212) 220-8700. Right next door to the Bronx Zoo, this is truly an oasis: more than 250 acres of grounds include the Hemlock Forest, 40 acres of the only woodland in New York left uncut since Indian days. The conservatory alone can take an entire afternoon. The grounds are open daily in the summer from 8 a.m. to 7 p.m. and in the winter from 10 to 5. The conservatory is open daily 10 to 4. The grounds are free. To visit the conservatory, the cost is $2.50 adults and $1.25, 6 to 16. Parking is $2.50.

 **Dining 23**_____

The Lobster Box/The Bronx, N.Y.

On our way to or from New York, we cannot count the number of times we have roared through The Bronx past the exit for City Island from the Bruckner Expressway or Hutchinson River Parkway and never realized what was out there. The same goes for our friends and acquaintances, who say "what?" when City Island is mentioned.

But for all the thousands who are unaware of City Island there are thousands who are. They pour out of New York City and the metropolitan area in droves

View toward Long Island Sound from Lobster Box.

each summer, seeking relief from the heat at Orchard Beach, riding horseback or hitting golf balls in a sylvan setting or wandering the streets ogling the boats, shops and passersby.

Visitors to the Bronx Zoo also could find City Island something of a refuge, with sustenance of appeal to the entire family at a choice of several dozen seafood houses and snackeries that dwarf the cottages along City Island Avenue.

The nicest, to our mind, is the Lobster Box, an island institution for 47 years. Perhaps it's because its facade is the only one that looks like a New England inn, its dark green awnings and white clapboard exterior true to its heritage as an 1800 Colonial mansion and the oldest landmark on City Island.

More likely it's because of the view of Long Island Sound, the lights of Queens and the Throg's Neck Bridge from the windows in the main dining room or the adjoining enclosed porch. On Wednesday evenings when the sailboats from the City Island Yacht Club hold their races, our informant said, the setting could not be more colorful.

And very likely it's because of the variety of lobster dishes. They number no less than 22, from plain to au gratin, Creole to thermidor. In addition, you can get shrimp 17 ways, as well as 13 other seafood entrees and seven "mini-menu" choices of complete dinners from $9.95 to $14.95. There's a hamburger plate among four items on the children's menu, but the only other sop to non-seafood eaters is the listing of two steaks and veal cutlet under "meats" in an inconspicuous spot on the menu.

Although the hustle and bustle outside must be something on a summer day or night, all is tranquil inside the Lobster Box. You enter through a New England-style reception area with lounging chairs, hooked rug and fireplace, pass through a nicely canopied lounge area with a corner art gallery, hanging Tiffany-type lights and a view of the open kitchen, and into the spacious dining room or, if you're lucky, the much-sought-after porch. The tables in both are spaced well apart and set with crisp white linens and candles in pewter holders. The rear windows of both rooms look onto the water, and most tables except those in the lounge get a view.

A basket of French bread, sesame bread sticks and large oyster crackers was served with our drinks, which were on the small side. The wine list is limited but half the 20 choices are $12; we enjoyed a Corvo white, a sprightly light wine from Sicily.

One of us sampled the lobster bisque that came with the table d'hote dinner. Served in a pewter bowl, it was thick and smooth and unusually good. Both of us got the chef's salad, brought to the table and served family style into two white bowls. A mix of greens, carrots, red onions and cherry tomatoes was tossed with a garlicky homemade French dressing.

The lobster in green sauce ("salsa verde") was chunks of lobster meat plus clams, mussels and shrimp in a spicy parsley sauce — a fine dish originating in the cuisine of Spain. Other appealing lobster variations include Creole (stewed New Orleans style), paella Mariscada, devilled with mustard and herbs, and Cantonese. Lobster prices were $22.50 to $23.95 a la carte and $25.95 to $27.50 for a complete dinner, which is a better bargain.

Our other entree was the day's special Atlantic redfish ($9.95), a bit plain for our tastes. It came with rice in a bowl, which curiously was served upside down in the midst of a side plate and then removed, the rice remaining in a mound.

The dinner included choice of desserts (all $3.50), anything from jello with whipped cream to peach melba and lemon chiffon pie. We tried the Galliano ice cream surprise, a cooling mix of ice cream with much Galliano and, the surprise, espresso beans on top.

Although this is a menu for the adventurous (appetizers like baked mussels oreganato and fresh calamari salad, shrimp dishes like fra diavolo or marinara), there are things like fried or broiled flounder ($11.50), halibut, salmon and swordfish. The mini-menu has seven complete dinners ranging from $9.95 to $14.95, the latter for two basic variations of lobster. Other bargains are the "earlybird specials," complete dinners served Tuesday through Friday from 3 to 6 p.m. for $9.95 to $14.95 (again for lobster).

About 20 items are on the lunch menu, the prices for which cover soup, salad and coffee as well. Seafood au gratin on toast points, mussels marinara or clams posillipo with linguini, shrimp oreganato, fish and chips, flounder mornay and California salad are among the offerings, priced from $5.95 to $10.95. The complete menu is also available at lunch.

Surely, there's something for every taste and price range at the Lobster Box. And, good as it is, there's far more than just lobster.

The Lobster Box, 34 City Island Ave., The Bronx. (212) 885-1952. Open daily except Monday from noon to 11 p.m. (closed mid-October to mid-March). Major credit cards. Reservations accepted.

Also in the Area

Anna's Harbor Restaurant, 565 City Island Ave., The Bronx. (212) 885-1373. A boat's bow forms the roof over the entrance to what appears at first glance inside to be a dark English pub, all stucco walls and beamed Tudor ceilings stretching endlessly to the rear. There, you find a spacious enclosed deck with large windows offering glimpses of boats and water. All is blue and white, from the blue citronella candles and tiny lights on trellises and trees to the linened tables. The entire place can seat 650, we're told, and in summer it does, when the airy deck appeals more than the darker, more formal main dining rooms. Seafood and Italian dishes comprise the oversized menu, starting at $11.75 for brook trout or bluefish to about $17 for seafood platters, reef and beef or bouillabaisse. Fourteen pastas are priced from $5.95 to $11.95. The dinner menu is available from noon on; a small luncheon menu offers entrees from $6.95 to $7.50 and a complete meal for

$6.95. Open daily, lunch noon to 3, dinner noon to midnight, to 1 a.m. on weekends.

Sammy's Fish Box Restaurant, 41 City Island Ave., The Bronx. (212) 885-0920. They've been adding for years to this ramble of rooms that began as a snack bar and multiplied through renovation and fire to seat 500 people amid an appealing mishmash of lighted aquariums, red neon lights, stained-lucite windows and whirring fans. You can dine outdoors under Cinzano umbrellas on a small front patio or on wicker fan chairs in the garden room. The Fish Box is the popular mid-ranger of Sam Cherwin's food empire, which also includes the Crab Shanty and the fancier Sea Shore at the other end of City Island. Here, pina coladas and strawberry daiquiris are de rigeur, surf and turf comes in 13 combinations (barbecued ribs and crab legs is one) and a five-course shore dinner ending in cheesecake or parfait is $24.95. Entrees are $9.95 (barbecued chicken) to $23.95 (lobster stuffed with shrimp or crab). Cold poached salmon served with avocado sauce ($7.95) is a winner on the lunch menu, which goes from $4.95 for a crab sandwich to $11.95 for lobster. Though the manager says the kitchen never closes, it's officially open daily, lunch Monday-Friday 11 to 3, dinner noon to 3 a.m.

Twilly's, 272 City Island Ave., The Bronx. (212) 885-9781. The sign outside intrigues: "Where the Not So Elite and Elite Meet." Inside is the funkiest ice cream parlor you ever saw. Originally called "The Hippies' Place," it looks it, with an unbelievable array of knicknacks, stuffed toys and such hanging from the ceiling and all for sale. Suburban matrons Nettie McKenna and Delores Lanzetta have made few changes in decor but were adding snack-food items like hot dogs, Twillyburgers, steamers and clams on the half shell for the summer of 1985. W.C. Fields is the inspiration for the place's name, as well as some of its exuberant sundaes and banana splits ($4.50 to $5.95) — the works, "Fields for President," a presidential amount of ice cream and toppings prepared with an assortment of fresh fruits, homemade whipped cream and crunchies for four or more, is $5 each. There may be no crazier place to enjoy a strawberry royale yogurt, a fancy pastry, specialty coffee or a beer or wine than at one of the marble-topped tables in the funky outdoor garden. Open Monday-Wednesday 4 to 11, Thursday-Sunday 11 a.m. to 1 a.m.; open from 11 a.m. daily in summer.

The Pizza Place, 286 City Island Ave., The Bronx. (212) 885-0744. If the kids crave pizza, this is the place, with five oilclothed tables along a brick wall and the usual assortment of pizzas (small, $5.75 to $9). A special Sicilian pizza is $7, or $1 a slice. You can get a broccoli and cheese calzone for $1.75 and any number of heroes for about $3; the roast beef with hot brown gravy for $3.50 is "one of my hottest selling heroes," the owner said. There's tossed salad but no dessert; for that, go up the street to Twilly's.

Outward Bound, 296 City Island Ave., The Bronx. (212) 885-0947. New in spring of 1985 was this cafe and deli with a display case full of delectables to take out — for boats, picnics or dinners back home, according to co-owner Lydia Landes. There are six gray and pink cafe tables and a beer license for dining inside. The pasta el pesto salad ($3.75) and chicken curry ($4.50) are popular, as are the five hefty sandwiches served on Jewish rye, golden raisin pumpernickel or Swiss peasant bread with a choice of homemade cole slaw, new potato salad or Greek salad (all $4.75). The soup of the day (escarole and bean when we visited) is $2.50, served with bread sticks and butter. Start your day with coffee or espresso and croissant; end with decaffeinated cappuccino and cheesecake. Open Tuesday-Sunday 10 to 7, to 10 in summer.

Daytrip 24

A Garden for Everyone

Brooklyn Botanic Garden/Brooklyn, N.Y.

Of all the trees that grow in Brooklyn, surely the most popular are the flowering cherries in the Brooklyn Botanic Garden.

On a busy Sunday in cherry blossom time, says museum president Donald E. Moore, 40,000 visitors may easily crowd into the 50-acre oasis in the center of Brooklyn. The double pink flowering Kwanzan cherry trees which form the Cherry Esplanade in the garden are the focus, but white cherries and a host of other varieties are also to be found.

If the cherry trees are the seasonal favorite, the Japanese Hill-and-Pond Garden would probably be the year-round winner in this garden, which is better described as "a garden of many gardens."

The Japanese Hill-and-Pond garden, with its delicate arched bridge, decorative Japanese portals and lanterns and splashing water feeding into a reflecting lake, was designed in 1914 by Takeo Shiota and is widely photographed.

But there are so many special attractions that it is no wonder well over a half-million visitors annually trek to the Brooklyn Botanic Garden. They don't come just to smell the roses, although roses are another prime attraction of this 75-year-old New York City landmark. The Cranford Rose Garden, the third largest public display of roses in the country (those in Hershey, Pa., and Hartford, Conn., are larger) boasts 900 varieties and some 5,000 plants, and is a special favorite in June and September.

One reason for the fame of the rose garden, we're told, was the presence for many years of internationally famed rosarian Peter Malins, who was a member of the BBG staff until his recent retirement.

Then there is the Shakespeare Garden, a brick-walled enclosure with a bench for contemplating the words of the Bard while surrounded by 80 of the herbs mentioned in his plays. Among those to be found in Brooklyn are aconite, chamomile, eglantine and gorse.

The Shakespeare garden seems appropriate in a place which has much to do with the English gardening tradition. The use of "botanic" instead of "botanical" in its name, for example, reflects a British preference, and at least once a month, according to Donald Moore, some titled member of the British aristocracy will visit. Recently it had been a Scottish earl, in search of some American trees that would be colorful at fall foliage time.

But there is the Oriental side to this garden, too. Not just the Japanese cherries and the Hill-and-Pond Garden, but the largest Bonsai collection outside the Orient, a collection revered by aficionados from around the world, is to be found in Brooklyn. Usually some 35 varieties are on display in the Conservatory, which also houses tropical plants, including palms and cacti of many varieties.

The Brooklyn Botanic Garden is world-famous for its magnolias and its crabapples as well. In fact, the garden's research facility in Westchester County has developed two patented hybrids which are known by gardeners around the globe: the Red Jade crabapple and the all yellow Elizabeth magnolia (the only truly yellow magnolia available). That facility also does research on plant diseases.

166

Japanese hill and pond garden at Brooklyn Botanic Garden.

All of this may sound a little complicated to the average person who's just trying to grow grass and a few flowers. The real secret to the Brooklyn Botanic Garden's popularity, however, is its very accessibility to the common gardener. There is, quite simply, a welcoming attitude, and programs that range from "the world's largest plant sale" in the spring to the country's first, and continuing, program which teaches children how to grow and cultivate flowers and vegetables in the summer.

The garden's Department of Information Services handles more than 1,000 plant-related questions which arrive in letters annually, plus an additional 2,000 to 3,000 telephone inquiries on a "hot line" service between 1 and 2:30 p.m. Tuesdays through Fridays — the number is (718) 622-4440.

Brooklynites form the largest group of visitors, not surprisingly. They use the garden as a retreat and it is only a small proportion who visit for scientific or botanic purposes. Rather they come to be refreshed and renewed among the beautifully kept grounds; to be amazed, in the spring, by the brilliance of the deep pink and white azaleas, or the gentle drooping wisteria blooms; to smell the roses; to sit on benches thoughtfully provided and feel removed from the intensity of city life.

The botanist, John Merle Coulter, who spoke in 1917 at the dedication of the garden's Administration Building, put it this way: "the mere presence of a botanic garden in a city is like having the spirit of nature as a guest, and all who become acquainted with the spirit are the better for it."

While the garden's prime ministry may be to its closest neighbors, it reaches out to gardeners worldwide. An active group of members includes people from all 50 states and the BBG mails material to people all over the globe. In fact its quarterly publications on garden-related issues are well-known and revered.

The permanent buildings in the park have not been the greatest of its charms. Despite the McKim, Mead and White design of the Administration Building, it is crowded, and the gift shop has much less space than it could use. The conservatory next door, where the tropical plants and Bonsai collection can be seen — plus the only frankincense plants in the Western Hemisphere - is likewise too small and in need of restoration.

The good news is that the future is bright for the BBG. A $21 million capital funds drive was expected to provide, by 1987, a splendid new conservatory granting much needed space and accommodating an expanded gift store as well. In the present conservatory's renovated Palm House will be situated a year-round restaurant. (At this writing a terrace cafe operates in yellow and white striped tents, weather permitting, with a limited menu.)

The vibrancy of the Brooklyn Botanic Garden is evident from a brief visit to its Administration Building — where almost everyone seems to be breathlessly running from one project to the next, and where changing art exhibits and auditorium programs are scheduled regularly. The garden's maintenance standards are refresh-

Location: 1000 Washington Ave., Brooklyn, N.Y. From the Brooklyn Bridge drive straight ahead onto Adams Street; go through a half dozen traffic lights until you reach Atlantic Avenue; turn left onto Atlantic and after about a half mile, take an oblique right onto Flatbush Avenue; drive up the hill to Grand Army Plaza and go two-thirds of the way around the rotary, taking a right onto Eastern Parkway. At the first intersection, turn right onto Washington Avenue. A large parking lot will be on the right at 900 Washington Ave. The garden may be entered directly from the parking lot, as may the Brooklyn Museum.

Open: Tuesday-Friday 8 to 6, Saturday, Sunday and holidays 10 to 6; closed Mondays except holidays.

Admission: Free.

Telephone: (718) 622-4433.

ingly high — with some 20 people directly involved in the horticultural work which is the heart and soul of the place.

A visit to the Brooklyn Botanic Garden is a special treat. You may be one of those people who wants to read all the fine print about the very well-marked flora and take notes for your own garden back home, or you may just want to stroll beneath the overspreading trees. You may want to pop in for a brief respite while in the neighborhood, or plan a whole day's outing. Whatever your preference, this still-free city space awaits you.

Also in the Area

The Brooklyn Museum, 200 Eastern Parkway, Brooklyn. (718) 638-5000. This museum, housed in a McKim, Mead and White landmark building, has a rich collection, including an extraordinary floor of period furnishings and decorative arts and good, if not huge, Egyptian and American Indian collections. The American paintings include works by Milton Avery, Mark Rothko, Helen Frankenthaler, Childe Hassam and John Singer Sargent, and Georgia O'Keeffe's "Brooklyn Bridge" is most unusual. We also appreciated the Francis Guy painting "Winter Scene in Brooklyn." The museum is located next door to the Brooklyn Botanic Garden and the two were once affiliated, but are now separate institutions. The problem with the Brooklyn Museum is that virtually everything is behind glass (including the period rooms), which is probably a necessity but annoying just the same. The gift shop is extraordinarily good; the formica-tabled cafeteria is depressing. Changing exhibits can be outstanding and you should check to see what's on at the moment. Open Monday, Wednesday, Thursday and Friday 10 to 5, Saturday 11 to 6, Sunday 1 to 6, holidays 1 to 5. Closed Tuesdays, New Year's Day, Thanksgiving and Christmas. Suggested contribution: $2, adult; $1, students; free to senior citizens and children under 12 who are accompanied by an adult.

 Dining 24_____

Raintrees/Brooklyn, N.Y.

Billing itself as "a cafe on the park," Raintrees, in the old Lewnes Ice Cream Parlor and Luncheonette at the busy corner of Prospect Park West and Ninth Street at the top of Park Slope, has a nice neighborhood bistro feel to it. People wander in and out, some stopping at the bar for a drink and a chat; a couple of people were even eating dinner alone at the bar the Wednesday night we were there.

Its expansive windows look out to Prospect Park across the street and a parade of promenaders, joggers and the like. The old stained-glass signs for the ice cream parlor are still over the windows, and the original floor of small white tiles remains.

Otherwise, the five-year-old establishment with what is generally considered Park Slope's best nouvelle cuisine is a far cry from its soda room past. The setting is attractive: Pink linens (with napkins tucked into the large globe-shaped wine glasses), bentwood chairs and votive candles in lalique-type vases; a painting of two huge pink tulips dominates the rear wall of the long and narrow space. At our May visit, pretty arrangements of dogwood branches and pink tulips in large bowls were on the back of the bar and on the grand piano that occupies part of the front. Taped music was a melange of blues, jazz and swing.

A basket of unwarmed French bread, good and chewy, was served with drinks,

Tulips on rear wall at Raintree's.

which at $3.75 each did not seem especially generous for the price, but the wine list was more reasonable, with several bottles under $15. Chantefleur for $9.50, muscadet for $12 and Macon-Lugny Les Charmes pinot chardonnay for $14.50 were a few.

The menu of six appetizers and thirteen entrees is augmented by several daily specials, including pasta primavera, pork chops with sour cream and capers, and baked brook trout topped with crumbs and a wine sauce.

Among appetizers ($4.75 to $5.90), mussels remoulade and snails in vermouth with roquefort cheese and pastry sounded good. We chose, however, a wonderful cream of mussel soup, thick and golden with saffron, and a special salad of duck with papaya slices. The latter, a bit light on the shredded duck but heavy on the papaya, was garnished with slivered endive, served atop spinach leaves, and had an interesting papaya dressing.

Our main courses were noisettes of pork a la Marc ($12.90), thick slices with a rich brown mushroom sauce, and shrimp with leeks and pernod ($14.75), a generous helping of tender shrimp with a mound of shredded leeks and a pernod-laced sauce. Both dishes were arranged like pictures on large white plates. Crisp cottage-fried potatoes and strips of zucchini and red peppers on side plates made another pretty picture.

Other entrees went from $10.90 for mussels steamed in cream, garlic and white wine to $16.90 for tournedos rossini. They included salmon with green herb sauce, scallops sauteed with shallots, swordfish with rosemary, roast duck with black currant sauce and broiled lamb chops with mango chutney.

Among desserts was a heavenly hazelnut dacquoise, almost toffee-like and nutty, plus strawberry cheesecake and walnut rum pie. Good brewed decaffeinated coffee accompanied.

Service by young waiters in bright suspenders and bow ties was friendly and professional.

Sunday brunch begins with a melange of fresh fruit topped with banana-poppy-seed dressing. The dozen entrees, priced from $6.90 to $11.90 (for steak and eggs au poivre), include interesting choices like eggs sardou, avocado stuffed with scallops, shrimp and crab, pain perdu (New Orleans-style French toast), Texas eggs and crabmeat benedict. The platter of sausages and pates includes the house country pate with mustard sauce and spinach terrine with English butter sauce, both of which are also popular as dinner appetizers.

Like several of Brooklyn's better restaurants, Raintrees does not serve lunch. "Tis a pity, for this probably would be our choice following a tour of the Botanic Garden or the Brooklyn Museum across Prospect Park. Meanwhile, we'll gladly settle for an early dinner or a leisurely brunch.

Raintrees, 142 Prospect Park West, Brooklyn, N.Y. (718) 768-3723. Dinner nightly, 5 to 10 or 11; Sunday brunch. Major credit cards. Reservations recommended.

Also in the Area

Restaurant Lisanne, 448 Atlantic Ave., Brooklyn. (718) 237-2271. A very special place, named for his daughter Liz and wife Suzanne, is run by personable Joel Wolfe in a high-ceilinged room topped by skylights in the heart of the antiques district. A few massed floral arrangements and blue overcloths over white linen brighten the generally spare off-white room with pressed-tin walls and ceiling. The blackboard menu changes nightly. When we visited, the five entrees ($12 to $18) were chicken sauteed with tarragon, calves liver with mustard, mesquite-grilled swordfish, veal scallops with basil and goose breast with orange marmalade. Appetizers include a morel timbale, American sturgeon caviar and Lisanne-cured salmon, $4 to $6. Desserts might be creme brule, walnut tarte or lemon mousse, all $3. Owner Wolfe prides himself on his interesting, fairly priced wine list, from a muscadet at $6 and a beaujolais at $8 to a few special vintages like Chateau cheval blanc at $100. The unusual all-day Sunday brunch offers everything from brioche French toast or cheese beignets to turnip gratin or leek and sausage pie ($4.50 to $10). Friday and Saturday dinners are prix-fixe, $22 to $30 for four courses, depending on choice of entree. Dinner, Tuesday-Saturday 6 to 9:30 or 10; Sunday brunch, 11:30 to 8.

River Cafe, 1 Water St., Brooklyn Heights. (718) 522-5200. We first tried this place shortly after it opened when the Circle Line tourboat guide pointed out a neat new restaurant operated by a couple of young guys on a barge under the Brooklyn Bridge. Expecting a casual spot, we arrived for Sunday brunch with our sons in tow. We gulped as we saw the tuxedoed maitre-d and our eyes widened as we gazed upon an utterly elegant room, mirrored around the sides, with huge and colorful bouquets on every table and another tuxedo-clad gent playing sophisticated melodies on a grand piano. But there was no escape, so we settled down to one of our pricier brunches ever. The second time we were there was for lunch, when we had the audacity to ask the price of the day's special scallops. "I don't know," professed our gorgeous waitress, obviously an aspiring Broadway star, "no one's ever asked." She ultimately returned with the word — $14 unadorned, with no vegetables, no salad. A friend at another table, who was treating an elderly aunt, asked to borrow $5 from us to cover the tip when she discovered that the bill exceeded her cash after her guest ordered dessert and that River Cafe does not accept Mastercard or Visa. Such are the perils for us suburbanites at one of New York's beautiful places, and what a place it is — particularly the view of the Lower Manhattan skyline from the dining room, the bar or the outdoor deck graced with redwood tubs of geraniums. Dinner is prix-fixe at $42, plus a $5 supplement for a couple of the 10 entrees, the fruitwood grilled veal chop and the sweetbreads when we were last there. Other choices included pan braised lobster and sea scallops with aromatics, red snapper with roasted oysters, bobwhite quails sauteed with pistachios, and loin and rack of lamb with onion tart and marinated artichoke. Start with lobster terrine or fresh California asparagus spears with wild mushroom dressing. At lunch, the place is filled with Wall Streeters who ride over on the cafe's special shuttle, an inboard cruiser called Tugboat Annie. Appetizers are $4.50 to $9, entrees $13.50 to $18 and desserts, $6. To mix with the beautiful people and enjoy the beautiful food and the beautiful view, many think it's worth it. Reservations are required, up to two weeks in advance. Lunch daily, noon to 2:30; dinner, 7 to 11:30. American Express and Diners' Club cards only.

Gage & Tollner, 372 Fulton St., Brooklyn. (718) 875-5181. What can you say, that hasn't already been said, about a restaurant that opened in 1879 and has been in the same location since 1889? The long, narrow, mirrored room retains its atmosphere of the Gay Nineties; the delicate old gaslight fixtures still work, and coats are hung on brass hooks between the mirrors, reminding us of Galatoire's in New Orleans. Waiters, whose uniforms bear insignia representing their years of service, are dignified, if perhaps absent-minded. Ours, an old dear, forgot our basket of bread, brought scallops instead of oysters, and left us to pour our own wine. The same menu, heavy on seafood, is served for lunch and dinner, making lunch a somewhat expensive proposition. We tried the soft clam bellies (done 16 different ways — we chose the seasoned fry, $10 and excellent) and fried oysters, $9. These were accompanied by cole slaw with the house dressing, kind of a cocktail sauce, and, when we finally got it, a basket of black pumpernickel and raisin bread, Irish soda bread and crackers. All other salads and vegetables are extra. We also sampled the corn fritters ($2), which were more like corn pancakes. They tasted drab alone — much better with a bit of maple syrup from the accompanying pitcher. Chowders and bisques, crabmeat four ways, scallops ten ways, lobsters devilled, thermidor, or in a cream stew, fresh fish like shad, snapper and bluefish in season are $9 to $17; steaks, chops (an English mutton chop with sausage, bacon and kidney is $14.50) and chicken round out the refreshingly un-nouvelle menu. For a less expensive lunch, you could go for an omelet or Welsh rabbit, $4 to $6. Desserts ($2 to $3.50) include lemon raspberry cake, apple crumb pie, rice pudding and caramel custard. Dining in this masculine place, with its intense aura of the past, is a very worthwhile experience. Monday-Friday, noon to 9:30; Saturday, 4 to 10:30.

Junior's, 386 Flatbush Ave., Brooklyn. (718) 852-5257. Calling itself "the heart and pulse of downtown Brooklyn," Junior's is a large and flashy deli, restaurant, bar and bakery. More of the award-winning cheesecake gets taken out than anything else; we picked up a small one ($6.50) and enjoyed it at home. Orange is the prevailing color of the decor; everything looks bright, clean and cheerful and tables are set with deli-proper bowls of cole slaw, beets, dills, tomatoes and hot peppers. Just about every kind of sandwich combination, bagels, dairy dishes, steakburgers and salad are listed, as well as full dinners ($9.20 to $16.20) that include corned beef and cabbage, Hungarian beef goulash on egg noodles, much seafood and steaks, many smothered with onions. Skyscraper ice cream sodas come in nine flavors; the myriad desserts include nesselrode whipped cream pie, bobka coffee cake and devil's food whipped cream layer cake. But you won't go wrong ordering, for $2.35, a piece of that faintly lemon-perfumed cheesecake. Open every day, 6:30 a.m. to 1 a.m., to 3 on weekends.

Tripoli, 156 Atlantic Ave., Brooklyn Heights. (718) 596-5800. Below the antiques district, lower Atlantic Avenue is lined with ethnic restaurants, most of them Middle Eastern. Among the best is this two-year-old establishment, its main floor restored to look like a sailing ship. Beyond the bar, you enter the ship through a hole in the bow. Ornate chairs flank canopied tables; other tables are perched on interesting niches on upper levels. A lavish mural of the sky goes up the walls and across the ceiling. Seafood is the specialty on the main floor; downstairs, used at peak periods, is like a Mediterranean grotto with Mideast-style booths, exotic lighting and, on Wednesday nights, belly dancing. The food is Lebanese, with an impressive variety at pleasant prices (dinner entrees $4.75 to $9.50 for Tripoli shrimp). The couscous is $7.50 and grape leaves stuffed with lamb and rice, $5.50. Nearly a dozen vegetarian dishes are offered at dinner and at lunch, when you can get a seafood omelet for $4.75 or an appetizer combination including hummus, baba, falafel, tabouli and grape leaves for $5.50. The seafood platter, complete with soup, Lebanese dessert and coffee (Arabic, if you wish), is $6.95. Lunch, Monday-Friday 11 to 3; dinner daily, 3 to midnight.

Le Parc Gourmet, 743 Carroll St. at Seventh Avenue, Park Slope. (718) 857-2600. On the second floor overlooking the heart of downtown Park Slope, Le Parc has a gorgeous setting, all forest green walls and carpeting, wood and chrome or green velvet chairs, lighted ficus trees and framed museum posters. Since its opening, the "gourmet" has been continually downscaled to the point where, in May 1985, a new all-day menu heavy on salads and sandwiches was being offered. Served in large glass salad bowls are chef, caesar, Nicoise and deli platter, $3.50 to $4.95. Besides burgers and sandwiches, you could order entrees like sole meuniere, scampi, veal piccata and chicken marsala, $6.95 to $9.95. Interesting desserts, all $2.75, include grand marnier chiffon and key lime pies. Open daily, 11 to 11.

The Ferrybank, 1 Front St., Brooklyn Heights. (718) 852-3137. A former captain at Gage & Tollner, James Strawder, and his architect son put together this striking restaurant in a former bank building just above the riverfront. Strands of beaded white lights hang from the ceiling; tables on the second floor overlook the main floor, and the bank's pillared columns still lend a formal air. The extensive menu begins with appetizers ($2.50 for celery and olives to $8 for lobster cocktail) and includes countless seafood entrees from $11 for bluefish to $17 for lobster thermidor, ending with a few beef and poultry dishes. Desserts, baked on the premises, include an Irish whiskey pie for $3.50. Dinner nightly, 5 to 10:30 p.m.

Charlie's, 348 Flatbush Ave., Park Slope. (718) 857-4585. All the oversized plantings and exotic statuary might give you the feeling of a museum, but otherwise the comfortable Victorian decor is home to a popular lounge and simple dinner fare, including hefty salads and pricy sandwiches, plus straightforward entrees like chicken marsala or veal piccata ($9.95 to $16.95). The two-page wine list is more interesting and varied than the dinner fare. Dinner from 5, Sunday brunch.

Daytrip 25

A Poet's Birthplace and Environment

Walt Whitman Birthplace and Old Bethpage Village/ Huntington and Bethpage, Long Island

The house in which America's famed poet, Walt Whitman, was born is now surrounded by mayhem and mall, only an acre left where once there were a hundred. This is congested western Long Island, home to hundreds of thousands of New York commuters, busy even on Sundays with car-choked highways and the rush of urban pulse.

The Whitman birthplace, built by the poet's father, is a quiet and simple spot amid the chaos. We can thank the Birthplace Association for dogged determination back in the late 1940s and early 1950s when the clapboard cottage was finally acquired and opened to the public.

Whitman's father Walter, after whom the poet was named, was a homebuilder and the 1815 house, just a stone's throw from busy Route 110 in Huntington, has some features that the average farmer might not have had in those days.

There are the windows — glorious large windows with 12 over 8 panes, bringing sun and sky into the small house. And there are the two huge cooking hearths — one in kitchen and one in the parlor — with a beautiful built-in cupboard next to that in the parlor.

Old galvanized nails hold together the wide-planked floors and there is a sturdiness and comfort despite the relatively few rooms.

Walt was born here on May 31, 1819, and lived in the house until he was four when his father, never as good a farmer as he was a house builder, took the family to Brooklyn where he thought he could make a better living.

The house contains almost no original furniture and only four precious Whitman pieces, but is furnished according to the period. A lovely christening dress, of the sort the poet would have been dressed in, is laid across the bed in the bedroom to the rear of the parlor. It is a rope bed, itself clothed rather majestically in a handsome blue and white spread woven by Sarah Seaman, who married a cousin of the poet's, Jarvis Whitman.

Then-rural Long Island was a formative place for Walt. Though he loved the city, and wrote eloquently about it, he also found special nourishment in nature, and he returned to spots on "the island" frequently during his early adulthood. In fact, in a period of some three to four years Whitman was a schoolteacher in the small villages of Long Island; the desk he used during one of those assignments is now in the kitchen to the right of the main door as visitors enter.

Other Whitman pieces in the house are a chair used by his mother, Louisa van Velsor, in the parlor; a secretary which belonged to his sister, Mary Elizabeth, in the upstairs room reserved as a library and museum store; and another desk probably used by Walt during his teaching career. Nineteenth century antiques lovers will find other interesting items, including kitchen utensils such as a lard press (our guide encouraged us to take it down from the wall and inspect its workings), old Bennington ware, candle molds and racks, and the like.

But you don't visit the Walt Whitman birthplace to gawk at the collection (which is interesting but not extraordinary) as much as to pay homage to the man. The

Walt Whitman's desk in kitchen of house.

members of the Birthplace Association are clearly interested in who Walt was and what he gave to posterity, and if your guide is as knowledgeable as ours, you will come away with a much better appreciation for this great (and long overlooked) American poet.

The birthplace serves not only as a museum, but as a center for activities such as poetry readings, scholarship and research, and annually, about the time of Whitman's birthday, a special birthday event is usually scheduled. At this time there is also a Whitman supplement printed in the Huntington newspaper, The Long Islander, which Walt founded. The poet was, during several different stints, editor of a number of Long Island and New York City newspapers.

He also was a nurse in military hospitals in Virginia during the Civil War, about which he wrote later. Perhaps more than anything, Whitman was a restless man, who had to keep returning to nature to refresh himself and provide the strength to carry on with the rest of his life.

When he was older, and after having suffered a paralytic stroke, Whitman spent a couple of years in recovering, which he recounts in his diary-like book, *Specimen Days:*

"It seems indeed as if peace and nutriment from heaven subtly filter into me as I slowly hobble down these country lanes and across fields, in the good air — as I sit here in solitude with Nature — open, voiceless, mystic, far removed yet palpable, eloquent Nature. I merge myself in the scene, in the perfect day."

Visitors will find the exhibit room on the second floor of interest. When we visited we viewed several pieces of sculpture — busts of Whitman — as well as photographs of the man. His long white hair and beard and his piercing, soulful eyes gave him an unusual look, and speak of a gentle nature and a fertile mind.

175

His poem, "Miracles," is reproduced on postcards at the house and you may buy some. Wrote Whitman:

> *Why, who makes much of a miracle?*
>
> *To me every hour of the light and dark is a miracle,*
> *Every cubic inch of space is a miracle.*
> *Every square yard of the surface of the earth*
> *is spread with the same,*
> *Every foot of the interior swarms with the same.*
> *To me the sea is a continual miracle,*
>
> *The fishes that swim — the ships with men in them,*
> *What stranger miracles are there?*

While the area around Walt Whitman's birthplace is no longer the country roads and natural environment which the poet sought and loved, from which he took some of the images for his famed *Leaves of Grass*, nearby in Bethpage the visitor can get a taste of what the area was like at the time of Whitman's life. The place to visit is the **Old Bethpage Village** restoration.

This is about a 10-minute drive from Huntington, and when visited on the same day as the Whitman birthplace, aids in the understanding of what the area was like.

Old Bethpage Village, which was begun in the late 1960s and early 1970s, is not unlike Sturbridge Village in concept, but much more dramatic in its setting. For here, surrounded by turnpike and turmoil, are more than 200 tranquil acres where the visitor finds horse-drawn carriages, a working farm, restored period houses, and tradesmen at work making shoes, shaping metal articles, sawing wood, making barrels.

The one original structure on the site — the Powell farm — with its picturesque, duck and geese-filled pond, and its pigs, oxen, horses, sheep and cows, was taken over by some foresighted Nassau County officials who saved, just about the time

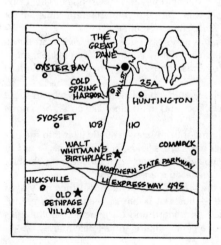

Location: The Walt Whitman birthplace is located in Huntington, N.Y., on Old Walt Whitman Road (which is just off Route 110). Take I-495 East (the Long Island Expressway) and Exit 49N or the Northern State Parkway (Exit 40N). Old Bethpage Village is reached via Exit 48 off the Long Island Expressway — from there follow the signs.

Hours: The Whitman birthplace is open year-round, Wednesday-Friday 1 to 4, Saturday and Sunday 10 to 4. The Old Bethpage Village restoration is open March-November, Tuesday-Sunday 10 to 5, rest of year until 4. Closed holidays except Memorial Day, Fourth of July, Labor Day and Columbus Day.

Admission: The Walt Whitman House is free. Old Bethpage Village costs $3 for adults, $1.50 for children.

Telephones: Whitman House, (516) 427-5240.

Old Bethpage Village, (516) 420-5280.

Horse-drawn wagon at Old Bethpage Village.

there was little left to save, this wonderful stretch of rolling land.

Since that time another 15 or so buildings have been moved from other Long Island towns and villages and slowly and painstakingly restored to their mid-19th century look.

Refreshingly uncommercial — in spite of the large contemporary brick administration building through which one enters — Old Bethpage Village is really what it purports to be: a page out of the past. Other than in the rather well-stocked museum shop, which is in the administration building, the only things available for purchase in the village are penny candy and cups of birch beer, obtained with special "money" which is purchased ahead of time. Otherwise, there is just walking around and looking to be done; if you want, and if the horse-drawn wagon is available at the time, you're welcome to climb aboard and take a ride.

Kids love the place, naturally, because they can scuff their shoes on dirt roads, run from house to house, and find the kind of freedom and interest that isn't available in the stuffier indoor museums. Visitors all receive a self-guiding map which takes them around the circuit, and they can stop in at whichever house or shop attracts them.

One of our favorite stops was at the Manetto Hill Methodist Church, where our guide (in period costume, as are all of the guides) told of the restoration of this simple and pretty little white church — whose congregation still returns annually for an Easter Sunday sunrise service. The one-room schoolhouse is fun (everyone sits in double desks and pays attention to the "teacher") and the Noon Inn is the place where travelers quench their thirst with the birch beer. The day we visited, a brisk but sunny Sunday in March, a costumed guide stationed on the second floor of the inn was explaining the intricacies of early American quilting.

Each month has special activities and days devoted to them. If you want to know in advance what you'll be likely to encounter, call or write for the calendar.

You can get lunch at the museum cafeteria, but it is stocked with mostly prepackaged, less-than-inspired items. Better to explore some of the interesting restaurants in the area or perhaps to pack a picnic.

 **Dining 25**

The Great Dane/Huntington, L.I.

A distinguished restaurant in a nondescript shopping center, The Great Dane was opened in February 1985 by Heidi and Ford Prime (he about a seventh-generation Huntingtonian and both with a fondness for Denmark).

"We have done very well since we opened," said German-born Heidi on our visit in May, "but this week has been simply insane!" We wondered if Long Islanders were starved for new restaurants since, after favorable reviews in the New York Times and Newsday a few days before, would-be lunchers were streaming in and being turned away from the small (42-seat) and sophisticated dining room as fast as they came in. Since the Primes had no plans to expand, they hoped things would return to normal soon.

The storefront room has been transformed into an oasis of chicness, without much in the way of decor. A greenish-gray dark carpet, foam green walls, a shelf with a black vase containing a striking floral arrangement, wall panels of carpeting hiding shelves on one side of the room and canvas panels displaying the banners of all four Scandinavian countries on the other make up most of it.

The shiny lacquered tables are a cinammon color with a small Viking ship logo in the corner; equally striking is the china with its bright blue border and flowers. Chairs are comfortable cane and chrome. Some of the tables are too close together for our taste, but everyone seemed to be having a good time when we stopped for a late lunch.

Those wonderful small open-faced sandwiches (smorrebrod) we remember with fondness from a trip to Copenhagen are a pleasant addition to the menu. You may choose one or more as an appetizer, or order a selection for a meal (it takes two or three to satisfy all but the daintiest of eaters). These are priced from $1.25 for apple, raisin and walnut, to $2.75 for smoked salmon, cucumber and dill or small shrimp with mayonnaise. Some are served on French bread, some on flat dark bread, and all go well with a Carlsberg elephant malt or an aquavit. We tried the roast beef with cheddar and crisp fried onions, and the smoked salmon — both were delicious and pretty as a picture. Danish saga cheese and walnuts, and roast pork with red cabbage, are a couple of others.

Many of the appetizers are the same at lunch and dinner — cold poached shrimp with dill mayonnaise, grilled chicken kabob with a spicy peanut sauce, fettuccine with sea scallops, and an acclaimed brie en croute with a tart lingonberry sauce. These are $3.75 to $6.75 and you are welcome to make a meal of just appetizers, at lunch or dinner. The soup of the day at our visit was a clear broth with several vegetables, broccoli, celery, asparagus and snow peas. It would have been better had the vegetables been cooked less, but was acceptable.

We loved the oriental chicken salad ($6.75), a heap of shredded chicken, vegetables and lettuce, topped with rice noodles, with the smoky taste of sesame oil permeating all. The French bread, Heidi's recipe that uses high-gluten flour, is some of the best we have tasted, chewy and crusty.

Other luncheon entrees are a spicy sauteed cashew shrimp ($8.50), fresh trout (raised in nearby Cold Spring Harbor) pan fried with hazelnuts and browned butter ($8.75) and spinach salad with scallops and grapefruit ($6.75). For more pedestrian tastes, a hamburger on French bread with fries is $5.25.

As for desserts ($2.25 to $3.75), not to be missed are the chocolate truffle cake with its thick layer of whipped cream, the candy-like pecan tart and the chocolate mousse of a perfect texture, served in a stemmed glass with minty whipped cream on top. Lighter appetites may go for the sorbet of the day — raspberry or lime when we were there.

At night, when there is candlelight, entrees are $10.75 to $16.75 and include pork medallions grilled with cracked black pepper, rosemary and garlic; duck breast with poached pear and port wine sauce, a butterflied and grilled leg of lamb, chicken breast Dijonnaise with apricots and New York steak grilled with bearnaise sauce. But you could just have a couple of the smorrebrod, if you wish.

A Sunday brunch menu offers fettuccine with sea scallops, tomato and coriander; scrambled eggs with smoked salmon, basil, scallions and cream cheese, almond French toast with grilled Canadian bacon, eggs benedict, crepes, roast leg of lamb and a few other items, from $7.75 to $13.25. The appetizers and desserts are the same as on the other menus.

The chef, Rob Francis, a young Culinary Institute of America graduate whose fare shows a partiality to dill, expects to change the menu seasonally.

A nice touch is that Le Petit Chateau, a red wine from nearby Hargrave Vineyard, is available for $2.50 a glass. Two other Long Island wines are available for $10.75 a bottle; other wines on the computer-printed list are in the $8.50 to $24 range. The wine theme is carried into the restrooms, with a stunning Pindar Vineyard poster framed on the wall in each.

Great Dane is great for both "grazers" and serious eaters. And the locals are finding it much to their liking. As a customer in the Downstreet Bookstore in Cold Spring Harbor told us, "My husband and I hardly ever eat out. But we've been to the Great Dane four times since it opened!"

The Great Dane, 215 Wall St. (Southdown Shopping Center), Huntington, N.Y. (516) 351-1218. Lunch, Tuesday-Saturday noon to 2:30; dinner, 5:30 to 9, Friday and Saturday to 10; Sunday brunch, 11:30 to 3. Closed Monday. Major credit cards. Reservations advised.

Also in the Area

Peche Mignon, 10 Elm St., Huntington. (516) 549-8311. The striking pink stucco house with the bright blue shutters and trim opposite a large parking lot at the edge of downtown Huntington is an oasis of country French cooking. Dinner only is served, but some highly regarded fare comes out of the kitchen. The eight entrees on the menu ($13.50 to $22.50) include sole stuffed with seafood in parchment, sweetbreads, boned coho salmon with vegetables and sorrel sauce, filet mignon forestiere and loin of lamb with a wine and shallot sauce. Appetizers run from $4.75 for pate to $9 for a parfait of fois gras with aspic; smoked Cold Spring trout and shrimp salad Fernande sound interesting. Dinner, Tuesday-Saturday 5:30 to 9:30 or 10.

Mediterranean Snack Bar, 360 New York Ave., Huntington. (516) 423-8982. The locals think very highly of Steve Soulellis's little restaurant, now in its 11th year. The long and narrow room has stucco walls, with a carnation on each blue-clothed table. A few of the tables are about two feet higher than usual, with high stools to match. The menu features mainly Greek dishes as well as other Mid-Eastern specialties like falafel. Stuffed grape leaves, souvlaki, kabobs and the like are $5 to $8; the latter price brings Steve's Special, a combination platter of souvlaki, giros, sausage, salad and pita bread. Moussaka is served with Greek salad for $7.50, and Greek pizza is a combination of spinach and feta cheese broiled on pita, topped with mozzarella cheese, $4.50. A blackboard lists the day's special

179

seafood dishes: shrimp Greek style was $10.95, stuffed flounder $10.50. Beer and wine (some Greek) are available. The baklava ($1.75) looks especially good. Monday-Saturday, 11 a.m. to 10 or 11 p.m.; Sunday, noon to 10.

Tucker's, 328 Main St., Huntington. (516) 271-3311. Tucker Frey, a CIA graduate, opened his food shop, featuring hundreds of cheeses and all kinds of coffee beans, in 1983. In back, at a few small round tables, he serves interesting lunches. A blackboard in front of the store lists the day's offerings; on our visit the soup was cream of asparagus with cheddar, and entrees included Cajun rabbit pot pie, Linden Tree chicken salad, asparagus and smoked gouda quiche, crabmeat and wild rice salad and strawberry rhubarb pie. At other seasons you might find oxtail barley soup, chili con carne with jalapeno corn sticks or a lamb and snow pea stew with saffron. The grilled brie and tomato on a croissant is so popular that it is kept on the menu almost all the time. Top price for entrees is $4.50. Wash it all down with cold or hot mulled cider. Tucker makes his own bread and croissants, and serves lunch from 11:30 to "whenever," he says, every day but Sunday.

Tee T's Landing, 96 New York Ave., Huntington. (516) 421-1330. The best view of Huntington Harbor is available from the awninged dining porch over the water at Tee T's, whose name could stand for "too-too." From the fancy landscaping to the elegant interior of this new stucco and wood restaurant, everything is on the high side, including the rock music from the band practicing upstairs during lunch, and the prices. Dinner entrees range from $12.95 for capon to $20.95 for Maine lobster pescatora. Luncheon entrees are $5.50 for omelet forestiere to $12.95 for broiled scampi, and include a couple of pastas and fried or marinated calamari from $7.50 to $9. The same appetizers at lunch or dinner are $4.25 to $6.95; desserts in the $4.50 range include hazelnut tart and chocolate mousse. Lunch, Monday-Friday 11:30 to 3; dinner 6 to 10, Saturday 5 to 11 and Sunday 3 to 10.

Lockwood's Ice Cream Parlor, Main Street, Cold Spring Harbor. The most interesting lunches in Cold Spring Harbor are said to be served at this old-time soda parlor, complete with a real soda fountain, painted floors and lettuce growing in flower boxes out front. Although most stop here for the ice cream, you can get lunch items like tomato and basil bisque, a broccoli, mushroom and cheddar quiche, a tart ginger chicken salad or a thymed tuna or devilled egg sandwich ($3.95 to $5.95). Open daily, noon to 5, Sunday 1 to 5.

Monterey Bay, 68 W.Main St., Oyster Bay. (516) 922-1427. California is in the name and the decor of this contemporary, casual establishment on the edge of downtown Oyster Bay. The menu is fairly standard, with dinner entrees from $10 to $14.95 (for seafood platter). More interesting were the luncheon specials when we visited: ambrosia salad, chicken cordon bleu with sauce chausseur, broiled blackfish scampi style and crabmeat quiche, $4.95 to $5.95. Open daily from 11:30 to midnight.

Index

Abraham Manchester Restaurant   79
Adamsville, R.I.

Al Forno   86
Providence, R.I.

Aldrich Museum   136
Ridgefield, Conn.

Altnaveigh Inn   97
Storrs, Conn.

American Bounty   147
Hyde Park, N.Y.

Andre's   134
Sharon, Conn.

Anna's Harbor Restaurant   164
The Bronx, N.Y.

Anthony's Pier 4   63
Boston, Mass.

Apricots   128
Farmington, Conn.

Arboretum   78
East Providence, R.I.

The Ark   92
Newport, R.I.

Arne's at Copley Place   57
Boston, Mass.

Arrowhead   5
Pittsfield, Mass.

As You Like It   52
Salem, Mass.

Audubon's Cafe & Restaurant   120
New Haven, Conn.

Back Bay Bistro   58
Boston, Mass.

The Barnacle   52
Marblehead, Mass.

Bartholomew's Cobble   13
Ashley Falls, Mass.

The Bayberry Inne   111
Branford, Conn.

Beekman Arms   148
Rhinebeck, N.Y.

Beinecke Library   116
New Haven, Conn.

The Black Pearl   89
Newport, R.I.

The Blacksmith Tavern   128
Glastonbury, Conn.

Blithewold   75
Bristol, Mass.

The Boston Brahmin   119
New Haven, Conn.

Boston Children's Museum   60
Boston, Mass.

Bricker's   22
Greenfield, Mass.

Bridge Street Cafe   72
South Dartmouth, Mass.

Britannia Spoon Company   116
Yalesville, Conn.

Bronx Zoo   160
The Bronx, N.Y.

Brooklyn Botanic Garden   166
Brooklyn, N.Y.

The Brooklyn Museum   169
Brooklyn, N.Y.

Bullock's   79
Warren, R.I.

Cafe Budapest   55
Boston, Mass.

Cafe Estoril   72
New Bedford, Mass.

Cafe in the Barn   76
Seekonk, Mass.

Cafe Lisboa-Acores   72
New Bedford, Mass.

Cafe Natural   141
Ridgefield, Conn.

Cafe Pomodoro   38
Worcester, Mass.

Call Me Ishmael   72
New Bedford, Mass.

The Candleworks   69
New Bedford, Mass.

Cap'n Nick's   120
East Haven, Conn.

Caprilands Herb Farm   93
Coventry, Conn.

Century House   113
Guilford, Conn.

Chez Bach   113
Branford, Conn.

Chowder Pot   112
Branford, Conn.

Charlie's   173
Brooklyn, N.Y.

Chester-Hadlyme Ferry   101
Chester-Hadlyme, Conn.

Chesterwood   10
Stockbridge, Mass.

Chez Claude   42
Acton, Mass.

Church Street Cafe   15
Lenox, Mass.

Ciao   44
Acton, Mass.

City Lights 85
Providence, R.I.

Cityside 65
Boston, Mass.

The Clark's 98
Willimantic, Conn.

The Coach Lite 7
Pittsfield, Mass.

The Computer Museum 59
Boston, Mass.

Coppola Brothers Italian Kitchen 150
Hyde Park, N.Y.

Cory's 158
Tarrytown, N.Y.

Country Inn at Princeton 38
Princeton, Mass.

Crabapple's 29
Sturbridge, Mass.

Crickets 65
Boston, Mass.

Croissant 71
New Bedford, Mass.

Culinary Institute of America 146
Hyde Park, N.Y.

Day's Catch 8
Pittsfield, Mass.

Deerfield Inn 20
Deerfield, Mass.

Denmarc 149
Poughkeepsie, N.Y.

A Different Drummer 45
Concord, Mass.

The Dock at Saybrook Point 105
Saybrook Point, Conn.

The Dock House 112
Guilford, Conn.

The Dragon 7
Pittsfield, Mass.

Duck Soup 8
Lanesboro, Mass.

Dudley's of Sparta 159
Ossining, N.Y.

Durgin Park 63
Boston, Mass.

Easy Street 150
Hyde Park, N.Y.

El Morocco 37
Worcester, Mass.

Eliza's 79
Bristol, R.I.

Elm City Diner 118
New Haven, Conn.

Embree's 13
Housatonic, Mass.

Emerson House 42
Concord, Mass.

Escoffier Room 146
Hyde Park, N.Y.

The Essex Institute 48
Salem, Mass.

Famous Bill's 22
Greenfield, Mass.

The Ferrybank 173
Brooklyn, N.Y.

Fiddler's Seafood Restaurant 104
Chester, Conn.

Fife 'n Drum 133
Kent, Conn.

Fine Bouche 102
Centerbrook, Conn.

Firehouse Cafe 37
Worcester, Mass.

500 Blake Street 120
New Haven, Conn.

Freestone's 71
New Bedford, Mass.

Frick's 92
Newport, R.I.

Friends & Company 109
Madison, Conn.

Fruitlands Museum 39
Harvard, Mass.

Gage & Tollner 172
Brooklyn, N.Y.

The Gallery Restaurant 157
Tarrytown, N.Y.

Gates 141
New Canaan, Conn.

Gelston House 104
East Haddam, Conn.

Gillette Castle 99
Hadlyme, Conn.

The Goodspeed at Chester 101
Chester, Conn.

Goodspeed Opera House 101
East Haddam, Conn.

The Great Dane 178
Huntington, N.Y.

Green Animals 87
Portsmouth, R.I.

Griswold Inn 105
Essex, Conn.

GuadalaHarry's 65
Boston, Mass.

Hancock Shaker Village 1
Pittsfield, Mass.

Hannah's 36
Worcester, Mass.

Harriet Beecher Stowe House 124
Hartford, Conn.

Higgins Armory Museum 31
Worcester, Mass.

Hill-Stead Museum 124
Farmington, Conn.

Historic Deerfield 17
Deerfield, Mass.

Holley Place 131
Lakeville, Conn.

Hopkins Inn 135
New Preston, Conn.

Horsefeathers 158
Tarrytown, N.Y.

Hot Tomato's 24
Northampton, Mass.

House of the Seven Gables 48
Salem, Mass.

Hurricane 83
Providence, R.I.

The Inn at Chester 104
Chester, Conn.

Iron Kettle 134
New Milford, Conn.

The Irvington Cookshop 158
Irvington, N.Y.

Isabella Stewart Gardner Museum 53
Boston, Mass.

Jacaruso's Trottoria 149
Rhinebeck, N.Y.

Jialih's 24
Northampton, Mass.

Junior's 172
Brooklyn, N.Y.

Keeler Tavern 138
Ridgefield, Conn.

John F. Kennedy Library 61
Dorchester, Mass.

Kent Falls State Park 131
Kent, Conn.

The Kitchen Shop Cafe 141
Ridgefield, Conn.

La Cuisine 112
Guilford, Conn.

La Difference 29
Hampden, Mass.

L'Americain 127
Hartford, Conn.

L'Amitie 30
Longmeadow, Mass.

The Landmark Cafe 64
Boston, Mass.

Laughing Brook 25
Hampden, Mass.

Le Bistro 92
Newport, R.I.

Le Chateau 140
South Salem, N.Y.

Le Coq Hardi 140
Ridgefield, Conn.

Le Parc Gourmet 173
Brooklyn, N.Y.

Legal Sea Foods 37
Worcester, Mass.

L'Entree 112
Madison, Conn.

The Lighter Side 23
Northampton, Mass.

Lily's Cafe 65
Boston, Mass.

The Lobster Box 162
The Bronx, N.Y.

Lockwood's Ice Cream Parlor 180
Cold Spring Harbor, N.Y.

The Lyceum 49
Salem, Mass.

Lyndhurst 154
Tarrytown, N.Y.

The Maharaja 86
Providence, R.I.

Main Brace 91
Newport, R.I.

Mansfield Depot 95
Mansfield, Conn.

Mark Twain Memorial 121
Hartford, Conn.

Maxwell Silverman's Toolhouse 37
Worcester, Mass.

Mediterranean Snack Bar 179
Huntington, N.Y.

The Milk Pail 133
Kent, Conn.

The Millicent Library 69
Fairhaven, Mass.

The Mission House 13
Stockbridge, Mass.

Monterey Bay 180
Oyster Bay, N.Y.

The Mooring 92
Newport, R.I.

Muldoon's Saloon 72
New Bedford, Mass.

Museum of Art, RISD 82
Providence, R.I.

Nathan Hale Homestead 95
Coventry, Conn.

Naumkeag 9
Stockbridge, Mass.

New York Botanical Garden 162
The Bronx, N.Y.

The Nickel Inn Cafe 45
Maynard, Mass.

No Fish Today Cafe 120
Waterbury, Conn.

No Name Restaurant 63
Boston, Mass.

Noah Webster House 124
West Hartford, Conn.

Noodles 16
Great Barrington, Mass.

Norcross Wildlife Sanctuary 26
Wales, Mass.

North Star 23
Northampton, Mass.

Old Bethpage Village 176
Bethpage, N.Y.

Old School House Cafe 140
Wilton, Conn.

Old State House 124
Hartford, Conn.

Orchard House 42
Concord, Mass.

Outward Bound 165
The Bronx, N.Y.

Panache of Hartford 127
Hartford, Conn.

The Parson's Daughter 127
South Glastonbury, Conn.

Paul & Elizabeth's 24
Northampton, Mass.

Peabody Museum 46
Salem, Mass.

Peche Mignon 179
Huntington, N.Y.

Phillipsburg Manor 154
Tarrytown, N.Y.

Plumbley's off the Common 23
Amherst, Mass.

Pot au Feu 85
Providence, R.I.

Prescott Farm 89
Middletown, R.I.

Provender 79
Tiverton, R.I.

Putnam Memorial State Park 138
Redding, Conn.

Quinton's 23
Northampton, Mass.

Raintrees 169
Brooklyn, N.Y.

Raphael's 85
Providence, R.I.

Reading Room 128
Farmington, Conn.

Red Lion Inn 15
Stockbridge, Mass.

Restaurant du Village 103
Chester, Conn.

Restaurant Lisanne 171
Brooklyn, N.Y.

River Cafe 171
Brooklyn, N.Y.

Roger Williams Park 83
Providence, R.I.

The Romagnoli's Table 64
Boston, Mass.

Roosevelt Sites 142
Hyde Park, N.Y.

Rosalie's 52
Marblehead, Mass.

Rudy's 135
New Milford, Mass.

Rue de L'Espoir 86
Providence, R.I.

The Rusty Scupper 45
Acton, Mass.

The Rusty Scupper 119
New Haven, Conn.

Sadler's Ordinary 98
Marlborough, Conn.

St. Andrew's Cafe 148
Hyde Park, N.Y.

St. Botolph Restaurant 58
Boston, Mass.

Sakonnet Vineyards 73
Little Compton, R.I.

Salem Cross Inn 27
West Brookfield, Mass.

Salem Maritime Museum 49
Salem, Mass.

Sammy's Fish Box Restaurant 165
The Bronx, N.Y.

Santa Fe 157
Tarrytown, N.Y.

Scibner's Downtown Oyster Bar 119
New Haven, Conn.

Scotland Yard 86
Providence, R.I.

Seamen's Bethel 69
New Bedford, Mass.

Seashell Cafe 105
Old Saybrook, Conn.

Seaside 65
Boston, Mass.

Seasons 65
Boston, Mass.

Serendipity 64
Boston, Mass.

Serino's at Short Beach 113
Branford, Conn.

Shaker Mill Tavern 16
West Stockbridge, Mass.

The Shaker Museum 4
Old Chatham, N.Y.

Shenanigans 127
Hartford, Conn.

Shuji's 7
New Lebanon, N.Y.

Singletons 58
Boston, Mass.

Slater Mill Historic Site 80
Pawtucket, R.I.

Sleepy Hollow Restorations 151
Tarrytown, N.Y.

Sloane-Stanley Museum 129
Kent, Conn.

Soup du Jour 52
Salem, Mass.

Soup to Nuts 30
Sturbridge, Mass.

Southern Cross 92
Newport, R.I.

The Sovereign 111
Branford, Conn.

Springwood Inn 150
Hyde Park, N.Y.

Standish House 125
Wethersfield, Conn.

Stonehenge 138
Ridgefield, Conn.

Struck Cafe 34
Worcester, Mass.

Sullivan Station 16
Lee, Mass.

Sunnyside 151
Tarrytown, N.Y.

Tammany Hall 51
Salem, Mass.

Tappan Hill Inn 155
Tarrytown, N.Y.

Tarrytown Boat Club 159
Tarrytown, N.Y.

A Taste of Paris 141
Ridgefield, N.Y.

Tee T's Landing 180
Huntington, N.Y.

The Pizza Place 165
The Bronx, N.Y.

Thimble Islands 106
Stony Creek, Conn.

Thompson's Chowder House 64
Boston, Mass.

Topsides Seafood Grill 51
Salem, Mass.

Tripoli 173
Brooklyn, N.Y.

Truc Orient Express 16
West Stockbridge, Mass.

Truffles & Such 8
Pittsfield, Mass.

Turner Fisheries 57
Boston, Mass.

Tucker's 180
Huntington, N.Y.

Twilly's 165
The Bronx, N.Y.

Valhalla at Quabog Country Club 30
Monson, Mass.

Van Cortlandt Manor 153
Tarrytown, N.Y.

Vanderbilt Mansion 145
Hyde Park, N.Y.

Vassar College Alumnae House 150
Poughkeepsie, N.Y.

Victoria Peak 149
Rhinebeck, N.Y.

Victoria Station 51
Salem, Mass.

Wadsworth Atheneum 124
Hartford, Conn.

C.W. Walker's Cafe 98
Willimantic, Conn.

Walt Whitman Birthplace 174
Huntington, N.Y.

Washington Irving Boat Club 159
Tarrytown, N.Y.

Westwoods Trail System 109
Guilford, Conn.

The Whaling Museum 66
New Bedford, Mass.

The Whistling Swan 29
Sturbridge, Mass.

Whitfield House Museum 109
Guilford, Conn.

Whitlock Farm 114
Bethany, Conn.

Wilbor House and Barn 75
Little Compton, R.I.

Wild Goose Grill & Rotisserie 65
Boston, Mass.

The Woodland 133
Lakeville, Conn.

Woodstoves 134
Sherman, Conn.

Worcester Art Museum 33
Worcester, Mass.

Worcester Science Center 34
Worcester, Mass.

Yale Walking Tours 116
New Haven, Conn.

Yesterday's 72
New Bedford, Mass.

Zanadu Garden Cafe 5
New Lebanon, N.Y.

The Zodiac 58
Boston, Mass.

About the Authors

Betsy Wittemann is a native New Englander who was introduced to daytripping by her family when she was quite young. Since that time she has explored widely and lived in both Athens, Greece, and San Juan, Puerto Rico, where she was associate editor of a Caribbean travel magazine. A journalist for several years on daily and weekly newspapers in Rochester, N.Y., and Hartford, Conn., she has written freelance travel articles for many newspapers in the Northeast, including the Boston Globe, Christian Science Monitor, Newsday and the New York Times. This book is her fourth collaboration with Nancy Webster. She resides with her husband and two children in Glastonbury, Conn.

Nancy Webster began her dining experiences in her native Montreal and as a waitress in summer resorts across Canada during her college years. She started writing her "Roaming the Restaurants" column for the West Hartford (Conn.) News in 1971. Her husband, who is a native upstate New Yorker, is a newspaper editor and guidebook publisher; they have traveled extensively throughout the country as well as New England and New York and co-authored the new book, *Getaways for Gourmets in the Northeast*. The parents of two college-age sons, they live in West Hartford, where her ever-expanding collection of cookbooks threatens to take over the entire kitchen.

Also by Wood Pond Press

Weekending in New England. The best-selling travel guide by Betsy Wittemann and Nancy Webster details everything you need to know about 18 of New England's most intersting vacation spots: nearly 1,000 things to do, sights to see and places to stay, eat and shop year-round. Published in 1980; fully updated and revised in 1984. 248 pages of facts and fun. $8.95

Getaways for Gourmets in the Northeast. This book by Nancy Webster and Richard Woodworth is for anyone who likes good food and wine. It guides you to the best dining, lodging, specialty food shops and culinary attractions in 18 areas from the Brandywine Valley to Montreal, the Finger Lakes to Cape Cod, Bucks County to Bar Harbor. Published in 1984. 306 pages to read and savor. $10.95

These books may be ordered from your local bookstore or direct from the publisher, pre-paid, plus $1 shipping for each book. Connecticut residents add sales tax.

Wood Pond Press
365 Ridgewood Road
West Hartford, Conn. 06107